T0322949

TRAVELLERS IN THE GREAT STEPPE

For my fair Rosamund

TRAVELLERS IN THE GREAT STEPPE

From the Papal Envoys to the Russian Revolution

NICK FIELDING

SIGNAL BOOKS · Oxford

First published in 2020 by
Signal Books Limited
36 Minster Road
Oxford OX4 1LY
www.signalbooks.co.uk

A catalogue record for this book is available from the British Library.

ISBN 978-1-909930-86-5 Cloth

Typesetting, pre-press production and cover design: Baseline Arts Ltd, Oxford
Main cover image © Potemin Anton
Printed in India by Imprint Press

CONTENTS

—ᴍ—

Traditional Kazakh
eagle hunter.

INTRODUCTION

—⚬—

I FIRST TRAVELLED TO CENTRAL ASIA DURING MY EARLY TWENTIES WHEN, like many others of that generation, I set off along the "Hippie Trail" eastwards from England to India and beyond. For a brief period in the sixties and seventies thousands of young people were gripped by the idea of finding places that had never been seen by our parents, of experiencing something more than the packaged, pre-processed and, above all, safe holidays that they had taken us on as small children. We left Europe with our creaky unbranded backpacks, gripping a copy of BIT's *Overland to India* guidebook – produced on a Roneo duplicating machine and full of useful tips culled from the letters to the editor from people who had done the same journey before – and made our way to the Pudding Shop in Istanbul and all places east. There were no published guidebooks of any description to the wilds of eastern Iran or the Afghan hinterland, or the tribal areas on the Pakistan border. There was barely even a good guidebook to Turkey.

Since those times the world has become a smaller place. Modern communications and transport have brought once remote places much closer – although many of the areas I visited then cannot be entered today because of war or political instability. Today, the gap year road trip is a rite of passage for many young people. There are websites devoted to it and the marvels of smartphones mean that you are never – and I mean *never* – more than a call away from family and friends. And that is fine. It is all that most people want. But it was always my dream to be out in the wilds, to be independent and to relish the chance of finding people with a different outlook on the world.

Sadly, those kinds of experiences are harder and harder to find. In Afghanistan I sat on the head of one of the giant Bamiyan Buddhas, now, alas, destroyed by the explosives of the Taliban. I drove through the Khyber Pass, something I have done since, but certainly would think twice about doing today. Later I walked for weeks through the beautiful and imposing Fann Mountains in eastern Tajikistan, visiting the Kulikalon Lakes and Iskanderun Lake, whose very name echoes that of the region's most formidable conqueror.

Ever since, time and again, I have been drawn back to these sometimes desolate and uninviting, sometimes overwhelmingly beautiful, places. Kyrgyzstan, a pristine jewel in the heart of Central Asia, amazed me. Song Kul Lake, set in a perfect extinct volcanic crater like a sapphire in a diamond ring, the views of the magnificent Tian Shan Mountains and the sense that things have continued much as they always had done, were more than sufficient reward. The remarkable Sulayman Mountain just outside the age-old city of Osh is said to hold the burial place of a Koranic prophet, but the tiny strips of cloth tied to every available branch of a tree or bush tell a much older tale, that of the shamanic traditions that shaped this land for millennia.

Further to the east I have spent time with nomads on the Mongolian plains in the Gobi-Altai region, where saiga antelope can still be seen and where wild rhubarb can be found in the rock crevices. To the north of there I have walked in the Western Sayan Mountains of Tuva, where the taiga is at its most glorious – rushing rivers, mixed forests and open-topped mountains that stretch forever. And in the Eastern Sayan Mountains of Buryatia I rode on horseback to the homeland of the reindeer-riding Soyots and the places known to the ancestors of Genghis Khan.

Of all these regions, perhaps the most inspiring for me personally is the Zhetysu/Semirecheye region of eastern Kazakhstan. Time and again I have returned, visiting the places associated with the remarkable English travellers, Thomas and Lucy Atkinson. They spent 18 months in total in this region from 1848 to 1849, during which time Lucy gave birth to their child. At that time, the Russians had only just built their first military bastion in the area and the Atkinsons were the first outsiders for well over 500 years to reach this beautiful region. When I first started travelling here in 2014, barely any outsiders had been there in years. The incorporation of the Great Steppe into the Russian

Empire and then the Soviet Union meant that travel in these mountains and valleys that lie along the border with China was far too sensitive to allow foreigners to visit.

However, as my interest in Central Asia grew, I realised that there *was* a history of travel to be written, one that had never been told before. Of course, when we speak of Central Asia, inevitably the first thing that comes to mind is the Great Game and the political and military machinations that absorbed and engulfed relations between Russia and Great Britain for much of the second half of the 19th century. That story, told so well by Peter Hopkirk in his many books, concerns itself with different issues to those of which I have written.[1] The Great Game itself was in essence about the borders between the Russian and British Empires, particularly along the line of the Amu Darya river that marks, at various points, the present-day borders between Afghanistan to the south and Tajikistan, Uzbekistan and Turkmenistan to the north. From a British perspective it was about whether or not Imperial Russia would attempt an invasion of India.

But my interest is in the vast regions that lie to the north of this fractious borderland and in particular in the Great Steppe – the central region of the vast Eurasian Steppe that stretches from the Hungarian plain almost to the Pacific. The Great Steppe stretches from the River Volga and the Caspian Sea in the west to the easternmost limits of Djungaria in the present-day Xinjiang region of Western China. To the north its limits vary with time; sometimes it is the Irtysh and Ural rivers, sometimes much further north. To the south the vast Central Asia plateau is watered by the Amu Darya and its sister, the Syr Darya – the Oxus and Jaxartes of old. In the far south on its borders lie the ancient cities of Samarkand and Bokhara, Khiva, Tashkent, Merv and Osh, all places with a written history than can be traced back to the most ancient of times.

But what of the Great Steppe itself, an area some have called the biggest field in the world? Those great regions where Genghis Khan marshalled his vast forces before heading westwards? Those vast bodies

---

1. See Peter Hopkirk, *The Great Game: On Secret Service in High Asia*, John Murray, London, 1990.

of water – Aral, Balkhash, Ala Kol and Zaisan – that barely saw a boat until modern times? And the great mountain ranges – the Altai, the Tarbagatai, the Alatau and Tian Shan? These are not names that reverberate through history. They remain much as they always have been – remote, unknown and jealously guarding their many secrets. This was a land of nomads, barren and harsh at its centre, but with rich grasslands fed by the many rivers flowing from these mountains.

In particular it was home to the three branches of the Kazakh confederation of tribes, people who had inhabited these regions for thousands of years, where they perfected the art of nomadic life. There they raised enormous flocks and herds of horses, cattle, sheep, camels and goats. Each year was punctuated by the same movements; a spring migration into the high pastures of the surrounding mountains where their animals were fattened and where they lived on horse milk and meat until the autumn. Then the return to a sheltered spot on the plains to wait out the bitter winter.

This was a society that kept no records other than the many epic poems and songs celebrating the stories of their great *batyrs* (warriors). Prior to the 20th century there are no local records. Here you will not find vast archives tucked away in some desert hiding place. Whatever is known is either within the local culture – desecrated and broken as it is by years of Soviet cultural vandalism – or in the voices of those outsiders who from time to time happened to pass through. Mostly they were on their way elsewhere – to India, China, Tibet – but occasionally there were visitors who took more than a passing interest in the lives of the steppe nomads. These are the voices I have sought to curate into this book.

This book makes no pretensions to be a comprehensive work. Some travellers – such as Marco Polo's father and uncle – I have included because their travels, even though their visits were fleeting, are not usually associated with the Great Steppe. Others, like Arminius Vambery, I have excluded because their writings are already well known. These gaps will not hinder the reader who is looking for new insights. In amongst them I trust the reader will find plenty of new stories about people whose journeys, precisely because they were in such remote and difficult terrain, are often little short of heroic. I have confined my choices to those who travelled since the time of Genghis Khan and to no later than the end of the 1920s. Arbitrary perhaps, but a line has to be drawn somewhere.

Here you will find the stories of those early papal emissaries who travelled with messages for the Mongols, believing that they could both convert them to Christianity and draw them into an alliance against the Muslims. Later came the traders and adventurers like Anthony Jenkinson and Jonas Hanway who thought they could divert the Silk Road to the north, out of the hands of their rivals in the Levant. And after the defeat of the Golden Horde we find the Russians taking an ever-increasing interest in the neighbouring territories to the south. A smattering of English travellers followed, including the rather odd John Castle and the extraordinary Reverend Henry Lansdell, not to mention the purveyor of "fake news", David Ker. Several remarkable francophone writers are added to the list, including two couples – Xavier and Adèle Hommaire de Hell and Charles-Eugène de Ujfalvy and his wife Marie de Ujfalvy-Bourdon. And that other remarkable couple, the Atkinsons, thoroughly deserve their prominent place in this book, as does the American diplomat Eugene Schuyler, whose book *Turkistan* is one of the great publications of the late 19th century.

Among the scientists, perhaps the most outstanding is William Bateson, a Cambridge biologist who in the 1880s spent 18 months wandering through the Great Steppe in search of tiny fossilised snails. Businessmen followed, including the butter-merchant and mountain climber Samuel Turner and the mining engineer J H Wardell. Who knew that before the First World War, much of Europe's butter came from the Great Steppe?

All these and others have found a place in this book. Their stories will, I hope, entertain and inspire you as much as they have entertained me over the years. I have made a conscious decision in this book to use the term "Kazakh", even when – as was usual in the 19th century and before – the term "Kirghiz" has been used in the original texts. In almost every 19th-century book on these regions you will find the Great Steppe described as "The Kirghiz Steppe". The reasoning behind the Russians' longstanding decision to call Kazakhs by the ethnonym of their near neighbours the Kirghiz is complicated and not entirely clear. Suffice to say that the Kazakhs always referred to themselves as Kazakhs. In terms of place names, it is sometimes difficult to be consistent as they have often changed so many times. Generally, I have tried to use the commonest and simplest version, unless indicated otherwise.

The narrative thread in this book, in so much as it exists, shows that far from being a desolate waste, the Great Steppe was well traversed by outsiders from the earliest times. The sheer physical difficulty of surviving in a landscape that was completely foreign to them, and the presence of predatory tribesmen on the lookout for potential slaves, meant that they were few and far between. Only a handful ever stayed for more than a few months. Those who survived generally had their local guides to thank, who knew that for those who had lived there for generations, the Great Steppe invariably provided all their needs, once the basic rules were understood.

The nomadic tradition was barely understood by Western visitors, for whom it was a completely unknown phenomenon. Those who thought about it at all either considered all nomads to be vagabonds and robbers, or, like Lansdell, saw them as living embodiments of the Hebrew patriarchs. Few Europeans had been migratory since ancient times and it was often regarded as feckless and irresponsible to move from place to place.

The descriptions by those who wrote more sympathetically about the nomads are remarkably consistent. Even in the earliest writings of Herodotus and others we can recognise the pastoral way of life as it has developed on the steppe. Descriptions written 2,000 years later barely differ in a single detail. What has changed is the outside world. Great events and social changes that took place thousands of miles away sometimes had a huge impact. The Silk Road ebbed and flowed according to the preoccupations of those who lived in the lands surrounding the Great Steppe. At various times Russia, China, an assortment of Central Asian kingdoms and even the British have played an important role in determining what happens in the heart of Asia.

Today, much of the steppe culture described by the travellers discussed in this book has been lost, mainly due to outside pressures. Vast areas that once supported large populations of both humans and their domesticated animals are now empty. New towns and industries are springing up. New roads and railways are linking up places that once were almost inaccessible. Modernity is arriving rapidly.

Nonetheless, the writings of these travellers are important as a history of times when little was recorded on the steppe. We may learn something more about the character of a historical figure when we hear incidents of their behaviour described in the form of anecdote by a traveller, even if he was an outsider and sometimes barely understood what was happening in front of him. For example, John Castle provides some insights into the character of Abul Khayir and almost 150 years later Henri Moser does the same for one of his descendants. In the same way we get pen portraits of several senior Russian army commanders from Schuyler, MacGahan and Mme de Ujfalvy-Bourdon. This is, at least, the raw material for history.

In writing this book I have tried to explain some of the historical events that have affected those living in the Great Steppe – not an easy task, as there is little study of this subject in the English language. And the disputes between the Russians and their neighbours and between the Bashkirs, the Kazakhs, the Turkomans, the Kyrgyz and the Kalmyks – not to mention the Djungars, the Dungans, the Nogai, the Mongols, the Uighurs and countless others – means that this is not a subject for the faint-hearted. Nonetheless, I hope that the writings referred to in this book have been put into the right historical context.

The reasons why outsiders travelled to the Great Steppe varied over time and in themselves provide a different kind of history. Some of these travellers, particularly the women, have been forgotten by modern readers. Hopefully this book will stimulate you the reader to track down some of the long-forgotten classics mentioned within.

Personally, I do not think the steppe culture described so vividly by travellers in these pages will ever fully disappear. The steppe is truly vast and can swallow whole cities with ease. Landscape has a close relationship with culture – and the former usually dominates the latter. Whatever happens, it will be many years before the Great Steppe finally gives up all its secrets. This book aims to provide just a glimpse of some of them.

*

In writing this book I have had help and support from many quarters. In the first instance I should like to thank H E Erlan Idrissov, Ambassador of the Republic of Kazakhstan to the United Kingdom of Great Britain and Northern Ireland, for his consistent support and encouragement for this project. His staff, particularly Ms Aigerim Seisembayeva and previously, Mr Askar Zhiymbayev, have also played their part. In Kazakhstan I have received support over many years from the Kazakh Geographical Society and its director, Mr Nurlan Abduov. Special thanks to Magzhan Sagimbayev for his support for my expeditions into the Djungar Alatau Mountains.

I would also like to thank Dr Emma Saunders, Science Archivist at the Department of Manuscripts and Archives at the University of Cambridge Library; Craig Bowen, Collections and Learning Manager at Canterbury Museums and Galleries, for help with materials on Henry Lansdell; Eugene Rae, Principal Librarian at the Royal Geographical Society, along with his very competent staff for their support over several years while working on the Atkinson Diaries; James Hamill, Department of Africa, Oceania and The Americas at the British Museum; staff at the Manuscripts department of the Bodleian Library in Oxford; Mark Adams, Senior Curator, Bird Group, Department of Life Sciences, The Natural History Museum; Laura Brown, Museum Archivist, Natural History Museum; Brian May, Managing Director, Berthon Boat Company Ltd, Lymington, Hants; Alexandre Akoulitchev, Gen Ramirez-Deffarges, Ruth Thornton, Brenda Stones, Vladimir Gostyevsky, Andrei Soldatov and Irina Borogan for reading and commenting on the manuscript; Thanks to Gen also for help in translating some of the French texts referred to in this book. Finally, I would like to thank my wife Ros for all her support over the past year while I have been writing this book. I could not have done it without her. I ask you, my readers, to forgive me for any errors that remain, for which I take all responsibility.

Nick Fielding
Oxford, November 2019

Overleaf: detail of Anthony Jenkinson's remarkable map of Central Asia.

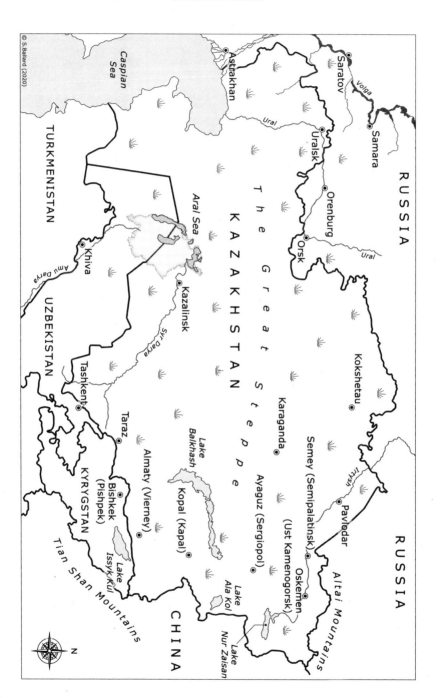

I

THE EARLY TRADERS
AND ADVENTURERS

—⁂—

IT IS HARD TODAY TO COMPREHEND THE IMPACT ON MEDIEVAL SOCIETIES
at the beginning of the 13th century of the great Mongol expansion
westwards across Asia and into the Middle East and Europe. At first
Europeans were incredulous and could not comprehend that there was
a ferocious military power greater than theirs existing in the world.
But as news of the humiliating defeats of European potentates filtered
throughout the western realms – particularly in Hungary and Poland in
1241-42 – the fear became palpable.

Desperate to halt the ruthless and unstoppable Mongol invaders,
Europe's temporal and spiritual leaders soon realised that they could
not be defeated militarily, but perhaps, it was reasoned, they could be
drawn into an alliance. Perhaps the Mongol leader Genghis Khan and
his successors could be persuaded to change the focus of their attacks
away from Europe and towards the enemies of Christendom in the
Middle East? Several attempts were made to create a Franco-Mongolian
alliance against the Islamic caliphates in the Middle East, against which
the European powers had sent several Crusades, with only limited
success.

It was widely believed that the Mongols would be sympathetic
to such an approach, given the strength of the Nestorian Church in
the East and rumours that at least one of the wives of Genghis Khan
was a Christian. Many Europeans believed the legend of Prester John,
alleged to be an Eastern Christian king who was predicted to come
to the assistance of the Crusaders in the Holy Land. Others thought

they would be able to make common cause with the Mongols against a perceived common enemy – the Islamic rulers of the Levant.

As early as 1220 tentative approaches were made to the Mongols by the papacy and by several of the European kings. Most of these approaches were prefaced by appeals for them to convert to Christianity, which were, in turn, met with uncompromising demands from the Mongols for submission and tribute. The Mongols hardly needed the support of European Christians, having already systematically subdued Islamic Persia and Syria, with great bloodshed and destruction. Christian Armenia submitted in 1247 and the Crusader state of Antioch fell before them in 1260. So worried were the Crusaders at Acre in the Holy Land in that year that they allowed the Egyptian Mamluks to pass through their territory unhindered, so that they could engage the Mongols at Ain Jalut, where they inflicted a significant defeat.

It was Pope Innocent IV who was most involved in trying to find common ground with the Mongols. His first missive, *Dei Patris Immensa*, was written in March 1245 and handed over to a Franciscan friar called Laurentius of Portugal for delivery. However, he disappeared *en route* to the Mongol homelands and was never heard of again.

The second letter, *Cum Non Solum*, was written in the same month and appealed to the Mongols to stop attacking Christians and asked them to spell out their intentions. It was carried by the Franciscan John of Piano Carpini. An Italian from a small town in Umbria, he was a companion and disciple of St Francis of Assisi. He was much travelled, having spent time in Saxony, Spain and Cologne propagating the Gospel. Carpini, who set out from Lyon, would have been in his mid-sixties at the beginning of his journey. He was joined by a Polish priest in Breslau and headed from there to Kiev and then across the Dnieper, the Don and the Volga rivers. Here, in April 1246 on the banks of the great river, he found the camp of Batu, the supreme commander of the Mongol forces on the western edge of the empire. Batu, in turn, sent Carpini on to the court of the Great Khan Ogedei at Karakorum.

The tiny delegation set out on its journey across the Great Steppe, crossing the Yaik (Ural) river, passing to the north of the Caspian and the Aral Sea, before heading up the Syr Darya river and then into Djungaria.

Precisely what route they took is not clear from Carpini's writing, but it is likely they passed through the Djungarian Gate – the gap between the Alatau and the Tarbagatai Mountains – to the east of Lake Ala Kol. They arrived at Karakorum on 24 August 1246, where they attended the election of the new khan, Güyük, grandson of Genghis Khan.

Güyük, of course, had little interest in these visiting friars in their poor clothing and offering little in the way of presents or tribute. In response to Pope Innocent's letter Güyük demanded his submission and a visit from the Western rulers to submit to his authority. As he wrote in his letter of reply: "You must say with a sincere heart: 'We will be your subjects; we will give you our strength'. You must in person come with your kings, all together, without exception, to render us service and pay us homage. Only then will we acknowledge your submission. And if you do not follow the order of God, and go against our orders, we will know you as our enemy."

Despite the uncompromising tone of Güyük's reply, two further papal letters followed, including that carried by Andrew of Longjumeau, a Dominican missionary, who was sent to Güyük Khan in February 1249. His route took him through Persia, along the southern and eastern shores of the Caspian and through the town of Talas, to the northeast of Tashkent. He and his companions arrived at the Mongol court, which was either on the Imyl river, close to Lake Ala Kol in the Zhetysu region of present-day Kazakhstan, or possibly closer to Karakorum itself. Here they found the Great Khan was dead, poisoned, it is said, by agents of Batu Khan, his rival. Andrew was sent back to the pope with a very dismissive letter. Very soon after Güyük's successor, Möngke, was elected in his place. The papal mission was yet another failure.

The best-known Western mission to the Mongols involved the Flemish Franciscan monk, William of Rubruck (Willem van Ruysbroeck) who travelled, not on behalf of a pope, but a king – and not as a diplomat, but as a simple priest. His travels to the Mongols took place between 1253 and 1255. Even before this he had participated in the French King Louis IX's crusade to Palestine, where he had heard about the Mongols directly from Andrew of Longjumeau himself. His remarkable report on his journey, in the form of a long letter to King Louis IX, is a fascinating document that provides a detailed source of information on the Mongols when they were at the height of their power.

Friar William was the first person from the West to write seriously about Buddhism and to describe shamanism as practised on the steppes, as well as providing information about the Nestorian Christian Church in the east. He also writes on geography, ethnography and nature and provides a vibrant description of Karakorum itself, including the Khan's palace and the various people he met there, who came from all over the known world.[1]

As with John of Piano Carpini, Friar William travelled via the *orda* (camp) of Batu close to the Volga before heading across the steppe towards Djungaria. From his writings it would appear that he travelled from the west via Talas until reaching the Alatau Mountains. In mid-November 1253 he and his companions then crossed a large river – probably the Ili – by boat. He passed a large town that he refers to as Equius, where there were "Saracens who spoke Persian". From here, he says, "we emerged onto a very beautiful plain, to the right of which lay large mountains and to its left a sea or lake fifteen days' journey in circumference. This plain is entirely irrigated, as much as one could desire, by the streams that flow down from the heights, all of which discharge themselves into that sea."[2] This sounds very much like a description of Lake Balkash, which is to the left if one is making a journey towards the east and which receives the waters of the Seven Rivers that flow from the heights of the Djungar Alatau. The estimate of the lake's size is, not surprisingly, inaccurate.

Friar William says that in this plain there were many towns, "but most of them destroyed, so that the Tartars might graze there, for there were most excellent pasturages in that country." On the plain they found a large town that he calls Cailac, "containing a bazaar to which merchants resorted in large numbers. We rested there for twelve days while waiting for one of Batu's secretaries, who was supposed to cooperate with our

---

1. See Peter Jackson with David Morgan (eds), *The Mission of William of Rubruck; His journey to the court of the Great Khan Mongke 1253-55*, The Hakluyt Society, London, 1990.

2. *Ibid*, p. 147.

guide in getting the business at Mangu Chan's court settled."[3] It was in this town that Friar William first came across "idolators", by whom he meant Buddhists.

Among the idolators of Cailac he mentions Uighurs, whose main territory was on the other side of the Tian Shan Mountains to the south. "All their cities contain Nestorians and Saracens intermingled," he says. In Cailac itself there were three Buddhist temples, two of which he entered. He seems at first to have mistaken the temples for primitive Christian churches, although the people he spoke to did not think of themselves as such. Certainly his description of one temple seems to be very close to a Buddhist shrine: "For there, behind a chest, which for them acts as an altar and on which they put the lamps and the offerings, I could see a statue with wings rather like St Michael and others resembling bishops with their fingers held as if in blessing." This does, indeed, appear to be a description of Buddhist deities and possibly a statue of the Buddha himself, often portrayed with his fingers raised in a blessing.

Friar William follows this with a description of the ceremonies he witnessed in the temples, which were aligned in an east-west direction and which contained many bells and statues. Some of the statues were large and he was told of one in a place called Cataia where the statue was visible at two days' distance – possibly a reference to the giant Buddhas carved into a rockface at Bamiyan in the 4th-5th centuries in central Afghanistan. The priests all shaved their head and beard and dressed in saffron colour and carried a string of beads, similar to rosaries. He says they continually repeated the words "On mani battam" – more correctly *Om mani padme hum*, a Buddhist chant that means "Om, the jewel in the lotus, Amen".

Friar William stayed in Cailac for 12 days. There has been confusion over the town's precise location, with some writers suggesting it was a town on the right bank of the River Ili, close to the town of Chingildi in the Qaratal district, west of Kopal. In fact, it has now been decisively identified as lying just outside the small town of Koilyk on the banks of the River Lepsy in the Zhetysu region, not far from Sarcand.

---

3. *Ibid*, pp. 147-8.

The site itself has been a UNESCO World Heritage site since 2014 and archaeologist Dmitry Voyakin has shown that its origin goes back at least 1500 years. In the 12th century it was the capital of the Karlyk khans and after about 1260 a political, academic and cultural centre for the Chagatai khanate. Besides the Buddhist temples, remains of which can still be seen, there is a mosque, a Manichean temple and a Nestorian Christian church, revealing that a wide variety of beliefs were tolerated by its rulers. It was probably destroyed in the 14th or 15th centuries.

The British couple Thomas and Lucy Atkinson, who spent almost seven years travelling in the remotest parts of Siberia and Central Asia, also came across the ruins at Koilyk during their travels in 1849 as they explored the river valleys of the Zhetysu region of what is now eastern Kazakhstan. In his diary entry for 15 July Thomas writes the following: "From the top of the pass we had a view of an old Kalmuck fortress on the opposite side of the river, one end of which had been washed away by the stream. It is an earth embankment, about 8 feet high. Its other dimensions are about 100 yards wide and 300 yards long, without any entrance gateway. About three versts distant there is a large barrow, but none near the fortress." They were terribly tormented by mosquitoes and the intense heat and quickly headed back up into the mountains to gain some respite.

Friar William and his followers left Cailac on 30 November 1253. Not far away they found a village inhabited entirely by Nestorian Christians. After another three days they came to Lake Ala Kol, so identified because Friar William mentions that there was a large island in the lake, known today as Ul'kun-Aral-Tyube. They left the lake in a southeasterly direction towards Lake Ebi Nor. He says: "Such a gale blows almost incessantly through the valley that people when passing are in great danger of the wind carrying them into the lake." The wind that passes through this area, known as the Djungarian Gates, is famous for its intensity.

From here the journey to Karakorum, where they arrived on 27 December, was comparatively straightforward, across what is now Xinjiang and then into Mongolia. A week later, on 4 January 1254 Friar William was given an audience with the Great Khan. He told him that he had come as a missionary and not as a diplomat, although on leaving Karakorum he admitted he had only baptised six converts. Famously, he took part in a debate with Buddhists and Muslims on the best form of religion. All the while he continued to make detailed notes of everything and everyone he saw or met. He stayed until July the same year and finally arrived back in Tripoli in the Levant just over a year later. During his stay he met numerous other foreigners, including the nephew of an English bishop, a French goldsmith and a French woman who cooked his Easter dinner.

In fact, there had been numerous European and Arab visitors to the court of the Great Khan, none stranger perhaps than Chaplain Robert, an Englishman captured in 1243 during the siege of Wiener Neustadt in Austria by the Mongols. The Englishman, it turned out, was the chief diplomat of Batu Khan, son of Jochi and grandson of Genghis Khan. His remarkable life story is told with much verve in Gabriel Ronay's wonderful book on the subject.[4]

A chaplain to one of the English barons opposed to King John, he had been banished from England and had fled to the Holy Land before making his way to the Crimea, where his language skills had endeared him to the Mongols, who found his knowledge of Western culture invaluable. He arrived in Karakorum in 1224, when Genghis Khan was still alive. By the time of the latter's death in 1227 the Englishman was already rising up the hierarchy and was likely responsible for the wording of the warnings issued by the Mongol court to Western rulers, concerning the dire consequences of not submitting to the Great Khan. He personally visited King Bela IV of Hungary twice to press home the message, but was rebuffed, resulting in the destruction of Bela's kingdom.

But the story of the Mongols was not just one of destruction. Their elimination of all competitors in Central Asia and Central Europe led to the establishment of the Pax Mongolica, a period of about 150 years in the 13th and 14th centuries during which communication and commerce flourished. There was no-one left to harass travellers and the Great

---

4. Gabriel Ronay, *The Tartar Khan's Englishman*, Cassell, London, 1978.

Khan's legal code ensured that travellers were unmolested on pain of death. After the papal envoys came the merchants and traders looking to buy the luxury goods – especially silk and spices – that could now be brought without hindrance from China along the various branches of the Silk Road.

Traveller-merchants such as Marco Polo, his father and uncle, had blazed the trail to China, at the same time shining light onto this largely unknown part of the world. Marco Polo himself, who left Italy for China in 1271, never travelled across the Great Steppe, choosing instead to take a more southerly route through Iran and then the Ferghana Valley and then rising up in the Pamirs to Kashgar. When he eventually returned to Europe in 1295 it was by sea. But in 1260 his father Nicolo and uncle Maffeo had travelled from the Crimea on the Black Sea before making their way across southern Russia to Sarai on the Volga, the residence of Barca Khan, the third son of Juji, Ghengis Khan's eldest son, where they arrived in 1261. From here, after a stay of almost a year, they travelled on to the city of Bolghar – which no longer exists – further down the Volga, below Kazan. Their route then took them to Ucaca or Ukek, another town on the Volga, after which they crossed the river and headed out into the steppes, where they met "Tartars" with their herds of cattle.

After crossing the desert, which would have taken at least two months, the brothers reached "a very great and noble city called Bokara", at that time a tributary city to Persia. It was ruled at that time by Borrak Khan, great grandson of Chagatai. Here they spent three years, until they met some envoys of the Great Khan himself, returning home from Persia, who told them that their master had never before met Latins and that if they would travel with them it would be very much to their advantage. Thus in 1265 they left Bukhara for the east. Although Marco Polo does not specify exactly the route taken by his father and uncle, it is likely they travelled through the Zhetysu region, along the foothills of the Djungar Alatau, to the Djungarian Gates, east of Lake Ala Kol. From there they would have struck east towards the court of Kublai Khan.

Even though Marco Polo did not cross the Great Steppe, he certainly came across steppe nomads, possibly Kazakhs, during his travels. This is clear from his very accurate descriptions of their mode of life: "The

Tartar custom is to spend the winter in warm plains where they find good pasture for their cattle, whilse in summer they betake themselves to a cool climate among the mountains and valleys, where water is to be found, as well as woods and pastures."[5]

"Their houses are circular and are made of wands covered with felts," he adds. "These are carried along with them whithersoever they go; for the wands are so strongly bound together, and likewise so well combined, that the frames can be made very light... They also have waggons covered with black felt so efficaciously that no rain can get in. These are drawn by oxen and camels and the women and children travel in them. The women do the buying and selling and whatever is necessary to provide for the husband and household; for the men all lead the life of gentlemen, troubling themselves about nothing but hunting and hawking and looking after their goshawks and falcons, unless it be the practice of warlike exercises. They live on the milk and meat which their herds supply and on the produce of the chase; and they eat all kinds of flesh, including that of horses and dogs, and Pharaoh's rats (possibly marmots or jerboahs-ed) of which last there are great numbers in burrows on those plains. Their drink is mare's milk."[6] Of this latter he adds that it is prepared "in such a way that you would take it for white wine; and a right good drink it is, called by them *Kemiz*". Today it is still made and drunk all over Central Asia, where it is called *kumyss*. It was first mentioned by Herodotus writing in the middle of the 4th century BC and by Strabo 400 years later.

Polo also outlines marriage customs and religion. Of the latter, he says these nomads believed in a Most High God of Heaven – usually identified as Khan Tengri – to whom they pray for health of mind and body. Another god, Natigay, was their god of the Earth and watched over their children, cattle and crops. Every yurt contained an effigy of him made from felt and cloth. Images of the head of house's wife and children were also to be found. Such beliefs existed in remote parts of

---

5. See Col. Henry Yule, *The Book of Ser Marco Polo, the Venetian, concerning the Kingdoms and Marvels of the East*, John Murray, London, 1871, vol. 1, p. 220.

6. *Ibid.*

Siberia until comparatively recently and effigies of the type described can be found in many ethnological museums.

Wealthy Tatars, says Polo, wear clothes of gold and silk stuffs, lined with costly furs such as sable and ermine, "in the richest fashion". Their weapons were bows and arrows, sword and mace. They wore armour made of tough buffalo leather and could live on their mare's milk for a month or more while on campaign. Their horses foraged for themselves. "Of all the troops in the world these are they which endure the greatest hardship and fatigue and which cost the least; and they are the best of all for making wide conquests of country." They could even ride for ten days when necessary without lighting a fire, living off blood from an opened artery of their horses. Every soldier carried ten pounds of dried milk with him which could be mixed with water and turned into a refreshing and nutritious drink. Even today such dried milk is still common in most of Central Asia for use as a snack when travelling.

There were, however, two drawbacks to the overland route to China as far as British merchants were concerned: it depended on peace in the many lands and amongst the many people through which the huge caravans of valuable goods passed; and second, the trade was in the hands of the Levant merchants and their Genoese and Venetian allies, who earned substantial profits by controlling access to the goods arriving from the East.

Nonetheless, in the 15th and 16th centuries European entrepreneurs, still very much familiar with the writings of such merchant-travellers as Marco Polo (who praised the wealth and grandeur of the lands of the Great Khan) were still lured by the wealth of the Far East, although the dangers of the overland routes had increased dramatically following the break-up of the Mongol Empire. Towards the end of the 15th century, explorers such as Christopher Columbus, Amerigo Vespucci, and Vasco da Gama all attempted to find routes to China, whether circumnavigating the globe westward, or sailing southeast, around Africa's Cape of Good Hope.

Another route, which often receives less attention, was the hypothesised Northeast Passage: accessing the east by sailing around the northern confines of Asia. It was the possibility of a Northeast Passage to Cathay that led a group of English entrepreneurs to finance an exploratory mission in 1553 under the command of two captains, Hugh Willoughby and Richard Chancellor. When the explorers rounded the northern coasts of Norway and Sweden, Willoughby and two ships were lost, but Chancellor managed to pilot his ship into the White Sea, thus "discovering" the northern Russian port of St Nicholas and, moreover, a direct sea route to Russia.

After attending Tsar Ivan IV's court in Moscow, where he received promising word that English merchants would be accommodated if they desired to trade in the tsar's domain, in 1554 Chancellor returned to England. By 1555 the English financiers received a royal charter making them an official company, usually known as the Russia or Muscovy Company. With the Company established, the English carried on a regular and direct trade with Russia via the northern route to the White Sea throughout the following decades.

Although the Company successfully established itself in Russia it did not lose sight of its original purpose – establishing direct trade connections with China. In 1556 another exploratory mission was dispatched to explore the waters east of the White Sea, but after reaching the island of Vaigach (off the coast of northern Russia) it was forced to turn back due to hazardous sailing conditions. It was perhaps the failure of this mission that led the Muscovy Company's directors to consider exploring overland eastern routes and the following year they dispatched Anthony Jenkinson to Moscow with instructions to seek a passage through the tsar's territory in order to explore routes to Central Asia, Persia and, ultimately, China. Conditions in Russia were favourable to this possibility because after several centuries of domination by the Mongols, the tsars had begun to reverse their previous defeats and expand into the territories of the Tatar khanates to the east, reaching as far as the north shore of the Caspian Sea.

After being granted a licence to travel, as well as receiving letters from the tsar addressed to foreign kings asking for his safe conduct, Jenkinson, a Tatar interpreter and two other company employees, Richard and Robert Johnson, left Moscow in April 1558. Not far from the point where the River Volga enters the Caspian they found their first nomads in the form of the Nogay Tatars. These derived their name from Nogai, grandson of Teval, the seventh son of Juchi, who founded the Golden Horde and was the son of Genghis Khan. By the end of the 16th century they were restricted to the steppes north of the Caspian and Black Seas, with occasional raids and forays northwards into the Russian homelands.

Jenkinson says that they lived in the open steppe, moving with their animals and households when fodder became short. "When they remove they have houses like tents set upon wagons or carts, which are drawn from place to place with camels and therein their wives, children and all their riches, which is very little, is carried about and every man hath at the least four or five wives besides concubines."[7]

As with other early travellers to the steppe, Jenkinson noted the Nogais' propensity towards horsemeat and horse milk. "Corn they sow not, neither do eat any bread, mocking the Christians for the same and disabling our strengths, saying we live by eating the top of a weed and drink a drink made of the same, allowing their great devouring of flesh and drinking of milk to be the increase of their strength."[8] At one point, close to where the Don and Volga come closest to each other, Jenkinson saw around a thousand camels drawing carts with felt yurts mounted on them from the Nogai horde of Khan Ismael, at that time an ally of the Russians against the Krim Tatars and the Khan of Astrakhan. From far off, he said, it looked like a town.

In newly-conquered Astrakhan – the Russians had annexed the city in 1557 – where he arrived on 14 July, Jenkinson noted the large number of starving Nogais, those who had fought against Tsar Ivan and lost. "At my being there I could have bought many goodly Tartar children, if I would have had a thousand, of their own fathers and mothers, to say, a boy or a wench for a loaf of bread worth six pence in England, but we had more need of victuals at that time than of any such merchandise."[9] He reports that the Tatars brought cotton, fine silks from Persia, mail for armour, bows, swords to trade, "But all such things in such small

---

7. See Edward Delmar Morgan and Charles Henry Coote, *Early Voyages and Travels to Russia and Persia*, vol 1, The Hakluyt Society, London, 1886, p. 52.

8. *Ibid*, p. 53.

9. *Ibid*, pp. 57-8.

quantity, the merchants being so beggarly and poor that bring the same that it is not worth the writing, neither is there any hope of trade in all those parts worth the following."

On 6 August, in company with a group of Tatar and Persian merchants, Jenkinson and his companions bought a boat, loaded it with trade good and four days later sailed out onto the Caspian Sea, becoming the first Englishmen so to do. They sailed to its eastern shore and on 7 October they landed at a place called Sellyzure or Shehr Vezir – since identified as Deu Kesken, on the southern skirt of the Ust Urt uplands, which lies between the Mangyshlak Peninsula and the Aral Sea. They then made their way to Urgench, where Jenkinson met the ruler, Ali Sultan, a Turkoman prince. All the people of this region were nomads, he says, with large herds of sheep, cattle and horses. The sheep had huge fat tails that weighed, he says, 60 to 80 pounds.

He also describes the way in which the locals used hunting birds to catch and kill wild horses: "The hawks are lured to seize upon the beasts' necks or heads, which with chasing of themselves and sore beating of the hawks, are tired; then the hunter following his game, do slay the horse with his arrows or sword."[10] As with the Nogai, he notes their love of horse flesh and *kumyss* made from horse milk.

Here, according to Jenkinson, they were among "the wild, predatory, inhabitants of the steppe, the Turkomans, who lived then, as they have done ever since, by rapine and plunder." Several attempts were made to seize his goods, but by December 1558, having followed the course of the Amu Darya for around 120 miles, his party had reached the Central Asian city of Bokhara, ruled at this time by Abdullah Khan, grandson of Janibek, who in turn was the grandson of Abu'l Khair who in the 1440s became the first khan of the Uzbeks and Kipchaks. In 1465 Janibek led a revolt against Abu'l Khair that led to the formation of the Kazakh khanate.

Jenkinson sets out all the information he could gather about trade and about the route towards China, noting the cities of Tashkent and Kashgar. He also mentions that the "people who war against Tashkent are called Kazakhs, of the law of Mohammed." This was true in that

10. *Ibid*, p. 73.

in the middle of the 16th century the Kazakhs occupied both banks of the Talas river and took the towns of Turkestan and Sabran and even threatened Bokhara. The fighting on the steppe was widespread during this period and as Jenkinson himself notes in reference to the Kazakhs and Kalmyks: "These two barbarous nations are of great force, living in the fields without house or town and have almost subdued the foresaid cities and so stopped up the way that it is impossible for any caravan to pass unspoiled, so that three years before our being there no caravan had gone or used trade betwixt the countries of Cathay (China-ed) and Bokhara and when the way is clear it is nine months' journey."[11]

Faced with the prospect of not being able to travel safely, Jenkinson and his party decided to return to Moscow, leaving Bokhara in March 1559 in a caravan of 600 camels. Ten days after he left a large army from Samarkand arrived and put the city under siege, although it was later defeated. Jenkinson arrived on 23 April at the Caspian shore where he found his original boat, which he boarded, along with a group of six ambassadors on their way to the tsar and 25 Russians who had been held as slaves in Bokhara. A month later they all made it to Astrakhan. He arrived back in Moscow in September 1559.

While waiting for a ship to sail to England in 1560 at Kolmogory in northern Russia, Jenkinson wrote a long letter explaining the incidents of his mission to his employers in England. It is one of the first European reports on the conditions of trade in Central Asia following the breakdown of the Pax Mongolica. It notes the various locations along the routes, the time it took to travel from one location to the next, the conditions, situation, products and merchants of the regions. In effect, it is a blueprint for re-establishing the overland route to China.

The company, it seems, was not convinced as in the following years, with a few exceptions, it focused its efforts on building trade with the Persian Empire to the south of Russia. Following Jenkinson's report, the Company in subsequent years dedicated less attention to the establishment of trade to the Far East and concentrated more on cultivating trade with Persia.

---

11. *Ibid*, pp. 91-2.

As for Jenkinson himself, he returned to the Caspian in 1562, but instead of heading east, he headed south towards Persia. After various adventures he returned back across the Caspian, reaching Moscow in August the following year, bringing with him raw silks and precious stones. He stayed for a while, helping to prepare a second Persian expedition by two of his associates. Further voyages followed until the sixth and last attempt by the Moscovy Company to establish trade links with Persia, which took place between 1579 and 1581. Jenkinson left Moscow for London in July 1564, arriving back at the end of September, having been away for more than three years. One final journey to Moscow took place in 1566, when he obtained a charter for the Company extending their privileges and giving them a monopoly over the White Sea trade.

In the end, the attempts by the Moscovy Company to open up the overland trade to the east via Russian and the Caspian Sea were unsuccessful, foiled by local warlords and the lack of central authority that gave free rein to the Central Asian nomadic raiders. The opening up of the sea routes to the east was the final nail in the coffin of this bold enterprise.

However, there was one remarkable, tangible achievement of Anthony Jenkinson's travels, in the form of the map he prepared of Russia and Central Asia. The original coloured and richly decorated map, which was 102cm x 82cm and designed to hang on a wall, was first published in 1562, following Jenkinson's first journey to the Caspian Sea. It was dedicated to its sponsor, Henry Sidney, and printed by a Dutch member of the Muscovy Company, Reginald Wolf. All the original small print-run seems to have disappeared not long after. It was only known to historians via a copy made by the great Flemish mapmaker Abraham Ortelius. Ortelius was making an atlas of the world and was sent a copy of Jenkinson's map which he included in the new atlas *Theatrum Orbis Terrarum*, published in 1570.

*

Having been lost to history, an original copy of Jenkinson's map turned up in Wroclaw in Poland in 1987 in remarkable circumstances.[12] During a visit to the cathedral library, the head librarian informed Krystyna Szykula, who was head of the University's Cartographical Collection, that a lady had brought in a 16th-century map. The lady was a retired teacher at a high school in Wroclaw. Before she brought it in to the cathedral, she had taken it to several major libraries, but no-one had shown any interest. She had used it for years as a teaching aid during history lessons. It had been folded twice and brought into the cathedral in a plastic bag. She told Ms Szykula, who bought it for the Wroclaw University Library where it is now a prize exhibit, that it had been a gift from a pupil, who had found it after the Second World War, probably in a cellar or attic.

After it had been conserved an announcement was made to an astonished audience at the 13th International Conference on the History of Cartography held in Amsterdam in 1989. Academic papers continue to be published on this remarkable survival.

The Wroclaw map, which was probably printed in 1567, is remarkable in that it shows all of European Russia, as well as lands to the east and south of the Ural Mountains. *Casakia, Samoyedia* and *Molgomzaia* are mentioned as also are references to *Mhoghol* and *Kirges*. Although the northern and western parts of the map were mainly based on existing maps, its eastern section is both new and reasonably accurate, with the exception of the Aral Sea, which is missing and instead represented by a body of water called the *Kitaia Iacus* – the Chinese Lake, shown with two rivers running into it – the Amow and the Sur, equivalent to the Amu Darya and Syr Darya.

Taskent also appears, as does the city of *Audeghen* (Andijan). It mentions by name five khans – *Kvrcot chan, Azim chan, Aphis chan, Alie chan and Blag chan*. There are religious, ethnographic, military and historical comments in cartouches on the map, as well as many drawings of native peoples, flora and fauna. One of the Latin inscriptions states:

---

12. For a full description of the map and its discovery, see Krystyna Szykula, 'Anthony Jenkinson's unique wall map of Russia (1562) and its influence on European cartography', Belgeo [Online], 3-4, 2008, http://belgeo.revues.org/8827

"*Turkmens empire is divided between five brothers, one of them, the leading one, is called Azim Khan, the next are designated Sultans. Only five towns or rather camps are subordinated to them.*"

It would be several hundred years before mapmakers returned once again to the Great Steppe. And then they came as traders, not emissaries.

—ແ—

Overleaf: woodcut from John Castle's book showing the interior of a yurt

2

JOHN CASTLE'S "MISSION" TO ABUL KHAYIR, KHAN OF THE JUNIOR HORDE

—⚍—

JOHN CASTLE WAS NOT YOUR AVERAGE ENGLISHMAN. In fact, he was barely English. Whether he ever spent any time in England is unclear. Some sources say that he was born in Prussia to an English mother and a German father from Hamburg and that he adopted an English persona in order to obtain favourable trade conditions. In some references he is called Cassell – a German spelling. And certainly it is true that the original text of his book was published in German in Riga in 1784. Signed original copies of his diary – which is still not publicly available – are held in a closed Russian archive. Those too were written in German. His book was not published in English until as recently as 2014.[1]

Very little is known about Castle's biography. He mentions that on his return from the steppe he found that a diary covering his time among the Bashkirs, whom he visited in the winter of 1735, a year before his journey into the steppes, had been stolen, along with drawings he had made of their villages. What he was doing there, at a time when they were in revolt against the Russians, is unknown. And what he was doing before travelling to the southern regions of Russia is equally obscure.

One thing is clear, Castle was never an official envoy of the Russians and his "mission" was the grand name he himself gave to his journey

---

1. Beatrice Teissier (ed.), *Into the Kazakh Steppe: John Castle's Mission to Khan Abulkhayir (1736)*, Signal Books, Oxford, 2014.

into the Kazakh steppes. In fact, the story of his visit in June 1736 to the Kazakh nomads of the Junior Horde sometimes reads like the script of a farce. It has something about it of the tall stories of Baron Münchhausen – the real one, not the fictional character – who, coincidentally, fought in southern Russia during the Russo-Turkish War of 1735-39. It is not that Castle lied; he seems to have been intent on putting himself at the centre of events in which he had no official role at all. The general tenor of his stories appears to be correct, but how a sometime artist and cartographer could become an official envoy from the tsars to the Kazakh hordes is a remarkable tale that owes more to human endeavour than official conferment. It was never likely to end well.

What is certain is that in 1734 he had joined the Orenburg Expedition, which had been sanctioned by a decree from the Empress Anna Ivanovna. The military expedition, which eventually lasted for a decade and involved around 10,000 troops and others, aimed to establish a fort and trading centre at Orenburg on the southern border of Russia as a means of securing it against raids by nomads from the steppes and as a precursor to opening up trade with Bokhara, gem-rich Badakhshan and India. It was also aimed at crushing the Bashkirs, a Turkic people settled between the Volga and the Ural Mountains who had been in near continuous revolt against the Russians ever since their territories had first become part of the Russian Empire in 1574.

Russia's aim was to build a line of such forts from Simbirsk in the west, all the way across the steppelands lying to the north of the Caspian Sea. The expedition, which was planned and executed by Ivan Kirillovich Kirilov, chief secretary of the Russian Senate, was prompted by the latest uprising of the Bashkirs, who had burnt Russian settlements and slaughtered settlers. Other objectives, to be effected by the numerous scientists and engineers who accompanied the expedition, included building a port on the Aral Sea, exploring the Syr Darya river and investigating natural resources in the region.

The original site of Orenburg, decided upon by Kirilov, was just over 900 miles southeast of Moscow and located at the junction of the Or and Ural rivers, although this site was abandoned after he died in 1739 because it regularly flooded each spring. As a result, a new city was proposed downstream on the side of a mountain. That too proved unsuitable and in 1743 the new city was finally founded at the confluence of the Ural and Sakmara rivers. The old settlement, located 160 miles upstream, was renamed Orsk Fortress. Orenburg became the main administrative and military centre for Russia in all its dealings with the Kazakh nomads. In 1755 it also became the base of the Orenburg Cossack Host who had been sent there from other parts of southern Russia to act as shock troops against the steppe nomads.[2]

Abul Khayir (c1680-1748) was the Khan of the Junior Horde (*Kishi Zhuz*) from 1718 until his death in 1748, a position he owed to strong support from allies in the Middle Horde (*Orta Zhuz*) and among the Bashkirs and for his military victories against the Djungars. He had been active in fighting against the Djungar Oirats (Western Mongols) for much of the first part of the 17th century, but overall the campaign had led to the loss of control over several cities in the south of the steppes, including Tashkent and Turkestan, and the deaths of thousands of Kazakhs. The Junior Horde itself was forced to move northwest towards Khiva and the Aral Sea – the so-called Barefooted Flight or Great Disaster ('*Aktaban Shubyryndy, Alkakol Sulama*' in Kazakh) of 1723 – which brought it into contact with the Russian authorities, who themselves were seeking to control the steppelands and settle them for agriculture.

Despite being elected as the main military commander of all three Kazakh hordes in 1726, with successes against the Djungars at the battles of Bulanty-Bileutinsk in 1727 and Anyrakay in 1728, Abul Khayir had been denied leadership of the unified horde and so returned to the western regions where the Junior Horde was located. Stuck between a rock and a hard place, the leaders of the Junior Horde had little choice but to enter into negotiations with the Russians, looking for protection from the Djungar Oirats and return of lands that had

---

2. Following the Russian Revolution, in the winter of 1919-20 this host, under its leader Ataman Alexander Dutov, made an epic 600-km journey, now known as the Starving March, from Ayaguz in what is now eastern Kazakhstan to the Djungar Alatau Mountains on the Chinese border. Hungry and frozen, about half of the 20,000 people who set off into the forbidding mountains between March and May 1920 died while attempting to cross into China, where the survivors were interned. Dutov himself was assassinated by a Bolshevik agent in Suiding, China, in February 1921.

been stolen from them, as well as water rights along the Ural and Tobol rivers, in exchange for loyalty towards the Russian Empire and defence of its borders from raids, as well as protection of trade caravans moving between Central Asia and Russia.

The first approaches to the Russians had been made in 1726 by Abul Khayir, who sent an ambassador to the Russian court. There was no agreement, so in September 1730 another embassy was sent to St Petersburg with a letter to the Russian Empress Anna Ivanovna asking for citizenship and protection. It was sent without consultation with other leading sultans, which would prove to have consequences later on. In March the following year the empress offered similar terms to those offered to the Bashkirs and Volga Kalmyks and sent Alexic Ivanovich Tevkelev (1674-1766), a Tatar who was translator of the Committee on Foreign Affairs, to organise the details.

Tevkelev, whose original name was Mirza Kutlu-Mukhammad – he Russianised it in 1734 – had originally worked as a translator for Tsar Peter the Great and in the intervening years had become an important figure, responsible for developing Russian policy towards the steppe nomads. It was his idea to create a new fortress at Orenburg and he became second-in-command of the Orenburg Expedition, with the rank of colonel. He was to do well out of his work for the Russian tsars. During his lifetime his family acquired around 250,000 hectares of land, making them some of the wealthiest landowners in the region. Tevkelev became Russia's first Muslim general in 1755 and eventually co-governor of Orenburg.

When he arrived at Abul Khayir's camp on the Irgiz river in October 1731 Tevkelev realised that there were disagreements amongst the Kazakhs about signing a deal with Russia. Abul Khayir, his sons Nurali and Erali and senior advisors nonetheless swore an oath of fealty on 10 October 1731, recognising that subservience to Russia offered stability to their 400,000 people, many of whom had been driven from their traditional lands around the city of Turkestan and the Syr Darya river by the actions of the Djungars. It was not the last time they would swear such an oath.

Abul Khayir, whose aim was to unite all the Kazakh tribes on the steppe, now sent emissaries to the Khans of the Middle Horde urging them to support Russian protection. Their leader, Khan Semeke, accepted the proposal and so his people were, nominally at least, now under the protection of the Russians. However, the Kazakhs were not regarded as citizens of Russia and, despite their oaths, were not necessarily loyal to the Empress. As Beatrice Teissier states: "For Abulkhayir the alliance was pragmatic, tactical and non-binding, not foreseeing the full colonization of Kazakh lands and certainly not the abolition of the khanship. Soviet historians and others have argued that it was the beginning of a binding association or union and on Abul Khayir's part a statesman-like, far-sighted move to 'civilise' and ultimately protect the Horde and the steppe by negotiating with the Russians."

Abul Khayir's pragmatism was clearly shown by his attitude towards the Bashkirs. When they rose in revolt against the Russians and the Orenburg Expedition in particular, the Junior Horde was cautious, but by early 1738 it was supporting them, despite an offer from the Russians of 60-100 roubles for every Bashkir head they could deliver. At one point Abul Khayir even attempted, unsuccessfully, to attack Orenburg.

However, in June that year once again Abul Khayir, his sons, deputies and the Sultans of the Middle Horde came to Orenburg to renew their oaths of loyalty. Hostilities with the Russians – and the Djungars – continued for many more years. In fact, it would be another 140 years before all three of the Kazakh Hordes were firmly under the control of the Russians.[3]

This, then, was the background to John Castle's mission to Khan Abul Khayir in 1736. Oaths had been sworn, but divisions within the Junior Horde and between it and the Middle Horde, and uncertainty about Russia's intentions meant that nothing was set in stone. Abul Khayir wanted to shore up his own position by relying on Russian military might, but could not be sure of the backing of his own people, let alone the Kazakhs in the Middle (and the Senior) Horde. The Russians knew about the divisions within the Junior Horde and they too were uncertain about their long-term intentions. Even after Castle's return, nothing was settled.

---

3. For more detail on this, see Martha Brill Olcott, *The Kazakhs*, Hoover Institution Press, Stanford, 1995, p. 31ff.

Castle says in his introduction to his journal – prepared for publication in 1741 but never published – that he made his "extremely necessary and happily completed journey" of his own free will "and purely for the best advantage of the Russian Empire". He refers to himself as "an Englishman and artist serving on the Orenburg Expedition". He adds that he undertook his journey entirely at his own expense and without support from anyone, while making it clear that he had not received what had been promised to him by Kirilov, commander of the Orenburg Expedition. He even mentions that Kirilov took from him a "noble stone" weighing 62 lb that he had found in Tatary – we never find out precisely what it was made of – and that he had sent 200 lb of meat to the Orenburg garrison when it lacked provisions in the winter of 1736 without receiving any compensation.[4]

So how precisely did this artist and adventurer end up as an emissary to the Kazakh khans? His adventure seems to have started as a result of his friendship with Erali Sultan, elder son of Abul Khayir, whom he met at Orenburg. Erali Sultan had taken part in the Junior Horde's embassy to St Petersburg in 1732 and had returned with the Orenburg Expedition in 1734. However, he was not allowed to return to his father's *aoul* (encampment) on the steppe, but instead was held as a hostage at Orenburg for the future good behaviour of his father, a not-uncommon tactic. He was not locked up, but nor was he allowed to leave the confines of the garrison. It was here that he met Castle and where, it seems, he played an important role in convincing the Orenburg commander, Lt-Col Jacob Fyodorovich Chemodurov, to allow Castle to visit Abul Khayir.

The immediate circumstance that led to Castle's journey was the arrival in Orenburg in June 1736 of a delegation from the Junior Horde with a letter for Chemodurov. They wanted to know if Orenburg was still being held or if there were plans to abandon the town. Castle says that he invited the envoys, along with Erali Sultan and a mullah, to his house where they told him that the Ottoman Turks in Constantinople had incited a coalition of Kazakhs and Kalmyks to attack the Orenburg Expedition, but that Abul Khayir was anxious to prevent

---

4. Teissier, *op. cit.*, pp. 20-21.

this by facilitating the appearance of a Russian envoy on the steppe, to demonstrate the latter's determination to crush any rebellion.

Despite what appeared to be a dangerous situation, Chemodurov was reluctant to send an envoy, but somehow Castle convinced him to allow him to visit the khan in order, he said, to paint his portrait. As soon as permission had been given, on 14 June 1736, he left the fortress at Orenburg, taking with him a young German apprentice called Dietrich Luftus and a Tatar servant called Kulben. The party also included the two envoys from Abul Khayir – Beybeck Augluck and Schag Bey – plus the adjutant, Kalbeck, along with Asan Abuys, an envoy from Janibek Khan from the Middle Horde, and another three young Kazakh merchants who had travelled with the khan's representative Bey Ian Bey during the previous winter and who had been robbed by the Bashkirs. Asan Abuys left the group after a couple of days to return to the Middle Horde.

Travelling towards the southeast of Orenburg, the party reached Abul Khayir's yurt on 19 June, although he was not there. Nonetheless many people came to visit Castle, by whom they were fascinated, particularly by his German clothing. Everything he had brought with him was gone through and several items quickly disappeared. "I was wearing English boots, with Bernkleder leggings beneath, which they drew off me completely with the greatest politeness," he wrote.[5] They thought his watch was alive and asked what kind of a creature it was. Thinking it was bewitched, they wanted to destroy it. His flintlock was also of great interest and even though he put it under a carpet and sat on it, it did not fail to attract the attention of the khan's 12-year-old son, who accidently set it off, with the result that it hit the leg of a horse standing several hundred paces away, breaking its leg. Although the tribesman had matchlock weapons, they had never seen a flintlock musket before.

More consternation followed when Castle's wig was accidentally disturbed: "Given that those present thought that I had changed my own growth of hair this way and were therefore afraid that I was able to change my whole head, they withdrew and wished to run away, which seemed very strange to me and I was obliged to ask my

5. *Ibid*, p. 31.

interpreter about it. He explained the reason to me with a great deal of laughter, whereupon I was unable to find any other way of reassuring them than that of removing my wig from my head and showing them this circumstance, whereupon they became so confident that they took the object in their hands and viewed it as something rather foolish, and tried it on each other with hearty laughter and afterwards I was frequently asked to show them this wig which they would then try on each other while laughing heartily and deriving a great deal of pleasure thereby, which provided me *justement* with the means of insinuating myself among them."[6]

Castle had brought with him many gifts – needles, knives, mirrors and other similar items – which he quickly dispensed. He was even obliged to hand over the buttons on his coat. Later, at dinner that night, more dignitaries arrived, and he was given *kumyss* – fermented horse milk – for the first time. The following night his fortune was told using a burnt lamb's shoulder bone – an old ritual that is still sometimes performed in rural communities in Central Asia. Castle drew a picture of this event in which the shaman or priest who performed the ritual declared at the end that he was not evil.

A young woman of around 20 also approached him at the meal, telling him in Kazakh that she was a Russian Christian who had been stolen from the town of Yaik (Uralsk) about ten years previously. She asked for his help in gaining her freedom. Castle says he could not help her but offered some tips on the direction in which she could escape. He says that a year later she arrived in Orenburg, where she married a Russian soldier.

Castle rode out the next day in the company of three of Abul Khayir's sons who reassured him that they stood by the oaths made to the Russian Empress. On his return he was asked to lodge with an old man who told him he had the ability to cool the air with incantations, even though he identified himself as a Muslim.

Finally, on 21 June, the khan arrived back at his *aoul*. Castle received a message saying that Abul Khayir would like to see him arrive on

---

6. *Ibid*, p. 32.

horseback in his German clothing, to which he consented. He was lodged in a white cotton tent, erected as soon as he arrived, and told to wait. Half an hour later he was led to the khan's yurt which, after an elaborate series of rituals, he was allowed to enter. There sat the khan, wearing a striped gown, with his brother Nyas Sultan and his two sons, along with many elders from the Horde. The khan made it clear that his main object was to ascertain the intentions of the Russians; were they about to leave Orenburg or not? If they were not, then he would forbid his subjects from joining in a Kalmyk uprising against the Russians that was in the offing.

Castle reassured him that the Russians had no intention of leaving Orenburg, just as they had none of leaving the Crimea, the region around the Sea of Asov or the Kuban. The people of all these regions had been obliged to bow before the Russian Tsar. After his long peroration, Castle was fed by the khan's own hands – a notable honour. After three hours the audience was over and Castle left the yurt in the company of 20 men, who tried – unsuccessfully – to prevent the large crowd outside from touching him for good luck.

The following day he travelled with the khan to the yurt of one of his concubines where again he was fed, while listening to music. During the journey they hunted with eagles: "On the way the Khan diverted me with the chase, which consisted of this, a bird that is even stronger than an eagle and is called *Pickurt* (*bercut*) in their language, for which a stand was set up on the front part of a saddle, on which it sat and when the occasion arose, given that we encountered many wild goats and horses, it would be released at different times and achieve this effect, whereby as soon as it reached just one of the wild prey, it would attack its eyes with its talons and blind it, and thereby furnish the occasion for killing it easily. And, although this bird was clearly unusually fierce, I felt even greater admiration because the Khan would straightway ride off on his horse, which he subsequently gave me, at those wild goats, and approach them at full gallop with the whip that he kept beside him and whip them off."[7]

---

7. *Ibid*, pp. 43-4.

Castle's description of the interior of Abul Khayir's yurt is both detailed and rare; not until Thomas Atkinson's journeys 120 years later do we find such interesting descriptions that are worth quoting at length:

The yurt that he was in was well supplied with fine Persian carpets lain on the ground, and he was sitting on his knees beneath which lay a fringed cushion of Buchar velvet. Above him hung a canopy of silken gauze, showing three-fold colours of red, white and gold. On the Khan's left hand sat his three wives, beneath a four-cornered hanging of this same gauze material. His oldest and true wife, the Sultaness, sat above them, dressed in a red silken cloth, richly decorated with golden flowers, in addition to which she wore a high ornament on her head, which resembled a Turkish cap and was embroidered with gold. The other two wives were dressed in red Buchar velvet, and each of their heads was embellished with a fine white cotton scarf, one of which in my estimation must have been at least 20 arsines long. On their feet they wore boots of green and very fine chagrille (shagreen).

Beyond the hanging a Kalmyk girl sat dressed in black *sammet* (velvet) and playing Russian songs on a *bandoir*. In front of the Khan himself, an old man was sitting beside a youth; the old one was playing on a Turkish balalaika and the boy on a Nogais violin with two strings. Three paces from Khan sat his elders, with a burning lamp of sheep fat set before them, in the centre. In the centre of the yurt stood a wooden container in the form of a washbasin, about four buckets in size, in which their drink, namely mares' milk, or *kumis*, was to be found. When I entered the yurt, the Khan gave me to understand that I should be merry that evening and that he had invited me to his tent for that purpose and he required me to sit down and gave me a drink out of his own hand.

The scene is captured in one of the drawings Castle made at the time.

Castle lists the gifts he brought with him, which included mirrors, knives, needles, "a gold-edged money bag containing a burning glass", a silver box and a gold-embroidered prayer cloth. But the most pleasing present was his portrait of Abul Khayir's son, Erali Sultan, which brought his mother to tears. As the evening progressed the khan became more and more tipsy and the conversation drifted from Castle's lack of wife and children to his thoughts about the khan's country: "… he asked me as a person who had been so far in the world, that I should honestly say what I thought of his country and whether I had ever seen a better one than his. This question would have been almost too difficult for me to answer, since I had encountered a perfect antechamber to Hell there, given that the same was without timber, without water, without grass and wholly without bread, is furnished only with hills and one must ride a great way before encountering one of these three most necessary things, though the last of these could never be found, in that they eat no bread at all."[8]

He used all his charms and diplomacy to answer the question. He also took out his paints and a piece of parchment he had brought for the purpose and began to paint the khan "with my finger and freehand, with such a happy outcome that the Lady Khan was pleased to let these words fall; that no drop of water could be more similar to another than my finished portrait to her husband."

The following day, 25 June, he rode to dinner with three khans from the Middle Horde, including Bukhenbay Batyr from the Shak-shak clan of the Arghyn tribe, who agreed to punish those who had stolen horses and camels from the garrison at Orenburg. Four days later, on 29 June, Castle met four envoys from Janibek Batyr who assured him that they would adhere to the oaths of fealty they had sworn to the empress. Further envoys from Janibek arrived who also gave him assurances of their loyalty. On 1 July a great dinner was held, to which were invited representatives of all three Kazakh hordes where two horses, two sheep and large amounts of *kumyss* were consumed and where further assurances of loyalty were given. Castle himself, it would seem, was not invited to the meal.

After the feasting had finished Castle was invited to the tent, where, he writes, he resisted drinking too much *kumyss* but his hosts were seriously inebriated before he retired to his yurt. Before leaving the

---

8. *Ibid*, p. 51.

company he wrote down, on their instruction, the names of all those who had sworn loyalty to the Russian Empire: Ammalik *biy*, Besh *biy*, Toktara *biy*, Umir *biy*, Urali *biy*, Koshkul, Tiule *biy*, Koshara *biy*, Asan *batyr* and Aik *biy*. However, he did not get fed: "When they had gone, I lay down to rest, but could not sleep from hunger, having asked the khan that same evening for something to eat, but had received the reply that there was nothing left, since 500 persons from among their elders had been fed. So on the occasion of this great feast, which had been ordered in honour of my arrival, I had to go to sleep hungry."[9]

No explanation is given for why Castle was barely fed after the first night during his stay with the khan. He says he was forced to eat roots and that someone later brought him some dried milk, but that generally he was starving. Yet other hospitality was offered, included two young girls, whom, Castle says, he declined on the ground that his religion "did not permit this sort of thing".

On 4 July, he was invited to the yurt of one of the khan's advisers, who gave him nine wolf pelts and four blue fox pelts for his interpreter. He then met the khan himself, who asked him to convey to Tevkelev that he wanted his own residence in Orenburg and that he wished to dedicate his three sons to the service of the empress. He said he would be able to bring more steppe people under the jurisdiction of the tsars and asked for a portrait. He also gave Castle and his interpreter a fine horse each and further fox pelts.

At 9am by his watch he set off, in the company of envoys from all three hordes – 14 people in all, whose names he provides – back to Russia. For the first five hours he saw nothing but yurt encampments and when he stopped for the night experienced for the first time the taste of *beshparmak*, a Kazakh horsemeat delicacy, usually offered to honoured guests.

Further adventures followed on the journey north. At one point, Castle came across a group of Kazakhs who seem to have taken part in the aborted attack on Orenburg, previously mentioned. He says he also came across a Bashkir, who fired 30 arrows at him, all of which missed.

9. *Ibid*, p. 58.

The Bashkir was then taken prisoner. He tells how the Kazakh envoys organised a special ritual when they became lost at some point; they knelt down facing each other with a fur blanket beneath them. In each hand they held an arrow with the tips directed towards their bodies. With the other end they touched the feather of the person opposite. After murmuring incantations, they waited to see which way the arrows would point. They then travelled in this direction, crossing the River Yaik (Ural) on their horses with their goods tied onto a raft that was dragged behind them.

Finally, on 17 July, Castle and his party arrived within sight of Orenburg. By this time they were on foot as their horses were too weak to carry them. They themselves had barely eaten in three days. At the outlying Sakmara fortress Castle asked the Cossack *ataman* (chief) to provide him with a convoy to Kirilov's camp 200 *versts* (a Russian measurement of 1.1 km) away or at least to send a letter. The *ataman* refused, saying he needed a written order. Even after he explained that he was with a group of envoys and that he was carrying a letter from Abul Khayir, the *ataman* would not budge.

At this point the Kazakh envoys were on the point of returning to the steppe and Castle was obliged to reassure the Kazakhs, buying them provisions of beer, brandy, sheep, mead, cooking pot, axes, boots, tobacco, powder and lead. On 20 July the party continued on its way, with Castle by now dressed as a Kazakh in case he was singled out by marauding Bashkirs. The following day, he met Captain Sowrin of the Pensich Regiment at the point where the Sakmara flows into the Yaik. Sowrin treated Castle and the envoys courteously. Envoys were sent to Kirilov, but returned, unable to pass through lines of hostile Bashkirs. Two Cossacks were then sent and finally, on 4 August, Castle received a letter from Kirilov saying that a convoy would soon arrive to escort him and the Kazakhs.

On 5 August the party reached Kirilov's camp 150 *versts* from Ufa, now the capital of Bashkortostan in southern Russia, where he handed over his pencil-written journal and gave a full report of his journey, explaining how there was a real chance that unless the envoys were listened to, up to 40,000 Kazakhs would join with the Bashkirs and Kalmyks to rise up against the Russians.

From here on Castle's story becomes rather confusing. Presumably he thought that by bringing a group of Kazakh dignitaries from the steppe to meet the Russians he was performing an important service, even a diplomatic breakthrough. However, that was not the way the Russians saw things. Kirilov, the commander of the Orenburg Expedition, led him a merry dance, refusing to pay him his "expenses" or to treat the Kazakh envoys with any seriousness. They were politely escorted back to the steppe. Castle was sent on a wild goose chase of several hundred miles from Orsk to Orenburg, Uralsk and then across the Volga to Simbirsk.

Castle met with Kirilov again on 27 October at Simbirsk, where the latter relieved him of the valuable semi-precious stones he had collected on his journeys. But of Kirilov's promise to send Castle to St Petersburg to make his report in person to the tsar, there was no sign it was likely to happen. "By then I felt that this care was being stretched pretty thin and that the said State Councillor was seeking to retain me on the pretext of having no money and permitting my outstanding wages to be paid out gradually in small amounts and only in sufficient quantity to allow me to live from hand to mouth, whereby I grew annoyed because I clearly saw that all his other servants were receiving their wages in full."[10]

By January 1737 Castle was clearly regarded as a thorn in Kirilov's side. On 13 March the State Councillor ordered Castle to travel to Samara. On the way his carriage fell through the ice into the Volga and almost all his possessions were lost, although he saved his journals. Kirilov now asked Castle to go as an envoy to India, clearly hoping to get rid of him once and for all. Castle refused. Kirilov died a few weeks later and his replacement, Commander Tevkelev, was even less sympathetic. Castle now had to ride back to Simbirsk to cash a credit note for his wages. Moreover, soon after arriving he was attacked by a sergeant and 16 men and taken to the police station in his nightshirt, bloodied and beaten. While he was there his lodgings were ransacked and most of his remaining possessions stolen.

Castle finally received some justice with the arrival of Vassily Nikitich Tatischev in August 1737, who was on his way south to take up the post

10. *Ibid*, p. 108.

of Governor of Astrakhan. Tatischev arranged for Castle's outstanding wages to be paid and gave him a further contract. Castle eventually stayed working for Tatischev – whom he called his patron – until June 1739, when he received an honourable discharge.

Castle probably spent the next year or so composing his Journal, in the form of a letter to the tsar, which was sent in August 1741. He says in the introduction that he was writing directly to the tsar because he could not be sure that Kirilov had sent his original report to St Petersburg. He also sent five portraits to the tsar, including those of Abul Khayir, his son Erali Khan, the Bashkir leader Aldar Iskeev and his daughter and one of a Tatar interpreter, all painted "just with my finger" (i.e. pastels), he says.[11]

That was the last that was heard of from Castle for a while. It is known that he had a brother and his father in St Petersburg, so it is possible he spent some time there. But the next time we hear of him is in 1743, when he showed up in Persia. Our informant is John Cook, a Scottish doctor who was attached to a British trading mission that travelled from Russia to northern Persia by land that year. Cook's character reading of Castle[12] is worth quoting in full, for the interesting perspective it offers on the man:

> One named Cassells, born in Prussia, whose father was a Prussian and his mother an English woman, gave himself out to be an Englishman; and, by virtue of the liberty which was granted to the British subjects to trade through Russia and Persia, by the court of St Petersburg, went to Persia in the year 1743, expecting some post or employment from Captain Elton, with whom he had been made acquainted when the captain was in Orenburg. The captain, however, would not encourage one of Cassels' disposition or incapacity, and Cassels would not accept of such terms as the captain thought proper for him.

11. These pastel paintings are now in the State Russian Museum in St Petersburg.

12. John Cook, *Voyages and Travels through the Russian Empire, Tartary and Part of the Kingdom of Persia*, Edinburgh, 1770, vol. II, pp. 515-8.

Cassels was a man of the most violent passions, quite ungovernable; very many instances of which I could give, which my design hinders me from doing. Cassels, in his fury, observed no moderation; neither justice nor honour could lay the smallest restraint upon his actions. He was so much transported with rage at being so unexpectedly disappointed that he applied directly to the Shah and accused Elton of crimes by which he might have risked either the loss of the Shah's esteem or suffered some remarkable disgrace. Mr Elton, with great composure and calmness, made the Shah sensible of his innocence and also of Cassels' madness; but pointed out the true cause; which as I said before was his being disappointed in getting a post under him, for which he was not qualified; letting the Shah know that he was only bred a painter: That he, (Elton) was of opinion Cassels had never been upon the sea, except betwixt Astrakhan and Enzilee.

The Shah was convinced by this, that Mr Elton deserved all the trust he had reposed in him; and would have ordered Cassels to be bastinadoed if Mr Elton had not interposed and protected him. Mr Elton did not rest here; but advised the Shah to employ him as his painter. The Shah ordered him to paint eight pictures and make them as like as possible. Cassels engaged for a price and fixed the time when all should be ready. But Cassels, enjoying a great salary and judging that when the pictures were ready, his salary would be withdrawn, was in no haste to finish his work. In short, he spent so much time that the Shah, having sent sundry messages for Cassels to bring the pictures, at last ordered him to be brought to the camp with his performances.

When he was brought before the Shah, he took notice of his breach of promise and also that thought the pictures had some resemblance, they had many faults and looked all younger that one which Cassels had presented to the Shah formerly. Cassels forgot himself so far that, it is said, he, upon this occasion, treated the Shah with such indignity that he ordered him to be strangled; which would have been put instantly in execution had not Mr Elton interposed and observed to the Shah that a mad man was not accountable for his actions or behaviour and that ill reports were frequently carried very far and lost nothing in rehearsing: That the Shah wanted foreigners both for his fleet and army; but an action of this kind would infallibly put a stop to any but madmen from coming into Persia. These and many other reasons which the captain made use of, saved the life of this madman.

After escaping with his life due to the intervention of Captain Elton, John Castle disappears from history. As Cook's little pen portrait makes clear, he seems to have been suffering from some kind of mania, one that allowed him to present himself as an important ambassador from the tsar and to argue with one of the most bloodthirsty tyrants in Persian history without considering the consequences.

Nonetheless, the three final sections of Castle's Journal are of great interest to historians and ethnographers alike. They contain his findings on the physical geography of the Kazakh lands to the southeast of Astrakhan, the customs and laws of the Kazakhs themselves and an essay on their rulers and their polity. These sections are free of the megalomania that characterises the rest of the journal and remain some of the best descriptions written of this obscure period of Kazakh history. He described the saiga antelope he saw in profusion, as well as wild horses, wild boar and many of the birds he saw. Considering that he was only amongst the Kazakhs for barely a month, he picked up a great deal of information. His description of a Kazakh family caravan is marvellous:

Each family has its own particular caravan, whereby their fairest daughter rides ahead on their best horse and leads the troop in this manner. She is dressed in a very costly dress, wearing a distinctive pointed bonnet with silver ornaments on her head, set with a special kind of red goose-feather, with a little bell hanging from it. After her follows a camel that she leads, whereby this one is always tied to the next, on which the carpets and other household goods are loaded. After this camel follows another with the children, then come the camels with the yurt and other things and, finally, the horses and sheep bring up the rear...[13]

Of Khan Abul Khayir himself, he says he was "of large and distinguished stature, white and ruddy of face, with something very amiable about it, as well as being very strong and forceful, in that no one in his entire nation can match him in stringing a bow." Castle claims that his prowess in battle led to his accession to the leadership of the Junior Horde, where he had command over 40,000 warriors, "but he does not enjoy any kind of sovereign rule, since his rule is subject to the approval of his elders and his orders ensure that which the elders have approved in carried out. His prerogative consists of this, that he may be highest person in the court of law, but he does not hold more than two votes, hence all public matters that arise, as well as his judgements, must also be approved."[14]

*

In the end John Castle's "mission" came to nought. Hostilities between the Russians and the various hordes of the Kazakhs – not to mention the Bashkirs and the Kalmyks – continued for many years to come. But his story also illuminates that fascinating period when not just the Russians, but many others, were trying to find out more about the largely unknown regions that lay to its south. In India, likewise, British interest in the vast hinterland of Central Asia was growing, not least because of the prospects of new areas of commerce.

Hard on the heels of the Russians, tough pioneers like Captain John Elton were busy selling their services to the Russia Company as voyagers willing to make the dangerous crossing of the Caspian, either to Persia in the south or eastwards towards Bokhara. As has been mentioned, Elton was sent by the Russian government in 1735 to assist in the Orenburg Expedition. He was supposed to explore Lake Aral, but was hindered by the Bashkir uprising from reaching the lake. He

---

13 Teissier, *op. cit.*, p. 132.

14 *Ibid*, p. 142.

then employed himself in surveying the southeastern frontier of Russia, particularly part of the basins of the Kama, Volga, and Ural rivers.

Returning to St Petersburg in January 1738, he quit the Russian service after being denied promotion. Instead he proposed to some of the British factors at St Petersburg to carry on a trade into Iran and Central Asia via the Caspian Sea. Together with Mungo Graeme, a young Scot, he obtained credit for a small cargo of goods to sell in Khiva and Bokhara. Leaving Moscow on 19 March 1738 they travelled down the Volga to Astrakhan where they embarked on the Caspian towards Karagansk.

At Karagansk the two men realised that the steppes were in turmoil and decided instead to sail for Rasht in Iran. Elton was able to sell his goods and also to obtain a decree from the shah granting the two men the freedom to trade throughout Iran. He persuaded the Russia Company to take up his scheme, and in 1741 an Act of Parliament sanctioning the trade was passed. The following year he organised the building of two ships on the Caspian, and Elton was placed in command of the first completed which carried the English flag – the first such vessel since the time of Anthony Jenkinson. Further north, however, there was growing concern at the news that Elton was building European-style ships on the Caspian for Nader Shah, the ruler of Iran. If true, it was inevitable that the Russians would withdraw support from the Company's plans for trading across the Caspian.

Anxious to know what was happening, the Russia Company sent the merchant Jonas Hanway to Iran to find out. He arrived in Rasht on the southern Caspian coast on 3 December 1743 and found that the stories were true. Elton had already built a ship of 20 guns for Nader Shah, and was soon appointed Admiral of the Caspian, with orders to require all Russian vessels to salute his flag. The Russian reaction was both immediate and severe. If Elton could not be curtailed from selling his services to the Persian shah, then the Russia Company would be put out of business.

In October 1744 the Russia Company, in order to placate the royal court in St Petersburg, vainly ordered Elton to return to England, but he declined, pointing lamely to a decree from Nader Shah forbidding him to leave Iran. Even offers of a pension from the Russia Company and a post in the Royal Navy had no effect. After Nader Shah was murdered in 1747 Elton narrowly escaped assassination himself, finding protection from several of the Iranian princes. Finally, however, in April 1751, he espoused the cause of Mohammad Hasan Khan Qajar, and was besieged in his house at Gilan by the rival faction. Here he was taken prisoner by the Governor of Gilan, Hajj Jamal Fumani, and soon after was murdered.

Much of Elton's story is told in his diary, parts of which were printed in Jonas Hanway's own account of his experiences trading across the Caspian, even though the diary is full of derogatory comments about Hanway – hardly surprising considering that it was Hanway who had informed the Russians about his activities.[15] Hanway himself writes of his argument with Elton, adding that Elton's anger with the Russia Company was due to the fact that it had caved in to the Russian demands to stop building ships on the Caspian.

Hanway mentions two other English traders who tried to develop a trade route that would have brought goods from Bokhara and Khiva, through Astrakhan and up the Volga to Moscow.[16] These were George Thompson and Reynold Hogg. These two men set out in February 1740 from St Petersburg to find out if the trade would be possible. By 17 June they has reached the Cossack garrison of Yaik (Uralsk today) where they changed from European to Tatar clothing and provided themselves with camels and horses and took on some Kalmyks and Tatars to help with the baggage. The local Cossacks categorically refused to join them, telling the Englishmen they were likely to be sold into slavery. A local Kazakh sent them two guides and they then joined other Kazakhs to make up a party of around 20 persons.

They left Yaik on 26 June and travelled due east at the rate of 60 *versts* per day through the desert landscape, wary of anyone they met on the road. On 11 July they fell in with another party of Kazakhs and six

---

15. See Jonas Hanway, *An Historical Account of the British Trade over the Caspian Sea with a Journal of Travels from London through Russia into Persia and back again through Russia, Germany and Holland*, Dodsley, Nourse Millar, Vaillant, Patterson, Waugh, Willcock, London, 1754 (4 vols.).

16. *Ibid*, vol. 1, p. 346ff.

days later arrived at the camp of Janibek Batyr, a Khan of the Middle Horde who treated them well: "This Tartar chief was sitting on a carpet in his tent; he rose and bid us welcome and making us sit down with him, he took a large dish of *kumyss*, which he drank and made us do the same. We gave him some small presents which he immediately divided amongst the company."[17]

The Kazakhs had a very extensive tract of land here, with Bashkirs to their north, Black Kalmyks and the city of Tashkent to the east and Karakalpaks and the Aral Lake to the south. "They live in tents made of wooden stakes and covered with a felt of camel's hair; these they fix or remove with great ease whenever they change their quarters and they never stay above two or three days in a place. They feed on horse-flesh, mutton and venison and drink fermented mare's milk to excess; so that they often intoxicate themselves with it. They have no grain, nor any kind of bread. When they go upon an expedition they take a small quantity of cheese, which they call *crute;* this being dissolved in water, is their chief sustenance during their journey. Money is hardly known among them; their riches consist in cattle, fox and wolf furs, which they exchange with their neighbours for clothes and other necessaries."

The two men stayed with Janibek until 8 August, when they found themselves about five days to the southeast of Orenburg. Here they joined a caravan of 60 Kazakhs and Turcomans and travelled on at the rate of about 50 *versts* a day. They passed by Lake Aral and the Syr Darya river. They found "an abundance" of wild horses, asses, antelopes and wolves and another creature they called a Jolbart, which they said was "not unlike a tyger". (In fact, it probably was a tiger.)

By 3 September they had reached the dry bed of the Oxus that had originally run between the Aral Sea and the Caspian, they were told, although it had long since been stopped up by the Tatars. Two days later they were in Urgench, which was entirely in ruins, with no building remaining other than a mosque. On 9 September they parted from the rest of the company and reached Khiva nine hours later, where they took lodgings in a caravanserai and where they paid a 5 per cent duty

---

17. *Ibid*, p. 347.

on their goods. However, trading conditions were not good as there was a rumour that Nader Shah, on his way back from India, might well pass through the city.

A few days later one of their Kazakh guides came to them in the middle of the night insisting that they should leave for their own safety. The party they had left on 9 September had been plundered by Turcoman raiders, with several of them killed. However, they decided to ignore him at which point he left, promising to return in the spring.

They noted that the trade in Khiva consisted largely of sales of Kazakh and Turcoman animal skins to Bokhara and Persia and the import of European cloth. Any profits to be made were out of proportion to the risks. They stayed in Khiva until 15 December, having witnessed the arrival of the Persians. Hogg stayed on in the city whereas Thompson travelled on to Bokhara, intending to return home through Persia and over the Caspian, north to Astrakhan. Hogg did not leave Khiva until April 1741. He was set upon by 17 Turcomans who left him for dead, before once again making it to Janibek's camp. He was absent, but Hogg eventually made it back to Orenburg, and then, the following spring, to St Petersburg.

As for Thompson, he made it to Bokhara by following the Amu Darya river. He gives a fascinating description of the city, noting that its products include wool, rice, cotton and rice. Soap, cotton yarn and calico were made there and people grew rhubarb. There was little sign of European commodities. Thompson stayed there until August because of reports that it was too dangerous to travel. He set off south, crossing the Amu Darya into territory subject to the Persians. On 22 September he arrived in Mashad in eastern Iran, which he found to be a rich city with 90 caravanserai, all in good repair. How he got home from there is unclear from Hanway's book.

Overall, Hanway's journey to Russia and then south across the Caspian marks the last time that British merchants showed any interest in Central Asia as a possible conduit for Silk Road goods from the East to England via Russia. The Russia Company collapsed in the wake of Elton's activities on the Caspian, but it would have done so anyway as the brigands of the steppe made it impossible to guarantee the safety of goods travelling by caravan, unless under heavily armed escort. It was just too risky. By the beginning of the 18th century the sea routes from Europe to India and China were well known and safer than either a crossing of the Central Asian steppes or further north on the sledging routes from Kiakhta via Irkutsk in Eastern Siberia back to European Russia – a journey that could only be undertaken in winter anyway due to the danger of floods and the bogginess of the ground in summer.

Commercial opportunities in the steppe would not attract Western Europeans again until the late 19th century, when agricultural merchants and mining companies found plenty of profitable business. The next group of travellers, who only touched the extremities of the steppe, were the scientists – Russians and others – about whom we will read later. But it was a remarkable English couple, Thomas and Lucy Atkinson, who were to provide one of the most comprehensive and significant descriptions of life of the steppe.

Overleaf: detail of lithograph
by Thomas Witlam Atkinson:
Sultan Souk and family

3

THOMAS AND LUCY ATKINSON
Across the Great Steppe to the Seven Rivers Region and the Djungar Alatau Mountains

—ᴍ—

BARELY KNOWN TODAY, THE ENGLISH COUPLE THOMAS AND LUCY ATKINSON travelled further and for longer in Central Asia than almost any other travellers before or since. Journeying from Moscow in the north in the late 1840s, they spent more than six years, mostly on horseback, riding throughout Siberia and Central Asia. During that period, they were in some of the remotest parts of the region for well over two years. They became the first Europeans in modern history to visit the Zhetysu region of what is now Eastern Kazakhstan, where they systematically explored the valleys of the seven rivers that give it its name. They arrived at exactly the moment that Imperial Russia was cementing its control over the region by building a line of Cossack fortresses along the border with China.

It was also almost exactly the moment that the Senior and Middle Hordes of the Kazakh tribal confederation agreed to accept Russian dominance over the region, a price they were willing to pay in order to gain some protection from the Djungar raiding parties that regularly crossed the ill-defined Chinese borders to prey upon their livestock and families.

Even more incredibly, Lucy Atkinson was pregnant when the couple set off for the steppe in February 1848. Nine months later she gave birth to her son, and from that moment the child accompanied them on all their journeys.

The fact that Thomas Atkinson was an accomplished watercolour artist added another dimension to their journey. Before the age of the camera, he was able to capture the essence of these wild and remote places better than anyone before or since. The portraits he made of prominent Kazakhs whom he met during his travels are unique. Thomas is generally known as a landscape painter, but his portraits of figures such as Sultan Sjuk, Sultan Boulania and Sultan Iamantuck and his family bring to life these characters who would otherwise have been lost to history. In a region such as nomadic Kazakhstan, where history was generally only recorded orally, these paintings are part of the historical record.[1]

Precisely why the tsars allowed the Atkinsons to travel in these remote regions, even as they were still grappling to bring them under military control, is a matter of conjecture. There is a suggestion that it may have been a mistake and that some military officials were later disciplined for allowing them to travel so far into Central Asia. But nothing was done to restrict their movements, either before or after the journey to the Zhetysu region. And they seem to have travelled unhindered – thanks to Thomas' passport that was officially approved by Tsar Nicholas I – during the whole of the six years they spent in Siberia and Central Asia. The tsars' preference for outsiders to run the Russian state – Baltic Germans, Scots and Poles were over-represented in mining, the military, inland waterways, engineering and many other professions – means that they were more comfortable with such people travelling through their dominions that they would have been had they been Russians.

ARRIVAL IN RUSSIA

In the summer of 1846, a rather unusual Englishman arrived in the Russian Imperial capital of St Petersburg. Well into his middle years, a little down at heel, but with an open face and an uncanny ability to get on with almost anyone, Thomas Witlam Atkinson was at a turning point in his life. For the previous six or seven years his life

---

1. For more on the Atkinsons, see my book, *South to the Great Steppe: the travels of Thomas and Lucy Atkinson in Eastern Kazakhstan, 1847-1852*, First, London, 2015, and my blog Siberian Steppes (https://siberiansteppes.com).

had been in turmoil, but now he had hit upon a plan. The stonemason turned architect, with a string of remarkable neo-Gothic buildings and churches to his name, was now about to embark on a new course in his life. After living abroad for the previous four years and facing up to the tragic death of his son, he had decided to travel to some of the most remote areas on earth – Siberia, Central Asia, Mongolia and northern China – armed with little more than a sketchbook. The architect had become the artist.

What prompted this practical Yorkshireman, born in 1799 in the small south Yorkshire village of Cawthorne, near Barnsley, to set off for such remote destinations as he approached his half-century? He was not an explorer by background, and until 1842 at least had led a comparatively sheltered life, with no indication at all that he had ever left the British Isles.

Nor was that the only remarkable thing about Thomas Atkinson. Soon after arriving in St Petersburg Thomas was to meet Lucy Sherrard Finley, a young, well-educated English governess employed by one of the grandest families in the Imperial capital with direct connections into the heart of the Russian aristocracy. Lucy was 29 and unmarried. From a Dissenting background, her family had come originally from the northeast of England where they had been involved in the Baltic trade for many years, running trading ships into St Petersburg and back again to England in the summer and then over the Channel to France during the winter.

At some point during the latter part of 1846, as he made his way around the salons of Imperial St Petersburg, Thomas and Lucy fell in love. But it was not simple. He was about to start out on a journey eastwards that was scheduled to last for several years. In the mid-19th century much of the region between the Urals and the Pacific Ocean, almost 5,000 miles away, was unknown, not to mention dangerous, inhabited by wild tribesmen and subject to greater variations in temperature than almost anywhere on earth.

Undoubtedly Thomas soon appreciated the advantages that would come from a relationship with Lucy. She spoke fluent Russian, whereas he did not. She was in the employ of a general in the Imperial Army who was also president of the Russian Geographical Society. And despite his loyalty to the emperor, General Muravyev-Vilensky was a scion of a family that had wholeheartedly thrown itself behind the reformers who supported the Decembrist uprising against the tsars in 1825. One of his cousins had been executed and others sentenced to a life of exile in Siberia. Yet another cousin was the Governor of Eastern Siberia, while another was a war hero. Lucy's connections to this remarkable family were to prove crucial to the success of her and Thomas' travels. Their marriage in the winter of 1848 in Moscow proved to be full of surprises.

But for now, Thomas, armed with a letter of introduction from the Earl of Westmoreland, British Envoy Extraordinary and Minister Plenipotentiary to Prussia, was intent on gaining permission for a journey he hoped would make his reputation as an artist. His first port of call was the British Legation in St Petersburg, where he was soon able to win over the British Minister Plenipotentiary to Russia, Andrew Buchanan. Records in the Bodleian Library include a letter from Buchanan to his superior in London, the future prime minister, Viscount Palmerston, dated October 1846:

Mr Atkinson, an English artist, who was recommended to the protection of Her Majesty's Legation by the Earl of Westmoreland, requested me some time ago to employ my good offices with Count Nesselrode (the Russian Foreign Minister – ed), with the view to obtain the sanction of the Emperor to a professional tour which he proposes making in Siberia and the Altai, and I am happy to say that, in consequence of his Imperial Majesty's orders, every facility has been afforded to Mr Atkinson by the Imperial authorities for the completion of his purpose. Mr Atkinson will be accompanied by an Englishman who has been for some time residing in this country.

They will visit Kiachta and intend to penetrate as far as possible into China. I have therefore called Mr Atkinson's attention to several points of political and commercial interest on which Her Majesty's Government might be glad to receive information and he has promised to bear them in mind and report upon them to

Her Majesty's Legation on his return to St Petersburgh. I have the honour to be, with the highest respect, My Lord,
Your Lordship's Most Obedient, Humble Servant.
Andrew Buchanan

Buchanan was not exaggerating when he said that "every facility had been afforded to Mr Atkinson" by the Russian authorities. The terms of the *ukase* (passport) granted to Thomas by the tsar meant that he was entitled to receive transport – carriages, sledges, horses, boats or whatever was available – provisions, Cossack protection and guides at any of the post-houses along his route entirely at the expense of his hosts. He was required to pay nothing in return. Over the course of nearly seven years, travelling a total of 40,000 miles, Thomas' expenditure was almost nil.

"I am deeply indebted to the late Emperor of Russia, for without his passport I should have been stopped at very government, and insurmountable difficulties would have been thrown in my way. This slip of paper proved a talisman wherever presented in his dominions and swept down every obstacle raised to bar my progress,"[2] is how in his first book Thomas described the importance of the document issued to him personally by Tsar Nicholas I.

It was a remarkable coup for an Englishman, at a time when tensions between Britain and imperial Russia were growing by the day. By 1854, only months after Thomas and Lucy – along with their son, Alatau, born during the course of their travels – returned to St Petersburg at the end of their wanderings, the two countries were at war with each other in the Crimea. Not until 1856 did Thomas venture back to England, to arrange the publication of his first book, which appeared two years later. That was followed by a further volume in 1860,[3] with a third volume planned, but which never appeared due to Thomas' untimely death in July 1861. Three years later Lucy also published a book, *Recollections*

---

2. See T W Atkinson, *Oriental and Western Siberia: A Narrative of Seven Years' Explorations and Adventures in Siberia, Mongolia, the Kirghis Steppes, Chinese Tartarty and Part of Central Asia*, Hurst and Blackett, London, 1858, p. vii.

3. T W Atkinson, *Travels in the Regions of the Upper and Lower Amoor and the Russian Acquisitions on the Confines of India and China*, Hurst and Blackett, London, 1860.

of Tartar Steppes, which is all the more remarkable for being one of the earliest (and best) travel books written ever written by a woman.[4]

All three books describe the incredible journeys made by the Atkinsons – surely the greatest husband-and-wife travellers of all time. And yet today, their names are barely known. Neither Thomas nor Lucy have received the plaudits they so richly deserve. This chapter concentrates on the journeys Thomas and Lucy made into Central Asia, in particular to what is today Eastern Kazakhstan, known in the mid-19th century as Oriental Tartary, the Kirghis (more properly Kazakh) Steppes and Chinese Tartary.

Until it was conquered by the Russians – a process that lasted the best part of 40 years in the second half of the 19th century – Central Asia was made up of a number of independent khanates. Bokhara, Kokand, Samarkand, Merv and others were the fiefdoms of numerous petty princes and tyrants. Thomas' arrival in Russia coincided with the first attempts by that country to seize the Great Steppe that stretched all the way from the Urals to China and to attempt to bring some kind of control to this wild region. This almost exactly mirrored similar events taking place in North America at the same time, where the US Cavalry and newly-arrived settlers were used to seize the traditional hunting lands of the plains Indians.

As Thomas declared in the introduction to *Oriental and Western Siberia*: "Neither the old Venetian nor the Jesuit priests could have visited these regions – their travels having been far to the south; nor am I aware that they brought back any pictorial representations of the scenes through which they wandered. Even the recent travellers, Huc and Gabet, who visited 'the land of grass' (the plains to the south of the great Desert of Gobi) did not penetrate into the country of the Kalkas; and the illustrations to their works were evidently fabricated in Paris."[5]

In contrast, Thomas made three substantial journeys into Central Asia, on the second one of which – by far the longest – he was accompanied by Lucy. He also sketched and painted his journeys, bringing back to England more than 560 sketches and completed watercolours of his travels. The Atkinsons were certainly the earliest European visitors to

---

4. Mrs Atkinson, *Recollections of Tartar Steppes,* John Murray, London, 1863.

5. *OWS, op. cit.*, p. vi.

much of Eastern Kazakhstan and their writings offer us a unique window into conditions and life on the steppes at this time. They met many of the leading Kazakh sultans on their journey, providing us with tantalising glimpses into a way of life that has long disappeared. Their accounts – and Thomas' paintings – provide some of the only descriptions of the people and places that existed prior to the arrival of the Russians.

And they were witnesses to history. As the Russians sent a Cossack expeditionary force of around 500 men south in the summer of 1848, along the line of the Tien Shan Mountains which marked the border with the Celestial Chinese Empire, Thomas and Lucy were only a few weeks behind, residing in their most southerly and remote bastion at Kopal for almost nine months. That was where in November 1848 Lucy gave birth to their son, named Alatau Tamchiboulac Atkinson, after the nearby mountain range and a sacred spring on the steppes close to the base of the mountains.

Until the spring of 1846 Thomas had been based in the north German city-port of Hamburg, where he worked on a number of architectural projects. There is no evidence that Thomas returned to England from Hamburg during the early 1840s. He had left England under a financial cloud, his business reputation in tatters. Hamburg at least offered him the chance to work as a jobbing architect, where he would not need access to credit. His son, suffering from a serious illness, had joined him but had died, aged only 22, in April that year. We are left to ponder on Thomas' state of mind during this period.

In only a few years Thomas appears to have lost his business, his wife and daughters and, tragically, his son. His decision to go to Russia, at the same time abandoning his profession and setting out to travel to some of the most remote and dangerous places on earth, seems to suggest a desire to get away from the pressures of the world.

Perhaps it explains his detached attitude to danger, set out in the introduction to *Oriental and Western Siberia*: "Mine is a simple narrative of facts, taken from journals kept with scrupulous care during the whole journey, often under the influence of great fatigue and amid the pressure of numerous difficulties. I suffered much both from hunger and thirst, have run many risks and on several occasions have been placed in most critical situations with the tribes of Central Asia – more particularly when among the convicts escaped from the Chinese penal settlements – desperate characters who hold the lives of men cheap. I have several times looked upon what appeared inevitable death, and have had a fair allowance of hair-breadth escapes when riding and sketching on the brinks of precipices with a perpendicular depth of 1500 feet below me."[6]

Others would have regarded his plan for travel in such remote areas as foolhardy in the extreme. If the "tribes of Central Asia" didn't get him, the climatic extremes of deserts and snowstorms would.

From Hamburg Thomas must have made his way to Berlin, then the capital of Prussia. His Hanseatic passport carried a visa that was also valid for travel to Berlin. One source at least states he travelled in order to find more work, not because of any decision connected to the death of his son. In her memoirs, Anna Maria Pickering says that Thomas decided to travel to Russia as a result of a meeting with Tsar Nicholas I: "On the Emperor of Russia passing through the city, he was so struck with his work that he sent for the architect, and at once engaged him to go to St Petersburg. He was employed for many years on Imperial works, both in St Petersburg and in other parts of the Russian Empire, including Siberia."[7]

This comment is slightly curious in that Thomas is not known to have built anything during the years he lived in Russia. However, it is quite possible that the story of him meeting the tsar is true. There were also other reasons that drew him towards Russia, and to Siberia in particular, not least his meeting in Berlin with the great German geographer and scientist Alexander von Humboldt, who had himself, in the late 1820s, travelled through the Urals and Altai Mountains of Western Siberia. In a letter written from St Petersburg in 1854, Thomas reminded the great man of their first encounter: "Sir, In 1846 you very kindly gave me a letter of introduction to Admiral Lutke…"[8]

---

6. *Ibid*, p. vi.

7. Spencer Pickering (ed), *Memoirs of Anna Maria Wilhelmina Pickering*, Hodder & Stoughton, London, 1903, pp 42-43.

8. Count Fyodor Petrovich Litke (1797-1882) was a Baltic German navigator, Arctic explorer, geographer and member of the Russian Academy of Science in St Petersburg. He was tutor to Tsar Nicholas I's second son Constantine and president of the Russian Geographical Society 1845-50.

The *Dictionary of National Biography* entry for Thomas suggests that Humboldt was a major influence. It states: "Inspired by Alexander von Humboldt's accounts of Siberia, Atkinson then moved to St Petersburg, after a short stay in Berlin. There, in 1846, he abandoned architecture as a profession for the pursuits of an explorer and topographical artist…"[9]

Thomas also received some support and encouragement from John Fane, the 11th Earl of Westmoreland and, from 1841-51 minister plenipotentiary at Berlin. Fane wrote a letter of recommendation to Andrew Buchanan,[10] *chargé d'affaires* at the British Legation in St Petersburg. It is likely that Thomas met Humboldt himself through the Fanes, as the latter is known to have been a friend of the earl and his wife Priscilla. Humboldt was just the sort of man that Thomas would look up to: a self-taught renaissance man, a household name in his lifetime and also a talented artist.

Thomas arrived in St Petersburg in the summer of 1846. The best clue to the date comes from a letter Andrew Buchanan sent back to Lord Palmerston, the newly-appointed foreign secretary, in the diplomatic pouch from St Petersburg to London. Dated from the end of October 1846, it reports that Thomas has asked Buchanan to make representations to Count Nesselrode, the foreign minister, "some time ago", suggesting at least a few months previously.

In *Oriental and Western Siberia*, Thomas recalls the course of events: "After due consideration I determined to apply to the Emperor for especial permission to travel and sketch, feeling certain that if this were granted, there would be no difficulties: if refused, I would not make the attempt. I wrote a letter, which was most kindly laid before His Imperial Majesty by Mr Buchanan, *Chargé d'Affaires*; and in three days received an answer from Count Nesselrode, informing me that the Emperor had granted my request, and that orders had been issued to the Minister of the Interior and other authorities to prepare for me all the necessary papers."[11]

Buchanan had not missed the fact that the Russians had offered Thomas unprecedented access to travel in parts of the Russian Empire

---

9. DNB, Entry for Thomas Witlam Atkinson. See https://doi.org/10.1093/ref:odnb/858

10. See https://en.wikipedia.org/wiki/Sir_Andrew_Buchanan,_1st_Baronet

11. *OWS, op. cit.*, pp. 1-2.

that few British travellers had ever visited. "Every facility", as set out in the special passport, meant that Thomas would have the same rights to horses, carriages, provisions, guides and Cossack protection, as an Imperial officer. He intended to use his newly-issued passport to travel right across the continent, as far as the Chinese border.

Count Nesselrode's reply to Andrew Buchanan still survives among the Atkinson family papers. Written in August 1846, it asks Buchanan to tell Thomas about the decision. A second letter from Nesselrode to Buchanan, dated 19 September 1846, notes that Thomas had offered some of his paintings from his travels in India, Greece and Egypt to the tsar, who graciously declined to accept them.

"My sole object," says Thomas, in the introduction to *Oriental and Western Siberia*,[12] "was to sketch the scenery of Siberia – scarcely at all known to Europeans. While thus employed, I passed out of the Emperor of Russia's Asiatic dominions; having been provided with an especial passport by command of His Imperial Majesty, Nicholas the First, which enabled me to cross the frontier, as well as to re-enter the Empire at any other points to which my rambles might lead me."

This was a privilege indeed. Other travellers took their chances on the post roads through Siberia, waiting for hours, sometimes days, for horses to be found and giving way if an official was travelling the same route. It is the first of many examples of Thomas making an impression on someone and perhaps winning favours that would be denied to another person. So often he got the best out of someone, whether the Cossack officers he met while travelling, the Decembrist exiles he met in Siberia or the governors of mines or of entire regions. Many of them went out of their way to help him and it stands as a tribute to the character of a man whom we can only know from the feint echoes that still resonate down the ages of his impact on other people.

The extent to which Thomas came to depend on this little scrap of Imperial paper can be gauged from his comments in *Oriental and Western Siberia*: "I am deeply indebted to the late Emperor of Russia," he wrote, "for without his passport I should have been stopped at every

---

12. *Ibid*, p. v.

government and insurmountable difficulties would have been thrown in my way. This slip of paper proved a talisman wherever presented in his dominions and swept down every obstacle raised to bar my progress."[13]

Buchanan must have realised that information gleaned by Thomas on his travels would be of enormous interest to his colleagues in Whitehall. Although not declared enemies at this point, within eight years Great Britain and Imperial Russia would be at war in the Crimea. Already tensions were growing between the two great powers as they struggled over the carcass of the decaying Ottoman Empire and to fill the power vacuum left in Europe by the defeat of Napoleon.

Nor was Britain a disinterested observer of Russia's Far Eastern southern neighbour, China. Only four years before, in August 1842, Britain had imposed the unequal Treaty of Nanking on the Qing rulers of China, forcing them to open their ports to foreign trade and to accept British-supplied opium. That was followed in 1844 by the Treaty of Whampoa that imposed similar conditions on behalf of France. Before long both countries would land troops in China and occupy the capital. The world was opening up for trade and the prospect of transporting Chinese goods to Europe overland was, for the first time, being considered.

As the Eastern and Far Eastern trade began to develop, so strategic considerations began to grow, not least in relation to India. Soon this preoccupation over who controlled what in Central Asia and its hinterlands would become known as "The Great Game" and would occupy the minds of politicians and diplomats in Europe for the following 70 years. Without realising it, Thomas was about to traverse some of the very lands that were at the heart of this often mystifying, but always engrossing, diplomatic duel.

Although he had been issued with an unusual passport, Thomas was not the first European to travel in Central Asia. By the 1840s there was no lack of travellers who had reached the Urals and then moved eastwards to Barnaul and the northern foothills of the Altai Mountain range in southern Siberia and from there on to Irkutsk and Lake Baikal. In 1840 the English magistrate Charles Cottrell had travelled

---

13. *Ibid*, p. vii.

from Moscow to Irkutsk and even as far as Nerchinsk, stating in his book *Recollections of Siberia*[14] that it was a journey "which we believe no other living Englishman has made, except two missionaries many years established in Selenginsk."

Other travellers included the Irishman Peter Dobell[15] and the remarkable Captain John Dundas Cochrane,[16] who between 1820 and 1824 had walked from Europe to Kamchatka on the Pacific Ocean and back again. Even the extraordinary blind traveller, James Holman, had reached Irkutsk in 1822, journeying alone and with only limited mobility. There he was suspected of being a spy and was seized by the secret police and deported to Poland. On his return to London he published an account of his travels.[17]

In 1840 and 1841 the great British geographer Roderick Murchison had been involved in two scientific expeditions to remote parts of Russia, including the far north and also the Urals and Altai Mountains. Both trips had received support from Tsar Nicholas I. Murchison's findings and detailed maps had been published in 1845, as *The Geology of Russia*.[18] In fact, it is quite possible that Thomas had read a copy of Murchison's book, as he visited many of the same places described by the latter, and in the same order. And even one of Thomas' illustrations for *Oriental and Western Siberia* bears a remarkable similarity to a drawing that appears in Murchison's book.

Alexander von Humboldt had also travelled in roughly the same areas in 1829 and his descriptions had no doubt enthused Thomas, particularly

14. Charles Herbert Cottrell, *Recollections of Siberia in the years 1840 and 1841*, John W Parker, London, 1842.

15. Peter Dobell, *Travels in Kamchatka and Siberia, with a narrative of a residence in China*, London, 1830 (2 vols.).

16. See James Dundas Cochrane, *Narrative of a Pedestrian Journey through Russia and Siberian Tartary, to the Frontiers of China to the Frozen Sea and Kamtchatka*, London, 1824 (2 vols.).

17. James Holman, *Travels Through Russia, Siberia, Poland, Austria, Saxony, Prussia, Hanover, & C. & C: Undertaken During the Years 1822, 1823 and 1824, While Suffering from Total Blindness, and Comprising an Account of the Author Being Conducted a State Prisoner from the Eastern Parts of Siberia*, Smith, Elder and Co, London, 1825.

18. Roderick Impey Murchison, *The Geology of Russia in Europe and the Ural Mountains*, John Murray, London 1845.

his descriptions of the Kazakh Steppes.[19] In an attempt to understand the volcanic activity that had shaped Central Asia, Humboldt had travelled to Barnaul in the Altai before heading south to Riddersk, Zyrianovsky, Ust-Kamenogorsk (modern-day Oskemen) and then to Lake Zaisan on the frontier of Chinese Djungaria, before returning to Orenburg.

The ambition of Thomas' proposed route caught the attention of Buchanan, who very explicitly suggested "several points of political and commercial interest" about which Thomas might like to tell Her Majesty's Government when he was next in town. Was it spying? Not in anything but the loosest sense. Thomas intended to travel in open view of the authorities, often in the company of Cossack guards. A trained spy might be able to make assessments of transportation movements or to know the regimental badge of every soldier he passed on the road, but Buchanan's pitch to Thomas was more akin to a call on his sense of nationalism, a typical request to pass on anything he thought might be of interest. As it turned out, he got more than he bargained for.

There was one other little mystery associated with Thomas' passport. It concerns the identity of the "Englishman who has been for some time residing in this country" who was mentioned in Buchanan's message as the person who would accompany Thomas on his journey. That turns out to have been Charles Edward Austin (1819-93). Austin, who came from Gloucestershire, was 20 years younger than Thomas and had trained as a railway engineer on the Great Western Railway, for whom he worked until the early 1840s. He subsequently moved to St Petersburg where he worked on steam navigation on the Volga, publishing a treatise on the then state of the river traffic and its management. The trip he started with Thomas was the first of two tours he made into Siberia.

Until the end of 1847 – Thomas' first year of travel – the two men were together as travelling partners and Austin is frequently mentioned in Thomas' travel diary for that year. Austin's obituary records that he was a good linguist, which could explain Thomas' decision to travel

---

19. For a summary of Humboldt's writings on Central Asia, see W Macgillivray, *The Life, Travels and Researches of Baron Humboldt*, T Nelson and Son, London, 1860, p. 348ff. Humboldt's main work on Central Asia, *Asie centrale, recherches sur les chaînes des montagnes et la climatologie comparée*, Gide, Paris, 1843, (3 vols.) has never been published in English.

with him.[20] In 1862 Austin presented to the Geological Society, of which he was a Fellow, some notes on his Siberian explorations. Sadly, these can no longer be located, although the Geological Society still holds a series of remarkable large-scale maps, drawn and coloured by Austin, of the area between Irkutsk and Nerchinsk in Eastern Siberia.

Thomas says that one of the first people he consulted about his proposed journey was Admiral Peter Ivanovich Ricord (1776-1855),[21] one of the founding members of the Russian Geographical Society and commanding officer of the Kamchatka Peninsula from 1817 to 1822, where he introduced the cultivation of potatoes. Ricord was Italian by birth but spoke perfect English, having served as a midshipman in the Royal Navy under Nelson. He had only ever travelled across Siberia on the Great Post Road, which passes to the north of the Altai region, but knew a great deal about the regions bordering the Pacific Ocean and Sea of Okhotsk. Thus Thomas lost no time once he was in St Petersburg in seeking out information that would be useful to him on his journey to the East.

In those first few days and weeks in St Petersburg, Thomas was already trying to make connections and to gather information about what he could expect to encounter on his travels. He was soon working his contact list, which included prominent geographers recommended to him by Humboldt in particular. We do not know exactly how he met Lucy Sherrard Finley, the 29-year-old Englishwoman he was later to marry. The fact that she was working in St Petersburg as a governess to the daughter of a Russian general, who also happened to be president of the Russian Geographical Society, may explain the encounter. Did Thomas meet her when he called upon General Mikhail Nikolaievich Muravyev?[22] Quite possibly. However the meeting occurred, it was to have a massive impact on the lives of both Thomas and Lucy.

---

20. Austin's obituary can be found in the Proceedings of the Institution of Civil Engineers http://www.icevirtuallibrary.com/content/article/10.1680/imotp.1893.20450

21. Thomas spells his name Rickardt.

22. Muravyev – later given the honorific name Muravyev-Vilensky for putting down an insurrection in Poland – was an important figure in mid-19th century Russia, scion of a famous family, many of whom had supported the unsuccessful Decembrist Revolt in 1825. Lucy's connections within the family were to serve her and Thomas very well during their travels.

Born in 1817 in Sunderland, County Durham, to Matthew and Mary Ann Finley, Lucy was the fourth child and eldest daughter of ten children. Her father was a schoolteacher, but he had probably started his career as a mariner. His father and grandfather, both called Robert Finley, had been master mariners. Lucy's grandfather Robert (1707-1806) was mainly involved in carrying coal from the coalmining and shipbuilding centre of Monkwearmouth on the north bank of the River Wear in Sunderland to London. He was also involved in the cross-Channel trade bringing French wines to the British market and he also made at least one trip to St Petersburg carrying hemp. It seems likely, therefore, that Lucy had heard tales of the frozen north throughout her early life.

Lucy's mother Mary Ann was born in Stepney in London's East End and she and Matthew were married at St Dunstan's in the East on 25 April 1810. Just north of the expanding docks of the Port of London, the area had long been associated with maritime trade and it is reasonable to suspect that Matthew had first visited Stepney and met Mary Ann while on a voyage down from Monkwearmouth.

In St Petersburg Lucy was one of many young Englishwomen who arrived to take up positions as governesses to the children of Russia's leading families. Her charge was Sophie, the only daughter of General Muravyev. Lucy would have been provided with a good wage and accommodation and would have had a status well above that of a house servant. With good fortune, she could save enough to provide her with an annuity in later life and perhaps, if she was lucky, she would meet a man and make an advantageous marriage.

We have already noted that Thomas was doing the social rounds in St Petersburg and was recorded by diarist Charlotte Bourne as a visitor to her house on at least three occasions early in 1847.[23] At some point a spark of romance seems to have been kindled between him and the unattached Lucy. Although nearly 20 years her senior, he would have appeared to her as a man of action, someone about to embark on a

---

23. *Russian Chit-Chat, or sketches of a residence in Russia, By a Lady, Ed. by her sister*, Longman, Brown, Green, Longmans and Roberts, London, 1856. Charlotte was employed by Senator Iurii Alekseevich Dolgoruki and his wife Elizaveta Dolgorukaia.

fabulously romantic journey, painting the wildernesses of Siberia and dealing with the ferocious tribesmen of the Steppes.

But for now nothing was to pass between the two. Thomas continued to make his preparations to leave and Lucy continued teaching her pupil the rudiments of French, English and Arithmetic. Before finally leaving for the East Thomas made contact with yet another source, this time a mining engineer introduced to him by the minister of finance, who had previously worked in the Altai. "From him I collected much valuable information relative to my route," says Thomas.[24]

THOMAS' FIRST JOURNEY TO THE ALTAI AND NORTHERN KAZAKH STEPPE

Early in the spring of 1847 Thomas Atkinson set off on the first leg of his journey from St Petersburg for Moscow, where he stayed for a few weeks. Thomas also met with the German-born Dr Sebastian Fischer, who until 1841 was head of the central military hospital at Qasr-el-Aini in Egypt and who was an expert on crustaceans. Fischer wrote letters of introduction for Thomas to Dr Friedrich August von Gebler (1782-1850), inspector of hospitals in the Altai region, with whom Thomas later spent many evenings in Barnaul. We will come back to him later.

After 15 days in Moscow, Thomas was off again, leaving for Ekaterinburg and the east on 5 March 1847. It would be almost a year before he returned. The rest of the summer was spent touring around the numerous mines and workshops of the Urals and completing a set of 12 paintings of the River Chusovaya, which can now be found in the collection of the Hermitage in St Petersburg. He also completed a number of paintings of Nevyansk and scenes in the Altai Mountains. By mid-July, he had completed his tour of the northern Urals and having reached Ekaterinburg, he then set off for the mines and forging mills in the industrial towns of the southern Urals.

One of the first things Thomas did on arriving in Barnaul on 4 August was to write a long letter to Lucy. He had written to her from

24. *OWS, op. cit.,* p. 2.

Kammensky *en route* from Ekaterinburg, leaving the letter with the post-house where it would have been picked up by a courier heading in the opposite direction, but he would have been anxious to tell her of his latest adventures. In fact, we can see from his 1847 diary that he wrote to Lucy 65 times during his year away from her. He notes in great detail the date of each letter he sent, giving each one a number, recording the place from which he wrote and the day on which he expected her to receive it in St Petersburg. Seldom did a week go by without a letter being sent – and presumably received, although none of these letters survive.

Sadly, we will never know precisely how Thomas courted Lucy via these letters from east of the Urals, but as they were the only form of communication available to the couple, we can be sure that they must have had an strong effect on her, as it was on the strength of what she read that she took the decision to give up her employment as a governess with the Muravyev family and to travel with Thomas in Siberia, despite the fact that she had barely ridden a horse in her life before this time.

After a few days' rest, on 8 August, Thomas and Charles Austin left Barnaul by *tarantass* (horse-drawn carriage) heading south, this time towards the Altai. They were beginning to leave the forests behind and enter into the steppelands. On 10 August at eight in the evening, after travelling along the valley of the Tchurish (Charysh) river, they arrived at Kolyvan Lake where Thomas, like many visitors before and since, was struck by the curious rock formations, which he sketched. Many of the great geographers, including the Germans Peter Simon Pallas, von Humboldt and Johann Friedrich Gmelin, also passed this way. "Nowhere else have I ever seen such beauty," wrote Pallas. Thomas returned to the lake on several occasions in later years to sketch and admire the views. About 40 miles to the south he could just make out where the foothills of the Altai merged into the Kazakh Steppe.

Steadily, the two men made their way southwards through the Altai region. At one point Thomas got his first glimpse of Bielukha, the biggest of the Altai Mountains, lying towards the south, its double peak surrounded by many other snowy crests. "Such scenes, and many others through which I have passed, offer most glorious studies to the lover of Nature, possessed of sufficient courage to woo her in these sublime regions when bedecked in her wild and gorgeous attire."[25]

It was now the beginning of September and snow had already fallen on some of the peaks. The party was now approaching the Bouchtarma river, which they crossed in a dugout canoe while the horses were swum across. On 2 September they reached Zyryanovsk, now in northern Kazakhstan, and rested up the following day, with Thomas and Charles Austin having dinner with the director of mines. This was then the most valuable silver-mining site in the Altai, but today is known mostly for lead and zinc, the silver having been largely worked out. More than 2,000 horses were employed in taking the silver ore to the smelting works in Barnaul, almost 1,000 km to the north.

Each day now the weather was deteriorating. It snowed on 4 September and the next day the ground was frozen hard, with a bitter wind. Two days later Thomas rode back to the Bouchtarma to sketch. The following day he was ill and stayed in town, writing a long letter to Lucy. On the 9th he was up at 4.30am to make a journey towards the Chinese border. His intention was to visit the lake of Nor Zaisan, but this was a sensitive area and he needed permission from the Cossack officer in charge of the region. Eventually the colonel commanding the district appeared and agreed that Thomas could pass the frontier and sketch wherever he wished but warned that the route he proposed to take was now blocked by snow in the mountains. Instead, said the colonel, he should get to Ust-Kamenogorsk and then head south into the steppe, following from one Cossack post to another until he reached the fortress at Kockbouchta.

From Zyryanovsk he reached the fort at Great Narym (Bolshenarymskoye), where all the inhabitants were Cossacks. That evening his party entered the Irtysh valley near where the Narym joins it. "The river once formed the boundary of the Russian Empire," Thomas noted almost wistfully. "The opposite banks is the Kazakh Steppe, which is gradually being absorbed."

On the 16th, for the first time Thomas visited a Kazakh *aoul* (camp) where, he notes in his diary, he found the chief "a very fine fellow".

25. *Ibid*, p. 210.

"He had us put into a yourt, carpets spread and gave us *koumis*[26] and afterwards tea. He arranged that some of his own horses should take us back and rode a little distance with us. He gave me a whip and I presented him with a knife. His son gave Austin a piece of voilock."[27]

The next day, having finished a long letter to Lucy, Thomas and Austin set off south at 1pm into the steppe. To the west about 20 miles away, the Monastir Mountains loomed over the steppes. Not far from here, they found several large tombs, consisting of a large basement about 12 ft square and eight feet high. On top there was a small pyramid. Nearby was what Thomas described as a temple – a platform some 17 feet high, oriented north-south with the granite bases of columns still visible He drew a plan of the place (now lost) and described the broken pottery he found in his diary: "I found many pieces coloured blue, some red and Austin found one striped red and grey. I also found parts of mouldings and some small ornaments in terracotta. It is somewhat difficult to see if a style of architecture has been employed. All the columns are gone and nothing left on the platform excepting the bases of columns and a few straight slabs of granite that may have been steps; in fact two are in their original position, one at the front entrance and the other I have marked on my plan. On the west side are lying four blocks of granite, one of which has a round hole made into it 15 inches in diameter and 15 inches deep. This may have been the altar on which the victims were immolated. The other three have formed a channel through the wall to carry off the water used in the sacrifice. Altogether this is a most interesting spot and one that affords matter for which speculation as to what people inhabited this place and erected such buildings; in all the valleys there are tombs, square masses of rough stone with a raised part in the centre."[28]

Speculation about the original builders of these tombs and monuments continues to this day. From his description, this temple

---

26. Fermented mare's milk and the preferred beverage for the steppe nomads. Only slightly alcoholic, it is the staple drink throughout the summer.

27. Felt, used by the Kazakh nomads to make their yurts, as well as boots and cloaks.

28. T W Atkinson, 1847 diary, RGS, SSC/143/1 [1847].

is probably the ancient Buddhist temple at Ablaikit, first described by Pallas.[29]

A few days later, having sketched at the Monastir Mountains, Thomas and Austin arrived at the *aoul* of Mohamed, a celebrated local chieftain, where they were amazed at the huge herds of horses and camels, along with sheep and goats. Mohamed himself came out to greet Thomas, taking his bridle and helping him off his horse. Once sat down, the first thing he and his three sons did was to ask to examine Thomas' pistols, which he removed from their holsters, stepping outside to give a demonstration on how they were fired. They had not seen firing caps before, having only used muzzle-loading rifles, and were deeply astonished.

Thomas provides a detailed description of Mohamed and his way of life,[30] noting his clothing, his hawk chained to a perch, the construction of the yurt, together with its fittings, the method of making *koumis* and the management of horses. He examined the horse tack in detail, noting the decorated harnesses and saddles, the ropes and thongs, the leather *tchimbar* (trousers) worn by Kazakhs and many other details. This is certainly one of the earliest and most complete descriptions of a typical Kazakh *aoul*, added to which, Thomas was able to describe the preoccupations of its inhabitants and their way of life. He counted 106 camels, more than 2,000 horses, 1,000 oxen and cows and 6,000 sheep and goats and remarks that the chief had two further *aouls* with even more animals.

The following day he set off to sketch at the Monastir Mountains, which he said the local tribes would not stay near overnight. The next few days were spent exploring the area and sketching wherever possible. One night he was awoken at about two in the morning by the sounds of confusion: "At first I thought it was the rumbling of an earthquake and instantly sat upright; the sound rolled on, approaching nearer and nearer. Presently it passed and the earth shook – it was the whole

---

29. The ruins at Ablaikit were first discovered by Cossacks in 1721. At that time more than 1,500 folios were found, most of them Tibetan or Mongolia Buddhist documents. These are now in the St Petersburg Institute of Oriental Manuscripts. See http://www.orientalstudies.ru/eng/index.php?option=content&task=view&id=2065.

30. See *OWS, op. cit.*, pp. 284-9.

herd of horses dashing past at full gallop. Now came shrieks and the shouting of men, from which I at once knew that robbers had invaded the *aoul*. It was but the work of a moment to seize the rifle standing close to my head and rush out of the yurt, when I beheld the Kazakhs with the battle-axes in their hands, spring upon their horses and dash off towards the place where we heard the shouting."[31]

Thomas had experienced his first *barimta* (raid). He picked up a gun and fired after the robbers as they galloped past with frightened horses scattering in front of them, and a group of men from the *aoul* mounted their horses to give chase. But they were quickly back having found that there were three times as many robbers and that they were prepared to defend their ill-gotten gains. "I deeply regretted it was not daylight," wrote Thomas. "Had it been so, some of these desperate fellows would have bit the dust, as they passed in one thick mass within pistol-shot; and the rifles would have brought them down at a long distance." The robbers had got away with about 100 horses. Undeterred, the next day he was off again, in the company of two Cossacks and three Kazakhs. He wore his pistols in his belt rather than in their holsters in case they came across any stragglers from the raiding party.

From Mohamed's *aoul*, Thomas decided to head back towards Ust-Kamenogorsk (Oskemen), stopping at another *aoul* on the way and avoiding heavy rain and sleet "so thick that we could not see any object at ten paces off". As was the case everywhere he visited on the steppes, Thomas was the object of much curiosity, with people seldom leaving him alone for long. The next day, with three Kazakhs and five spare horses to allow the riders to change and ride fast, they set off again towards the northeast and the Irtysh, about seven hours away. After enduring several soakings, he felt a fever coming on and by the time the party reached Ust-Kamenogorsk he could not even get onto his horse without assistance. A doctor was called and once again he went through the cycle of sauna baths and bleeding. It was another 11 days before he was strong enough to get up.

---

31. *Ibid*, p. 298.

After a hard journey via Riddersk and Zmeinogorsk, Thomas reached Barnaul on 1 November. The city had been built at the junction of the Barnaulka and Ob rivers, its streets laid out on a grid. Around 9,000 lb of silver were smelted there annually, as well as almost all the gold mined in Siberia. The latter was cast into bars and every year sent in six caravans to the mint at St Petersburg. It was the administrative centre of the mining industry and the *Natchalnik* – director of mines – lived there, along with the heads of the major departments. According to Thomas, the town's leading citizens were not poor: "I must say that the mining population of the Altai are more wealthy, cleanly and surrounded by more comforts than any other people in the Empire."

In Barnaul Thomas was to meet a man who became a good friend in the short time they knew each other. Dr Friedrich August von Gebler (1782-1850), a German intellectual and correspondent and collaborator with von Humboldt, was inspector of hospitals for the Altai and was also a distinguished naturalist and collector. He supplied specimens of birds and insects to several museums, including the British Museum in London. He had also travelled extensively through the Altai and had collected a huge herbarium of around 1,200 Altai plants, 15 of them previously unknown. His *Overview of the Katun Mountains, the Highest Peaks of Russian Altai*[32] for the first time described the Mount Belukha glaciers and contains the first map of the region. He located the source of the River Katun and also founded the museum in Barnaul. He was awarded three orders of the Russian Empire for his botanical and entomological discoveries.

Gebler was certainly regarded highly by Thomas, as contained among surviving family papers in the Dahlquist Collection is a handwritten 13-page manuscript, probably written by Lucy, entitled "Survey of the Katun Mountains, the highest peak of the Russian Altai by Dr Frederick Gebler". This manuscript is a translation of part of Gebler's paper, none of which had never been translated into English, either before or since. Presumably Lucy was able to make the translation during one of several stays in the city. Speaking of Gebler, Thomas says he "spent many happy

---

32. Published as vol. III of *Mémoires des Savants Etrangers*, St Petersburg, 1837.

hours in his company during my first winter in Barnaul. On his journey of inspection to the different mines he had visited many interesting places in the Altai and from him I gathered much information relative to my journey in these regions."[33]

Thomas had now almost completed his first year of travel. Having journeyed east from St Petersburg he had visited the Ural mining districts, the impressive Altai Mountains and the northeast of the untracked Central Asian steppes. If anything, at this point he was an explorer of Central Asia. Once on horseback and out on the steppes he appears to have been in his element, taking whatever chances he could to visit areas never before visited by Europeans and enjoying the company of the nomads he met on the way. He related to the tribal leaders he met with humanity, showing none of the arrogance or superiority that mars other narratives. He also seems to have been very happy with the opportunities he found for sketching the great vistas and scenes of wild nature that greeted him along his route. Already at the end of this first year he must have had a sketchbook full of ideas that he could bring to fruition over the winter.

While staying in Barnaul Thomas wrote to Lucy at least once a week back in St Petersburg. Their romance was flourishing. At some point towards the end of 1847 – the exact date is not known – Lucy and Thomas decided that they should meet up again. What we know from his diary is that he left Barnaul in a sledge lent to him by the inspector of mines, Colonel Sokolovsky, on 13 January, travelling non-stop via Tomsk, Kiansk and Ekaterinburg and arriving in Moscow on 7 February, after an absence of 11 months. He immediately wrote to Lucy in St Petersburg and she arrived in Moscow at nine in the evening on 16 February. Two days later, in the chapel of the British consulate, they were married.

The entry in the books states: "Thomas Witlam Atkinson, native of Silkstone in the county of York in England, widower, artist by profession, of the English church, and Lucy Sherrard Finley, spinster, late resident in St Petersburg, also of the English church, were married according to the rites and ceremonies of the Church of England this 18th day of February."

---

33. OWS, *op. cit.*, p. 331.

The witnesses to the wedding were Basil Kapnist, Lisa Kapnist and Euphrasia Morrison. Basil and Lisa were the son and daughter of Ivan Vasilievich Kapnist, who was the civilian Governor of Moscow and therefore an important public official. The Kapnist family was related to the Muravyevs by marriage and it seems likely that Lucy knew them because of her position in the Muravyev household. She refers to them in her own book as "our friends the Kapnists". That was the reason they decided to attend the wedding. Lucy says she stayed at their grand mansion on Tverskoye Street in Moscow prior to the wedding.

THE JOURNEY TO THE ALTAI AND THE KAZAKH STEPPES

We can only begin to imagine what was passing through the minds of Thomas and Lucy as they left Moscow in Colonel Solokovsky's sledge on 20 February 1848. Lucy had given up a secure position with one of the grandest families in Russia, through whom she had met many of the most prominent figures in the Imperial court. She was now intent on spending the next few years travelling through the wildernesses of Siberia and the Kazakh Steppes with a man she barely knew. She was not at all used to such a life, having had no experience of horses or living rough. But something about Thomas had undoubtedly caught her imagination and she did not stint in her commitment.

We do not know if she had to be persuaded to travel with Thomas, or if she was a willing collaborator in a journey that was to last for the following five years and take them to some of the remotest (and bleakest) places on earth. From everything she wrote in her own book, she seems to have been full of enthusiasm for the journey and seldom departs from a narrative that suggests huge enjoyment and satisfaction with the adventurous journey, although her joy is often tempered with sadness and concern for the plight of the political exiles, whose families she had got to know – including the Muravyevs themselves – during her previous eight years in Russia.

As for Thomas, for most of his first year he had travelled with fellow Englishman Charles Austin, who knew the ropes and spoke some Russian. But they had gone their separate ways, with Austin heading for Irkutsk, whereas Thomas, after travelling back to Moscow to meet and marry Lucy, wanted to return to the steppes. Was Thomas willing to marry Lucy – albeit bigamously – because she would be able to make his journey much easier? Before seeing Thomas' diaries that thought had occurred to me, and other writers have suggested a utilitarian motive for his decision to marry Lucy. But he is so warm towards her in the diaries that it is difficult to believe that it was not a love match. After all, how did he know she would not be a drag on him, asking to go back at the earliest opportunity and creating all kinds of problems once they got into the remote areas? She had no experience of rough travel, and had barely been out of a city before. Thomas was taking a huge risk and it makes much more sense to conclude that he was willing to travel with her because he loved her and because she wanted to travel with him, rather than believing he took her along simply because she could be useful to him.

The first stage of their journey, to Ekaterinburg, was scheduled to take them 12 days and nights of near-continuous travel in the sledge borrowed from Colonel Sokolovsky. On leaving Moscow on 20 February they travelled east via Petooshka (today Petushki) on the left bank of the Klyazma river, and then on to Nijni Novgorod. Their efforts to get back on the road quickly were thwarted by the town's governor, Prince Ourosoff, and his wife, who insisted that Thomas and Lucy stay at least until nightfall when the roads would freeze over again and make it easier for the sledge to move. They eventually got going at 10pm, their sledge running on the ice of the Volga. A sledge in front of them had gone through the ice, but they were luckier, although Lucy soon found that the bitter wind had begun to cut her face and lips, and took to wearing a muslin cloth over her head in the open sledge.

After more adventures on the road, including becoming stuck fast in the snow, they arrived at 4pm on 27 March in Omsk where the local police master treated them very badly and directed them to a common lodging house on the outskirts of the town. They survived the night, and the following day went to see Prince Pyotr Dmitrievich Gorchakov (1790-1868), the Governor of Western Siberia, to present their papers. Gorchakov asked to see Thomas' paintings which were shown later in the evening to a large gathering.

Thomas presented one of his pictures to the prince and promised to send him another large painting showing a view of the River Irtysh. The prince asked to be forgiven for not inviting Lucy, explaining that it was because he had no other women available to join the party. The next day the prince specifically requested that Lucy should come to dinner, even though he only had his staff in attendance. He also agreed to allow the couple to travel south through the steppes to the newly-founded town of Kopal in the shadow of the Alatau Mountains, generously providing Thomas with a map of the steppes and a letter of introduction to the Governor of Tomsk.

As they approached Tomsk, the snow was becoming thinner and thinner. They finally arrived on 4 April, glad not to have to travel any further on the broken *trakt,* which Lucy said reminded her of sailing over a rough sea. They were put up in the governor's residence even though he and his family were in Barnaul. With the roads now in very poor condition, they were stuck in Tomsk for more than a month, until the roads had dried out sufficiently to pass on to Barnaul. The only public dining room in the town was run by a German giantess and a dwarf albino who had once been part of a travelling circus: "These two, weary of the life they were leading, agreed to marry and settle down, she being an excellent cook, and he a good hand at making port wine", wrote Lucy.

They eventually left Tomsk on 3 June at 8am. Before leaving, their friends the Asterhoffs presented Lucy with a beautiful rifle made by Orloff in St Petersburg. By this time most of the snow had gone and now the countryside was covered in the most beautiful wild flowers – "globe anemone, forget-me-nots, deep blue iris and many others." When Thomas had passed this way in February there had been 43 degrees of frost. Now the main problem was flooding. Often they were moving along through water that reached up to the axles of their carriage. When they eventually reached the valley of the Ob on 6 June – 18 June according to the Old Calendar – they could see it had overflowed the banks and in places was more than 20 km wide.

Lucy says that they had been plagued by mosquitoes as they approached the Ob, made much worse for them by the lack of a breeze and their slow progress due to the flooding. In desperation for some wind, Lucy suggested that Thomas should try the "sailor's remedy" (urinating into the sea) when overtaken by a calm. This he did and in no time a strong wind had sprung up, which turned into a fierce storm that prevented them crossing until the following day – and even then it took three hours. They spent the night huddled in their carriage. "It gave us something to laugh at, and I made a promise never to be caught meddling with the wind again," wrote Lucy.

On 7 June, once they had crossed the Ob, it was a comparatively short ride to Barnaul, where they made for the house of Thomas' friends, the Strolemans, who were delighted to put them up for as long as they wanted. The next day a series of introductions began, where Thomas showed off his new wife to the friends he had left almost six months before. There was Madame Anosov, the wife of Major-General Pavel Petrovich Anosov, the Governor of Tomsk, and Madame Sokolovsky, wife of the director of mines for the Altai, along with Madame Kavanko. That evening General Anosov and Colonel Sokolovsky returned from their trip. Lucy presented the colonel with one of Thomas' pictures of Kolyvan Lake in the Altai as a thank-you gift for the loan of the sledge which Thomas had used to travel to Moscow and back. The next day General Anosov was presented with a watercolour of the Ouba river. "The General said I had painted Siberia as it is, that there was nature in all my works and not fancy," Thomas recorded in his diary.

Thomas left Lucy in Barnaul for several weeks while he and Colonel Sokolovsky went on a snipe shooting expedition along the River Mrassa and then on to the upper part of the River Tom, where the colonel was due to inspect the gold mines. She knew that Thomas was due at some point to make a trip to Lake Altin Kool (now known as Lake Teleskoye) and the other women of Barnaul tried very hard to discourage her from making the trip. "They say it is ridiculous," she wrote, "the idea of my going, as the gentlemen get thoroughly knocked up who have ventured so far; however, I have a little wilfulness in my disposition, and am determined to try, and it will be rather odd if I do not succeed. One lady says I may be able to ride one or two days, and she will even give me three, but more it is impossible to do; so they expect me to return alone."[34] How wrong they were!

On 9 July, two days after Thomas returned from the Mrassa river, they set off from Barnaul for Biysk and then on to Lake Altin Kool. Before leaving Thomas arranged to meet Colonel Sokolovsky in Zmeinogorsk

---

34. *Recollections, op. cit.*, pp. 46-7.

and left their spare baggage with him, carefully listed in his diary. Thomas lost his *tchube* (fur cloak) on the way, but a Cossack sent back to search for it found it lying by the road. In Biysk they were met by Colonel Keil, commander of the Cossack detachment, who was very helpful and provided useful information on the steppes. His wife, deputed to look after Lucy, was less endearing: "From her I would defy anyone to gain information upon any subject, excepting it might be dirt! And on this point, I fancy her information would be original."

On leaving Biysk the Atkinsons travelled along hills that overlooked the valley of the River Bia, which flowed out of Lake Altin Kool. It was a hard journey. Their next stop was Sandhyp on 12 July, which was occupied by Cossacks and their families only. From now on they would have to travel on horseback as the track was too difficult for carriages. This meant jettisoning yet more of their clothing and equipment, to be picked up on their return. The following day as they left the village they were followed by the Cossack women. Lucy recalled: "One old woman with tears had entreated me not to go, no lady had ever attempted the journey before. There were Kalmyk women living beyond, but they had never seen them. In the early part of the day she had offered to let her daughter go to take care of me; however, when the daughter came in, a healthy, strong girl, some thirty-five summers old, she stoutly refused (to my delight) to move; the mother tried to persuade, and did all she could, it was of no use; and I was left in peace."[35]

Lucy relates that she brought a beautiful side saddle with her from Moscow but when Colonel Sokolovsky had seen it, he had warned her against its use, saying it would be no good in the mountains. Instead, he lent her one of his own, about which she had no regrets: "At times, we have had ledges of rock to ride round, where, had I had a side-saddle, my legs would have been crushed to pieces or torn off. At times, I have had to lift my feet on to the saddle, there being barely room for the horse to pass between high masses of rock. Then there were passes to ride over, formed by the granite mountains, in places quite perpendicular down to the Bïa. Our horses have stood on many points, where we could see the

---

35. *Ibid*, p. 53.

water boiling and foaming probably 1,000 feet below us; just imagine me on one of these places with a side-saddle!"[36] So, unusually for the time, she rode *en cavalier*, wearing trousers rather than a skirt.

The next day, they rode until eight in the evening, at which point their Cossacks built them a *balagan* – a kind of lean-to shelter. Lucy records that by hanging a sheet up at the open side, she was able to undress. She was less impressed by Thomas' habits and soon told him so: "I now found that Mr. Atkinson had been in the habit of sleeping amongst these wandering tribes without doing so. I told him, without undressing I should soon be knocked up, and advised his following my example, which he did, and continued doing so with benefit to himself."

By this time, in early July, Lucy must have known that she was pregnant. And yet she never mentions the fact in *Recollections* until the birth has actually occurred. Did she keep it secret from Thomas, anxious in case he sent her back to Barnaul? That seems likely, as his diary too mentions nothing about her pregnancy. For the first few days on horseback she found the going hard, but, as she says, "I determined to conquer this weakness." Soon she was riding like a veteran.

Their party now consisted of a *talmash* (camp organiser and translator), a Cossack and five Kalmyks, plus eleven horses. By Wednesday 14 July they reached a Kalmyk village beyond the River Lebed, having travelled 65 *versts* that day. The next day, as they neared the summit of some high granite rocks, Lucy's horse stumbled and she almost fell, but managed to keep her seat, much to the admiration of the Kalmyks. After 50 *versts* they reached another Kalmyk village where they witnessed a remarkable scene. As they sat eating dinner, they saw a young girl running towards the River Bïa, pursued by a man on a horse, with others following on foot. As soon as she reached the riverbank, the young girl threw off her headdress and leaped into the water, where she was swept downstream. Two men following along the bank jumped in and one of them pulled her out, still alive. It transpired that the man on horseback was her brother and that she had jumped into the river to

---

36. *Ibid*, p. 54.

avoid being married off to an old man she did not love. The young girl survived, but the Atkinsons never found out who she married.

A similar event occurred the following day, but this time Thomas was asked to exercise the Judgement of Solomon. In a Kalmyk village they found a group of men surrounding an old woman, and, a short distance from them, a group of girls assembled around a very pretty young girl of about 16, who appeared quite unconcerned, and was busy cracking nuts. She was the woman's daughter and the six men were all suitors, one of whom the mother thought a good match.

Thomas was asked to decide the case, with each man pleading his cause. Lucy says that the most eloquent of all was an old man who spoke of his possessions, his lands, his herds of cattle, his position as the chief of the village, and finally of the great love he had for the young girl. Thomas listened as all the speeches were translated and then asked the young girl to step forward. He asked her, through the interpreter, which of the suitors she preferred. She resolutely rejected all of them, as a result of which Thomas suggested that it would be better for her to remain with her mother until she found the man she wanted to marry. "The lovers retired satisfied, since no one had obtained more favour than the other," wrote Lucy. "The young girl thanked Mr. Atkinson by a smile, but the mother looked disappointed, as she had pleaded for the old man, whose age appeared more suited to the mother than to the daughter, he being the old woman's senior by many years."

A day later, on Saturday 17 July, an incident occurred that was undoubtedly a great test for Lucy. Faced with very steep cliffs, they decided to take the horses around a point that jutted out into the river, which here was a torrent. There was a narrow ledge, but even so, the water was up to the horses' saddle-flaps. One step away from the rock was deep, fast water. As Thomas records in his diary: "All passed well except Lucy. The Cossack who led her horse did not keep him close to the rock. In two or three steps he was in deep water and swimming. Our guide saw this and called to the Cossack to hold the horse just by the bridle or they would both be lost. Lucy sat quite still (tho' the water filled her boots) and was drawn round the point and landed in safety. This was truly a most dangerous place."

Lucy recalled that an old Kalmyk woman who had joined the party screamed out as she languished in the deep water. But her calmness and decision to sit still as the Cossack grabbed hold of the bridle saved her. Thomas makes no mention of this event in his book, merely stating that "after a difficult and sometimes dangerous ride on horseback over a wild mountain region, we made our first night's lodging in a *balagan* on the Altin Kool or Golden Lake,"[37] but his diary notes make clear his admiration for Lucy over this incident. Not for the last time did his published narrative lose something through his decision not to tell anyone about Lucy.

They reached the lake that evening, just as the sun was setting and camped close to where the River Bia debouches from the lake and near the present-day village of Artybash. It was a magical moment for Lucy: "It was one of the most lovely scenes that could well be imagined; a bright sun shed its light over lake and mountain; the water was calm and shining like molten gold, in which the rocks, trees, and mountains were reflected as in a mirror, redoubling the beauty of the scene. We sat on our horses looking at this picture for a long time, enraptured by its beauty. It repaid us well for all our toils, and, when contrasted with the rugged scenes we had passed over, this was like enchantment; and still more so as I looked around, for mountains rose up on every side, with apparently no outlet: it was as if we had been dropped down from the clouds into fairy land."[38] This painting also complements the sepia-tinted lithograph entitled *Altin-Kool, Altai Mountains* that appears in *Oriental and Western Siberia*.[39]

To this day, Lake Teletskoye, as it is now called, is regarded as one of the great natural beauties of the Altai region and is part of a World Heritage site. Almost 80 km long, 5 km wide and surrounded by high mountains, it is over 365 m deep in parts. Lucy was almost certainly the first European woman ever to visit the lake.

That evening Thomas and Lucy took a boat to the other side of the lake to a headland from where he could sketch. On their way back Thomas

---

37. *OWS, op. cit.*, p. 363.

38. *Recollections, op. cit.*, p. 62.

39. *OWS, op. cit.*, opposite p. 363.

decided to start playing his flute, which he carried with him throughout his travels. The sound of the flute had an almost magical effect on the local Kalmyks, many of whom had arrived to look at the strangers. As soon as he got out of the boat, Thomas was surrounded by them, begging that he should continue to play. "The power he gained over these simple-hearted people by his music was extraordinary," wrote Lucy. "We travelled round the lake in small boats, it was a tour of eleven days, and in all that time he never once lost his influence; like Orpheus, he enchanted all who heard him; without a murmur they obeyed him in everything; indeed, there was often a dispute to ascertain which might do his bidding; and there was no lack of hands to spin the line which was required to sound the lake."

By now their party consisted of two Cossacks, the *talmash* and 11 Kalmyk boatmen, and the next day they set out to explore the lake in five canoes, some of them fastened together. They were caught in one of the many storms that sweep across the lake and had to put in for safety. It was an unpleasant surprise for Lucy, who said she had never experienced anything like it before. Their campsite was recorded by Thomas in a remarkable painting that is now at the Royal Geographical Society – although unfortunately it is not on display. *A night scene at our encampment on the Altin-Kool, Altai Mountains*[40] shows Thomas and Lucy resting under an open-sided shelter, while their Kalmyks are gathered round a raging fire. Lucy described it thus: "We went for a short walk along the shore; on returning, and as we drew near our bivouac, one of the wildest scenes I had ever witnessed came into view. Three enormous fires piled high were blazing brightly. Our Kalmyk boatmen and Cossacks were seated around them, the lurid light shone upon their faces and upon the trees above, giving the men the appearance of ferocious savages; in the foreground was our little leafy dwelling, with its fire burning calmly but cheerfully in front of it."[41]

Lucy took the opportunity to improve her marksmanship in the forests surrounding the lake. She now had four weapons: a small rifle

---

40. RGS, 700114. The painting, along with three others held by the RGS, once belonged to Sir Roderick Murchison.

41. *Recollections, op. cit.*, pp. 66-7.

given to her by Mr Tate, the Orloff shotgun presented to her by Mr Asterhoff and a pair of pistols she kept in her saddlebags. When she shot a squirrel, a Kalmyk begged her to allow him to have it for his supper, which she agreed to as long as she could have the skin. She says that the Kalmyks were not too fussy about what they ate, even eating the odd lynx that Thomas shot.

One night around 20 Kalmyks came into their camp and sat around the blazing fire. Soon their arms were slipped out of their fur coats and they sat with their entire upper body exposed, their queues hanging down from the back of their heads. At one point a brawl almost broke out over some small pieces of coloured silk Lucy had given to some of the men, not helped by the fact that many of them were drunk. The couple were relieved when, shortly before midnight, the group upped and left.

Lucy was clearly enchanted by the lake and remarks that in years to come they would recall the happy times they had experienced there. This was her first real experience of outdoor adventure – riding horseback, camping in the wild, relying on the countryside for food – and she relished it. She would never lose her enthusiasm for rough travelling, even under the most difficult circumstances. After 11 days, having thoroughly explored the lake and completed a circumnavigation, they set off back along the Bia river, making a raft at one point and then gliding gracefully back to Sandyp.

Their next objective was to be the Kazakh Steppe, where they hoped to reach the distant settlement of Kopal far to the south. First, they travelled via the Katun river valley through the mountains on a journey that took almost three weeks, often riding well above the snowline. At one point they got their first views of Mount Bielukha, the grandest of the Altai Mountains, "looking like a ruby encircled by diamonds", is how Lucy described the peak. This was very difficult and dangerous terrain, but the horses were magnificent, despite the fact they were unshod.

Having reached the village of Kokshinska late at night, Lucy was exhausted: "I had been so many hours on my horse, and had passed over such frightfully difficult roads, that when we stopped, I was actually obliged to be led, for I could not stand, my limbs were so benumbed. After lying on the bench in the cottage for a few seconds, I recovered. There was no possibility of giving way to fatigue on this journey; I had all kinds of duties to perform. The next day, after bathing, I was all right again. I have generally been able to bathe every morning and evening this summer, and sometimes in the middle of the day; without doing so, I do not believe I should have accomplished the journey half as well."[42] A young girl in the village refused to believe that they had come down the mountainside at night, saying it was near impossible, even during the day.

Their intention was to travel on to Mount Bielukha and get as close as possible to the summit. But on 3 August they reluctantly decided to turn away, hoping to return another day. By now snow was starting to fall and they would certainly have perished if they had pushed on. Instead they continued to descend the Katun and then across the Yabagan Steppe, where they found a Kalmyk *aoul* and a shaman, who beat his drum for them. Thomas sketched him, although the old man thought that his spirit was in danger of being captured.

After many days riding through the mountains, finally on 26 August they made it to Zmeinogorsk, where they stayed at the house of Colonel Gerngrose, who was known to Thomas and who was director of the silver smelting works. For the first time since Barnaul Thomas and Lucy slept in a bed: "Oh what a luxury it seemed to be, and how I enjoyed it", Lucy wrote.

A week later, at 7pm on 2 September, they set off once again, heading for Semipolatinsk (now Semey in Kazakhstan). By midday the next day they were on the banks of the River Irtysh, crossing it by moonlight that night. It was 6am on Saturday 4 September when they reached Semipolatinsk, where Thomas showed his letter from Prince Gorchakov to the police master, who said he had already received orders from the prince. The following day they began what was to become an epic journey, heading for the distant Cossack outpost of Kopal, 1,000 km away to the south.

Why Thomas had chosen Kopal as his destination is not clear. He may have heard about it from some of the military officers they met on the way. Or it may have been suggested by Colonel Sokolovsky or General Anosov, who would have known about the Cossack expedition the previous year that first reached the small encampment lying on the plain beneath the

---

42. *Ibid*, p. 76.

Alatau Mountains. They had sent a battery of mountains guns to protect the encampment and only weeks before a larger expeditionary force of Cossacks, together with their wives and families, had set off on the long march southwards. It was not an easy journey and several of the Cossacks had died on the way, as Thomas and Lucy were to see for themselves when they came upon their graves in the steppes.

Whatever the reason, they were now well on their way. Thomas was, by this time, already a seasoned traveller having followed much of this route down to the Kazakh steppes the year before. He was confident and experienced. For Lucy, though, it was a completely different experience. Although she had now been in the saddle for two months, travelling hundreds of kilometres across very rough terrain, this was still new to her and her pregnancy must have made this a particularly hard journey. And yet she showed no signs at all of backing out. In fact, very much the opposite. She appears to have relished the journey and only seldom loses her sense of fun and adventure on what was to become the toughest journey of her life.

Thomas and Lucy set off south from Semipolatinsk in what is now northern Kazakhstan across the vast steppes towards the Alatau Mountains on 6 September 1848. The road then, as today, runs almost due south through a desolate landscape of scrubby grass, rocks and salt lakes.

The travelling was hard and they managed only five *versts* an hour and had to stop frequently to rest the horses. Lucy says that at times it required eight horses to drag the carriage out of the bogs, which had been made worse by overnight rain. On the 7th they saw the Arkat Mountains – also known as the Monastir Mountains – in the distance and by midday had made it to the Cossack picquet, where Thomas sat down to sketch. A lithograph of his drawing can be seen in *Travels in the Region of the Upper and Lower Amoor*. Little has changed in this area in more than 160 years. There are few habitations, the road is poor and there are few, if any, signs of cultivation. The nomad yurts, visible in Thomas' watercolour, are long gone, although the return to Kazakhstan in recent years of Kazakhs who had fled across the Tien Shan to China, has seen a small influx of people who still lead a semi-traditional lifestyle.

On 9 September Thomas and Lucy arrived in Ayaguz, a fortress and home to 800 Cossacks, but now without artillery, which had been sent further to the south. The commander was away, but once again the officer in charge had already been informed of their impending arrival. In the morning they got ready to move out, this time on horseback, leaving their carriage in the care of a Cossack officer. Now, in addition to Cossacks, they were accompanied by a group of Kazakhs, who Thomas said had a "strong and wild appearance". The terrain was now sand and low hills, with little vegetation. That night they slept in a Kazakh *aoul* on the bank of a small stream in a yurt erected for them under the direction of their Cossack Peter. Their host was a wealthy Kazakh who decorated the yurt with *voilock* (felt cloth) and beautiful carpets. A sheep was killed and cooked in a large cauldron. Thomas says this was the first place they saw sheep being milked.

On Friday 10 September camels were added to the Atkinsons' baggage train for the first time, which now consisted of three Cossacks, five Kazakhs, plus the Kazakh host and his attendants. From here on the land took on an even more desolate character, with no trees or bushes or any sign of vegetation. West of them lay a large saline lake, which Thomas names as Yakshe Kessile-Tuz, surrounded by red vegetation indicating its salinity. This lake, which now exists largely as a saltpan, is one of many vestigial lakes that are the remains of a watercourse that once linked the giant Lake Balkhash further westwards to Lake Sassykol ("smelly" lake) and Lake Ala Kol and also to Lake Ebi Nor in Western China.

At this point, Thomas' host appears to have lost the way. "Our host was now at a loss which way to proceed to find an *aoul*," he says in his diary. They rode on, coming across many tombs, several of considerable size and built in stone in a conical form. Some of these tombs can still be seen in the same region. Travelling this road in the summer of 2015, I was surprised at the shapes and sizes of these tombs. They were not built by the Kazakhs, said Thomas, but by a people "swept away ages ago".

In some places, efforts have been made in recent years to repair and replace the ancient tombs that can be found along some of the old trade routes. Just outside Kapanbulak, for example, can be found the Mausoleum of Kengirbay Zhandosuly, also known as Bi Ata. Born in 1735 and a member of the Argun tribe of the Tobkyty clan of the Middle Horde, his life is celebrated in many local poems and songs. The first mausoleum was built in 1825. This was replaced by a newer edifice in 1996 and construction of a magnificent new limestone building began in September 2015.

In his second travel book, *Travels in the Region of the Upper and Lower Amoor,* Thomas recalls that the journey from Ayaguz south to the River Bean and the Kara Tau Mountains that marked the southern boundary of the Kazakh Steppes took him about ten days.[43] It was, he says, the boundary between the pastures of the Great and Middle Hordes – two of the three hordes (*jus* in Kazakh) that make up the population, even today. He passes over these ten days briefly, noting only that the country "varied greatly in its aspects; arid steppes were frequently crossed, on which the grass was withered by the sun and the only patches of green were the salsola (saltwort) bordering the numerous salt lakes."

In fact, this journey was almost a complete disaster and it is only by the slimmest of chances that Lucy, now more than six months pregnant, made it at all. To find the full story, we have to rely on Thomas' diaries and a few references in Lucy's book.

Lucy writes that the Cossack women she met in Ayaguz advised her strongly against attempting the journey south to Kopal. Her response was remarkable: "They had heard of the great horrors and miseries endured by some of the wives of the Cossacks who had but lately crossed the steppe with their families on their way to the new fortress. They were convinced I should die ere I reached the place. I laughed at their fears, and assured them that it would cause me much anxiety to be left behind, and, even though they told me that death would be my lot if I went, still I was firm to my purpose. You know I am not easily intimidated when once I have made up my mind. I started on this journey, with the intention of accompanying my husband wherever he went, and no idle fears shall turn me; if he is able to accomplish it, so shall I be. I give in to no one for endurance."[44]

The ladies of Ayaguz prepared bread and salt for Lucy, plus little meat pies and an enormous water melon. She set off with "a great waving of caps and handkerchiefs". At their first stop Lucy was to have her first experience of the real steppe life: "Herds of cattle were seen in every direction, men and boys on horseback engaged driving them towards

---

43. *Amoor, op. cit.*

44. *Recollections, op. cit.*, p. 88.

the aoul, and a still stranger sight, women busy milking the sheep." It must have been an overwhelming sight, later sketched by Thomas.

Having described the hospitality of the Kazakh chieftain already mentioned by Thomas, she depicts the difficulty of the journey. Soon after leaving the chieftain she said they had difficulty finding drinking water. "I was completely parched with thirst. Several hours past and still no sign of water; at last, I observed a beautiful lake shining in the distance; to describe to you the joy I felt is impossible, no words of mine can give an adequate idea of my feelings."

Unfortunately, the "beautiful lake" turned out to be a mirage.

Soon after, they came upon a camel train which had left Kopal, far to the south, to collect salt. But they too had no water and were looking for somewhere they could find some. Thomas and Lucy's party soon after changed direction and then another disaster almost occurred when Lucy's horse bolted and she only avoided a nasty fall by grabbing its mane and holding fast to the reins. Another lake turned out to be saline. Women in a nearby yurt brought her milk and later mutton. The Atkinsons set off eastwards, in the direction of Lake Ala Kol, where they were assured they would find good water, but once again, on reaching the next *aoul* the water turned out to be little more than a brackish pool.

Lucy recalls that after leaving here their path was over marshy ground with tall reeds and bulrushes, followed by very high grass and swampy soil. At times they were up to the saddle-flaps in mud and water and then had to deal with a camel which lay down and refused to get up. Although they are not precise on the location, it sounds very much like Lake Sassykol, the large lake to the west of Ala Kol, which has miles of reeds and bogs on its banks.

By 13 September Thomas and Lucy could see for the first time the snowy peaks of the Alatau Mountains far to the south. "It is a day I shall never forget", wrote Lucy – and for good reason. They set off at 7 in the morning. Their Cossack Peter told them the ride would be 40 *versts*, although Alexae, the second Cossack, said it would be double that distance until they reached a place with good water. Both were wrong by a good margin. By 4pm that afternoon it was clear that they were no closer to their destination and so they began to eat the melon Lucy had been given in Ayaguz. For Lucy, this was the first time she had ever tasted melon: "It appeared to me the most delicious thing I had ever tasted in my life."

But still the journey went on, *verst* after *verst*. None of the Cossacks appeared to know where they were and even the Kazakhs could only point towards the distant mountains 40 or 50 *versts* away. As the sun began to sink, they kept on going, searching for any sign of habitation. By 2am the following morning there was still no *aoul* in sight and things were getting desperate. Lucy, by now freezing and exhausted, could scarcely hold the reins of her horse, having only a dress on. Her warm jacket had fallen from her horse earlier and not been noticed as missing until it was too late to go back. She lay down on a bearskin while Thomas put his fur-lined *tshuba* over her. He also gave her a glass of rum. After 30 minutes or so she began to revive. One of the Cossacks said they must remount immediately, otherwise they would all be lost. The horses would not go forward after the sun rose unless they first got to water.

With the *tshuba* tied over her, Lucy managed to move on for another two hours before once again dismounting and beginning to walk. Thomas persuaded her to get back on the horse again for another hour. Again she tried to dismount, telling Thomas to go on and bring water back for her. "My husband now held me by the hand, in the other I kept the reins, but that was all, I had no power to guide my poor horse." In his diary, which appears to be the source of Lucy's account of the whole saga, Thomas says that Lucy told him to let her die there on the steppe. "I now began to fear she would sink under this fatigue," he wrote.

As the sun began to rise, and in order to encourage her, Thomas told Lucy he thought he had heard a dog bark, a sure sign of nearby human settlement. "I told Lucy. She said I only fancied so or wished her to think so and go on, but she said it was impossible." She struggled on, but was now very weak. Soon after he heard the dogs again. "No music ever sounded so sweet in my ears and when Lucy heard them she cheered up and we went on," Thomas wrote in his diary. "At 5 o'clock we got to an aoul belonging to a mùllah. He did all that he could for us. Tea was soon made which we drank with infinite delight, but Lucy could eat nothing."

Not long after they were joined by one of the Cossacks he had sent forward earlier in the night to try to find the *aoul* they had been searching for, but who had also missed it. They eventually found it a few hours later and decided to halt there for the day to recover from what must have been a terrible ordeal, particularly for the heavily pregnant Lucy. Later that day Thomas reflected on the journey, which had totalled around 150 *versts*, sustained only by watermelon and a tot of rum: "The Cossacks were wrong in not ascertaining if water could be procured on our route, as the want of this when riding over the hot sand was severely felt by both of us – in August a party of Cossacks on their march to Kopal had crossed this part of the steppe. Several had died on the road. We saw their graves. These caused sad reflections as it might have been our case. We should (never) have been put into the sand without anyone knowing who or what we were."

Despite not mentioning this event in any of his public writings, in his diary Thomas is highly respectful of Lucy: "I can't speak too highly of Lucy's courage and endurance during 22 hours on horseback, frequently riding very fast in the day and then riding through the nights across such a desert. Here we might have been plundered and overpowered had some of the bands of *Baranta*[45] known of our march. Our arms were all kept in readiness and several would have bit the dust ere we had been taken. The part we rode over in the night was a most singular place. There must have been thousands of the conical mounds. Frequently we crossed them and at other times rode round their bases. I should like much to see this place in the daylight – still I have no wish for another such a ride under the same circumstances."[46]

What is most remarkable about the story of Lucy's brush with death is its omission from Thomas' book, *Travels in the Regions of the Upper and Lower Amoor*, which contains the description of his and Lucy's journey to Kopal in 1848. Despite the drama, Thomas could not include it because of his fear that his bigamy would be discovered. There is

---

45. Thomas' usage is wrong here. A *barimta* (Atkinson mistakenly copies this as *baranta*) is a raid carried out by mounted Kazakh horsemen, usually on the *aoul* of a rival, and in order to steal animals to settle a dispute. It is not a collective noun for robbers. And his use of the term 'bit the dust' (for the second time) is a very early usage of this phrase, more usually associated with Hollywood Westerns.

46. 1848 diary, entry for 14 September 1848.

little doubt that his book would have been even more dramatic than it was already, but all references to Lucy had to be resisted. Ironically, the absence of any mention of Lucy – or indeed of his son Alatau – in either of his books has led some critics to believe that Thomas was callous or egotistical. But his diary entries, which seldom fail to mention Lucy and which, time after time, show his deep love and affection for his very brave wife, prove that this was not the case.

Even now when they had reached a resting place with fresh water, the journey was not over. It was a further two days on horseback until they could reach the banks of the Lepsou – a journey over rolling low hills and deep sand in which the horses often sank up to their knees. The camels were left far behind, but after six hours the party began to make firmer ground. Both Thomas and Lucy mention the large numbers of *kurgans* (barrows) scattered across the steppe, as well as straight canals, some still containing running water and which date back many hundreds of years.

INTO THE DJUNGAR ALATAU

By Thursday 16 September the Djungar Alatau Mountains were now plainly in view, their snowy peaks catching the early morning sun. The Atkinsons were riding parallel to the mountains at a distance Thomas calculated as 100 *versts*. The strong wind from the mountains whipped up the sand around them, creating dust devils: "We saw several times during our ride columns of sand carried up by the wind. Sometimes five and six were seen, each turning round its own axis and moving slowly over the steppe. They sometimes rose to a great elevation. When seen with the sun shining upon them they appeared like pillars of smoke. But when seen looking towards the sun they were dark whirling masses. I was anxious to get to them but never succeeded. They were often from six to ten *versts* distant."[47] As they came within sight of the Lepsou, Lucy gave her horse free rein and galloped towards the banks. "I drank freely of it and I thought it the sweetest water I had ever tasted in my life," she wrote.

47. 1848 diary, entry for 16 September 1848.

They now rode southwards, parallel to the Djungar Alatau Mountain chain, but still on the grassy flatlands that stretched way out into the desert towards Lake Balkhash. They crossed the River Bean that marked the boundary between the territory of the Great and Middle Hordes and noted the many *kurgans* and extensive earthworks in the area. One, located on the Lepsou, Thomas describes as a parallelogram "about 700 yards in length and 300 in breadth. The earth walls are now about 12 feet high and have been considerably higher; their thickness is about 16 feet at the bottom and nine feet at the top. This enclosure was entered by four gates, one being in the centre of each side; but the eastern end has been partly destroyed by the river which is gradually cutting down the bank."

This was, in fact, the ancient city of Koilyk, which is mentioned by some of the early travellers to the Zhetysu region – see Chapter 1. This city, which flourished until the 17th century, is now a UNESCO World Heritage site, having been excavated by archaeologists, who found the remains of Buddhist temples, mosques and a Nestorian church, revealing that the city's rulers supported religious freedom.[48]

Thomas and Lucy were now entering the Zhetysu, known in Russian as Semirechye – or Seven Rivers region.[49] These rivers, which all flow into Lake Balkhash, originate in the glaciers and lakes of the Alatau Mountains. Bounded by Lake Ala Kol to the northeast, Balkash to the north and west and the Alatau Mountains to the south, much of the Zhetysu region, with the exception of the river valleys, is dry and inhospitable. During the Atkinsons' time the tribes of the Great and Middle Hordes would spend the summers with their huge herds of animals in the *jailoo* (alpine meadows) of the Alatau Mountains, returning back in the autumn to the shores of Lake Balkash, where they would settle in for the winter.

The Atkinsons' route from the banks of the Lepsou to Kopal is not clear from either of their accounts. Thomas refers to a group of mountains

---

48. See Chapter.1.

49. The seven rivers traditionally associated with the Zhetysu are: the Ili, the Karatal, the Bean, the Ak-Su, the Sarcan, the Bascan and the Lepsou.

in front of the Djungar Alatau as the Karatau. This name is no longer in use, but there is a group of hills that sits to the southwest of Lake Ala Kol, which fits their description. Between this small range, which lies to the south of the modern town of Usharal, and the Djungar Alatau there is a wide valley – the Ghilderagharagi – which Thomas describes entering after crossing the mountains. He describes a hard journey where they could only ride single file and where eventually they had to dismount and lead their animals up a narrow ravine towards the top, from which they had a very clear view of the Alatau chain, with its snowy peaks.

Thomas knew the Russians were building a fort somewhere on the River Kopal, but was not sure of the exact location. He kept moving towards the main Alatau chain, noting the Ak-su and Sarcan rivers. It seems likely that his group made their way up what is today known as the Hasford Pass, from where far below him he would have been able to see the gorge from which the Ak-Su pours out of the mountains. The entry to the pass today is just outside Zhansugurov, which was once called Abakumovsky after the Cossack commanding officer at Kopal. From its highest point you can see the villages of Suyuksai and Arasan, which are on the old Cossack post road that once linked Kopal (and later, Almaty) with Ayaguz.

Thomas says that on 20 September, just at dusk, they reached a group of yurts, "to the great astonishment of the Cossack inhabitants". This was the new settlement of Kopal. The officers, who explained that their expedition had arrived a month previously, welcomed the Atkinsons, who spent the rest of the evening giving them the latest news from Europe.

In the morning Thomas found some of the Cossacks, of whom there were around 500, busy throwing up the earthworks for a V-shaped military bastion facing out into the steppes. Others were preparing timbers to make log cabins. He tells us that the first Cossacks had arrived in the region four years previously and had built an artillery platform at the mouth of the gorge from which the River Kopal sprang from the mountains. In those days it had taken 42 days of route-marching to reach the camp, although this had been reduced to 18 days by the time Thomas and Lucy arrived.

The impending arrival of winter meant there was an added urgency to the work of the Cossacks. Many had brought their wives and children with them and now they had to make shelters. They used whatever was available, taking stones from the river gorge to build the walls and making roofs from tree trunks covered with nine inches of earth. Instead of glass, they used Chinese silk, strained onto frames.

In August 2014 I saw the original Cossack bastion at Kopal for the first time. Its V-shape is still clearly visible, as are the large ditches in front of it. There is still some trace of the buildings that were once within the bastion and even the most cursory inspection turns up artefacts that date from the 19th century. We found old hand-sewn leather boots and plenty of brass cartridge shells – although the latter probably dated from the early 20th century. For several years, until the establishment of Vierney (Almaty) in 1854, this was the most important military outpost in the Kazakh Steppe and even then, one of the remotest points in the Russian Empire. It was to be home for Thomas and Lucy – and an unexpected arrival – for the following eight months.

By the time they reached Kopal, Thomas and Lucy had already travelled very substantial distances. Lucy calculated it thus in a letter to a friend, as recorded in her book: "Since I left you in February last, I have travelled in a carriage 6,267 versts, on horseback 2,040, in boats and on a raft 760. This is the distance we have gone in the direct road; but I have done much more, having been on several excursions on horseback; for instance, the very evening after our arrival here, we went on a trip of 17 versts.

"This year my husband has travelled 10,705 versts in a carriage, 2,290 on horseback, and 1,490 in boats, exclusive of divers excursions for sketching of 40 or 50 versts distance; so, you see, the ground we have gone over is immense: –

	Versts	English miles
My husband in all direct travelling	14,485	About 10,864
I the same	9,067	" 6,800

Despite the prospect of a further ride north of well over 1,000 km, it seems that the original intention of Thomas and Lucy had been to return from Kopal to Barnaul in the Altai before the winter set in. However, their plans were disrupted by two major events. The first was a weather event. Well before the end of October, winter arrived with a vengeance. Snow began to cover the shelters the Cossacks had been digging into the earth. By November the *bourans* – harsh Siberian winds laden with snow – began to blow off the steppes, sometimes lasting for days at a time, "during which," wrote Thomas, "men could not proceed twenty paces from their dwellings." On the morning of 23 November, a huge gale began which soon transformed into a hurricane, "sweeping the snow into clouds like flour, rendering it almost dark at midday".

Overnight the weather deteriorated even further and the Cossack commander, Captain Abakumov, told Thomas that it would get even worse. Already the primitive huts in which most of the soldiers were living were covered by deep snow. As soon as passages were cleared, they were filled again. "At length each party became prisoners in their dwellings, from which they could not proceed five paces. They had now great difficulty in cooking; and those most distant from the kitchen found it a constant labour to keep up a communication with that necessary establishment. When the snow became deep enough, a gallery was formed in it and then they passed to and fro without difficulty."[50]

The *bouran* lasted until 4 December – 11 days in all. It must have been all the more terrifying for Lucy because barely a month before, on 4 November, she had given birth, two months prematurely, to a baby boy.

—∞—

Overleaf: Thomas Atkinson's watercolour of The Acsou River gorge in the Djungar Alatau Mountains.

---

50. *Amoor, op. cit.*, p. 94.

4
EXPLORING THE DJUNGAR
ALATAU MOUNTAINS
The Atkinsons in the Zhetysu

—⟋ⵉⵉⵉ⟍—

ACCORDING TO A STORY TOLD TO THOMAS, not a great deal of thought had gone into the siting of the bastion at Kopal. Referring to events that had taken place in the early 1840s, he writes: "A brace of generals, with a numerous staff, were sent into the steppe to determine upon the site of the new fort. Stores and creature comforts of all kinds accompanied the two heroes, among which champagne was a prominent item. A strong guard of Cossacks formed their escort and numerous cooks and bakers were also attached to the expedition. A party of Cossacks and cooks were always sent on in advance to select the place for encampment and to prepare a sumptuous entertainment and strict orders were given that the day's march should not be a long one."[1]

Thomas says that after reaching the easternmost valley of the Lepsou river, a beautiful spot near the town of Lepsinsk, the generals and their entourage decided to stop for a few days. From here they moved on westwards to the River Kopal, more than 600 km south of Semipalatinsk, but found it so desolate that they decided to halt at this point and order the construction of a fort. With that, says Thomas, the generals returned to the north.

Soon after this, in the summer of 1846, an advance party of 70 Cossacks and 80 artillerymen arrived under the command of Cossack

---

1. T W Atkinson, *Travels in the Regions of the Upper and Lower Amoor and the Russian Acquisitions on the Confines of India and China*, Hurst and Blackett, London, 1860, p. 95.

Captain Nukhalov and built a gun emplacement in the mouth of the gorge out of which the River Kopal burst from the Djungar Alatau Mountains. When the main body of Cossacks arrived in late August 1848 under the overall command of the regular Imperial army officer, Captain Abakumov, they started building a V-shaped bastion about 400 m from the river, on rising ground. At that time, says Thomas, "not a single tree was visible and scarcely a bush could be found, except on the banks of the river, and even there they were few."

Kopal was one of four Cossack encampments founded in the region, the others being Kargaly, Topalevsk and Arasan. These defended villages acted as post-stations for the regular military despatches that were sent up the line to Omsk in Western Siberia every Monday. In total there were 12 picquets (military posts) between Ayaguz and Kopal, each with two pairs of horses.

The first problem encountered at Kopal by Mr Loganov, the Cossack engineer officer, was the lack of nearby timber. The nearest source was more than 20 miles away, close to the gorge of the Aksou River, from where it had to be cut down and transported by bullock carts back to the fort. First to be built were the fort, the storehouses and the hospital. Only then could the individual Cossacks begin work on the hovels in which they would have to live that first winter with their women and children. Thomas says most of these rooms were 12 ft square, in which two families totalling up to ten people, would have to live. Many simply dug pits, which they covered with branches and earth.

At first Thomas and the heavily pregnant Lucy were given a yurt in which to stay. After a few weeks, the garrison commander obviously took pity on Lucy and just before Alatau was born, the Atkinsons moved into a two-room house. "I now often think what would have become of me had we been in a yurt when I was confined. I believe both I and the child must have died," she wrote.

Life was not entirely grim at Kopal. Lucy notes that at the end of September and beginning of October she and Thomas would take long rides around Kopal and in the evenings would assemble with Baron George Gotthard Moritz Ernst Wrangel, a Livonian (German-Baltic) army officer in the tsar's service who was district commander and whose yurt was next to that of the Atkinsons.[2] From 18 January 1848 Baron Wrangel, then 32, was appointed officer in charge of the Great Kazakh Horde. Lucy gives a wonderful description of her first meeting with the baron, who had received a sabre wound whilst fighting in the Caucasus and still bore the scar:

> Baron Wrangel, the governor, was much surprised at seeing a lady enter, and perhaps also at my appearance, for, to say truth, I was not very presentable. On our journey I had mounted camels and bulls as well as horses, but the last day, having a stream to cross to enable me to reach a Tartar encampment, I found it too deep to ford pleasantly, as the water would reach to my waist. Whilst hesitating what was best to be done, a Kazakh, who had followed us down the bank, without ceremony walked into the water, and, placing himself before me in a stooping posture, patted his back, and signed for me to mount, which I at last did, and crossed on the man's back.
>
> We found the Baron sitting cross-legged on a stool, with a long Turkish pipe in his mouth, a small Tartar cap on his head, and a dressing-gown, à la Kazakh. Mr. Loganov, the engineering officer, and the topographer, were dressed in exactly the same way. They all gave us a most cordial welcome: we sat chatting till a late hour. The tent in which we found the party assembled was very large, and used as the common sitting-room; each had a small one for a sleeping apartment, one was allotted to us, and another was used as a kitchen: thus we formed quite a little colony.[3]

The other officers were: the troop commander, Captain Abakumov, and Captain Loganov, the engineer; Captain Izmaelov, the commander of the Cossacks; Captain Tochinskoi, his second-in-command; two young lieutenants, one of whom was a surgeon. There was also a topographer and a quartermaster.

---

2. Baron Wrangel had previously been adjutant to Prince Gorchakov at Omsk, with the rank of major, after a distinguished military career in the Caucasus and elsewhere. He died at Sooru in Estonia in 1878.

3. Mrs Atkinson, *Recollections of Tartar Steppes*, John Murray, London, 1863, p. 111.

Food in Kopal was basic: no vegetables at all, no butter or eggs. Mostly they ate meat and rice, with coarse, black bread, which "even Mr. Atkinson had some difficulty swallowing". Lucy did not drink the brick tea that was usually on offer in Kazakh yurts, although Thomas usually did so, if only so as not to hurt the feelings of his host.

Despite the lack of culinary choice, it appears to have been a jolly place. In the evenings the officers would gather together to be entertained by Baron Wrangel's inexhaustible fund of entertaining anecdotes. He would accompany Thomas's flute-playing on the guitar and evenings would often end with the singing of the Russian and English national anthems.

On at least one occasion, there was a grand ball to celebrate the arrival of some of the officers' wives from Semipalatinsk. Lucy provides a wonderful description of her preparations for the ball: "Having but one dress besides my travelling one, I drew it forth and looked with dismay at its tumbled appearance. I had a small iron with me fortunately, the only one in Kopal, so I despatched our Cossack to and fro to the kitchen to have it heated. Thus, with a flannel petticoat for an ironing blanket, and a box for a table, I managed to make it decent, and forthwith I commenced my toilet. The guests were bidden for five o'clock, but our host begged of me to be ready earlier to receive his lady visitors. In the midst of my dressing a *bouran* arose; I was obliged to rush to one side of the tent to hold it down, my candle was blown out, leaving me in total darkness. Mr. Atkinson ran outside to call the men, who were heard screaming and running in all directions, as the kitchen, with all the delicacies for the coming feast, was being nearly swept away; at last, with ropes and beams of wood, it, as well as our tent, was secured. With some difficulty I got a light, and resumed my dressing; in the meantime, I received three notes to hasten operations."

As soon as she was ready, Lucy entered the main house where the ball was to be held. She found the baron in full uniform, but the grandest man in the room was his Kazakh bodyguard, Yarolae: "He wore a magnificent new dressing-gown, a splendid shawl round his waist, and a tall-pointed silk cap, and red boots; altogether he looked and felt superb." All around the room were newly constructed stools, with a carpet-covered dais at one end. Here Lucy, as hostess, took her position, while Yarolae announced the entry of the first ladies: "Walking like a prince into the centre of the apartment, he announced, in a voice like thunder, 'Madame Ismaeloff and Madame Tetchinskoy.' The contrast between them and the gaily-attired Kazakh was too striking. The former lady was a soncy-faced old body, with a bright shining skin, a clean dark-coloured cotton dress, a white collar which reached to her shoulders, a white cap with a very full border, a lilac silk shawl, and brown worsted gloves, completed her attire; her companion, a small person, had a similar dress, but instead of the shawl she wore a pink satin mantle, trimmed with white lace. They came up to me, each giving me three kisses, and took a seat on either side of me, without uttering a word. Yarolae was again off; the next visitor was proclaimed by the roaring of a bull. The door was thrown open very wide, and 'Anna Pavlovna' was announced. My gravity was this time sorely tried, and more so as I glanced at the Baron; his face was irresistible, he went forward to shake Anna by the hand; her deep-toned sonorous voice resounded through the room."[4]

This lady was a tall and rather stout woman, dressed in a Russian *sarafan* (peasants' dress) a coloured cotton shawl, shoes but no stockings. A bright red cloth was bound round her head. "As you may imagine, she was gloveless, but what an arm and hand she had! Big enough to knock down anyone who approached her ungraciously."

The final two ladies were from Biysk and, says Lucy, "had more pretensions than the others". "Madame Serabrikoff had on a woollen dress, and the other a faded green silk, with a patch in the skirt, of another colour; this latter visitor found means during the evening of telling me that she had not expected the ball to take place so soon, otherwise she would have had her polka ready to wear; it was a beautiful blue satin, which had been presented to her on leaving Bisk."

To begin with the Russian ladies sat bolt upright, trying to look stately, until they had had a drink or two, when there was an almost immediate transformation. Lucy reproached the baron for offering Chinese spirit, but he told her that they all expected it and would not be happy if no drink had been offered.

---

4. *Ibid*, pp. 114-5.

As for Thomas, he spent his days sketching the scenery around Kopal or out in the mountains, exploring the remote valleys and ridges to the south of the town. On fine days he was able to get out on horseback and hunt with Captain Abakumov or some of the other officers. He describes setting off south with a party of 17 on one occasion to cross the Myn-Chukur ridge behind Kopal and cross into the valley of the Kora river. Even today this is a very difficult journey, but at that time it must have been very dangerous indeed. However, it is worth it for the scenery alone.

On reaching the top of the ridge, Thomas described the view below: "As we stood looking into the depth, probably 5,000 feet below us, the river appeared like a band of frosted silver; we could also hear the roaring of the water as it rushed over its rocky bed... This side of the valley was exceedingly abrupt; indeed, in many parts the precipices were perpendicular; in other places the declivity was so steep that neither man nor horse could maintain a footing, nor were there either trees or bushes growing on any part. The opposite side, facing the north, was well wooded, the trees extending from the bank of the river upwards, till they diminished at the snow line."[5] Little has changed in the intervening years.

Thomas was deeply struck by the beauty of the Kora Valley, as he devotes almost two chapters to describing it and to recounting the folklore associated with it. On particular mystery concerns the five massive stones he describes in the valley standing on their ends. One, he says, was 76 ft high, while the others were from 45 to 50 ft high. Close by was a massive pile of stones, 28 ft high and 42 ft in diameter and which appeared to be a huge tomb. According to one of his Kazakh guides, the Kora Valley (the name itself means "sealed" valley) was once the home of powerful genies who constantly feuded with other genies in the Tarbagatai region to the north. There followed a huge battle between the rivals, which was only settled when Shaitan himself made an appearance and crushed the genies, burying them beneath these huge stones. Hence the meaning of the name.

I spent several days trying to locate these standing stones, but could not find them, although there are other massive stones in the valley. One local source said that there had been many landslides and earthquakes

---

5. *Amoor, op. cit.*, p. 100.

in the region and that it was likely the original stones had long since been toppled over and broken up. Perhaps… or perhaps they remain to be discovered?

Thomas travelled extensively in the Kora Valley, visiting all the side valleys, lakes and glaciers, sketching whenever he could. The entire valley is about 90 km in length. At its western end now is the industrial city of Tekeli, but no entry can be gained there because of the valley's steep sides. At the other end are the great Tronov, Bezsonov and Sapozhnikov glaciers.

Thomas was certainly very happy travelling through this valley, noting on 4 October 1848, for example, that he had experienced "one of the most lovely mornings I had ever beheld". The following day he awoke to find very different conditions, with more than a foot of snow, which was continuing to fall. It was time to leave. A great storm rolled in and it took the group three days to get out of the valley. From the top, looking to the north, the steppes looked peaceful and Kopal was still basking in the last vestiges of autumn warmth. But they had been lucky and they knew it. Undeterred, Thomas and a smaller party set off shortly after to visit the valley of the River Bean, about 20 miles to the east, where he had been told of the existence of a huge cavern.

Thomas also spent time in Kopal working at his paintings. He notes that his first work was a large watercolour, which soon after he sent to Prince Gorchakov by courier, as he had promised to do. "While dabbling in my colour-box, discomfort and even hunger were forgotten and the occupation enabled me to smile at the disasters of a stormy winter and to enjoy the amusements of my companions," he wrote.

Chief of whom, of course, was Lucy. Soon enough the day of Lucy's confinement approached. She made light of the circumstances surrounding the birth of her baby boy. In *Recollections of Tartar Steppes* she teased her anonymous correspondent about why she had not written: "But you are already asking what excuse I can make for the two last weeks. Here I have a little family history to relate. You must understand that I was in expectation of a little stranger, whom I thought might arrive about the end of December or the beginning of January."

By these calculations, Lucy had become pregnant only weeks after setting off with Thomas from Moscow, following their wedding in

February. That must have seemed like a lifetime ago. Since then she had travelled thousands of miles by carriage, horse, camel and even on the backs of bulls. She says she had hoped to be back in Barnaul for the birth and therefore had not prepared for the event, "when lo and behold! On 4th November, at twenty minutes past four pm, he made his appearance. The young doctor here said he would not live more than seven days, but, thank Heaven, he is still alive and well. He is small, but very much improved since his birth. I shall let him get a little bigger before I describe him. He is to be called Alatau, as he was born at the foot of this mountain range; and his second name Tamchiboulac, this being a dropping-spring, close to which he was called into existence."[6]

The young military surgeon told Lucy the premature birth was due to "excessive exercise on horseback", surely one of the great understatements of all time. Lucy added that no-one should have any illusions about the doctor: "Doubtless, seeing I speak of the doctor, you imagine we have a competent one here. Far from it, he is but twenty-three years of age; theoretically he may be clever, practically certainly not. When my husband applied to him in my case, he declared he had not the slightest knowledge of anything of the kind."

Lucy admits that it was fortunate that Thomas was at home, as he had returned only the evening before, having been absent two days on a shooting expedition. However, it is unclear that he attended the birth himself – very unlikely during that time. She says she does not know what she would have done without the help of Madame Tetchinskoy, one of the recently-arrived officers' wives, during what must have been a terrifying night following the birth: "During the night the *bouran* was so terrific that not a sound scarcely could be heard within doors. I never closed my eyes during that night; my heart was lifted up in thankfulness to the Creator for all His mercies to me. Had this event occurred one short week earlier, and on such a night, what should I have done? The child was enveloped in furs and placed on a leathern trunk against the stove to keep him warm; the woman was stretched on the floor wrapped in a sheepskin. I lay on my bed, hearing the poor infant, when there was

---

6. *Ibid*, pp. 105-6

a moment's lull in the storm, moaning. I screamed to the woman to give the poor little thing to me, but not a sound did she hear; at last, after about two hours I managed to awaken her, and make her understand; she took up the poor babe, and poking it at me like a bundle of straw, down she was again immediately; the instant the child touched me, it ceased its moaning. They had placed in its mouth a piece of muslin, containing black bread and sugar dipped in water, and, indeed, this was all he had till the third day, when he received his natural food."[7]

It turned out that Madame Tetchinskoy was not quite as respectable as her married position suggested. In fact, she had previously been condemned to receive a hundred lashes for "destroying her infant ere it saw the light" and, wrote Lucy, "probably at this moment she would not have been alive had not a Cossack come forward and offered to marry her before she had undergone the sentence, and he received fifteen lashes instead of her – such is the law. They are living very happily together: to judge from all I have seen, she is a very kind woman, willing to oblige when she can."

Alatau's birth was a major event in Kopal. Other children had been born that month, but not one survived; others who had been born on the journey across the steppe all died. Alatau was the only one who survived the winter. In the old Cossack cemetery in Kopal you can still find some of the gravestones put up at that time to commemorate the many people who died during the early years of the town.

During the winter more than 100 people died and Thomas described the pitiable scenes: "It was truly heart-rending to look upon their miserable families when the storms were raging; some were seen trying to shelter themselves under strips of *voilock* and others were lying down to sleep in corners of half-roofed rooms... First the children sank under this severity and were carried in numbers to the graves; the poor miserable mothers, worn out by anxiety, fatigue and bad food, next fell victims to the fatal maladies which assailed them. I have often watched the mournful processions wending their way to the fill selected for the cemetery, about two miles distant from the fort and when they have passed have turned away with

---

7. *Ibid*, pp. 117-8.

gloomy foreboding for the future. The endurance of the Cossacks lasted a little longer, but their turn was approaching."[8]

*

Having seen all the gravestones at the old cemetery in Kopal, I began to wonder where they had come from. They are not typical Orthodox grave markers, but many are long, thin stones over two metres in length. The mystery was solved by my good friend and translator Vladimir Gostyevski, who lives in the nearby town of Tekeli. Vladimir noticed one of Thomas' drawings of Kopal showing a large *kurgan* (barrow) at a distance. The *kurgan* is still there, but something is missing. When Thomas drew the *kurgan* it was surrounded by large, long, thin stones, doubtless placed there in antiquity. Now they are absent. Could the grave markers be the same stones, with writing crudely carved by a mason in the camp during those dreadful early years? I have little doubt that this is the case.

And what about the name of the child? Alatau Tamchiboulac Atkinson is surely one of the most distinctive names ever carried by an Englishman. Alatau is the name of the mountain range through which the Atkinsons spent so much time travelling and which they were the first Europeans to explore in any detail. Its basic meaning is "variegated" and refers to the vegetation. And Tamchiboulac is the name of the spring near where the child was born and in which he was bathed almost every day of his life until the age of eight months. It was a brave decision to give such names to the child, but they were carried with pride by their bearer throughout his eventful life. He too had an adventurous career and in 1870 migrated from England to Hawaii, where he became director of education, editor of the *Hawaiian Gazette* and was eventually responsible for organising the first census of the islands. He died in 1906. The name was passed down the generations and there are still descendants today named Alatau.

Today, the Tamchiboulac Spring at Kopal is still famous throughout the district. People come from all around to fill bottles with the water,

---

8. *Ibid*, p. 153.

which, they say, contains all the naturally occurring elements in the periodic table. At any time of day you will find people there, in the deep glade where water pours from the rocks in front of you. It has clearly been in use for hundreds, if not thousands, of years, a place where clean, life-giving water can always be found.

Some people believe that even the name of the town, Kopal, is linked directly to the spring. They explain that in Russian, the sound of water dropping to the floor is written onomatopoeically as *kapali-kapali-kapali* and that this is the origin of the name. Others link it to the name of a famous *batyr* (warrior) prince, but this question has never been finally resolved. Close by, at Arasan, is another famous spring whose waters are known throughout Kazakhstan for their healing powers. Both springs source their water from the Djungar Alatau.

*

Lucy got up for the first time the day after Alatau was born, walking about the room for a few minutes. The following day she was up after breakfast and stayed up the whole day. And from then on she was up every day. To start with, Thomas and Lucy were living in a traditional yurt, with a felt door and a fire in the centre. As Lucy wrote: "Thus in fine weather a yurt is no despicable accommodation, but Heaven protect you when a *bouran*, or even a moderately fresh breeze, arises. Here in Kopal I have been awoke out of my sleep by the wind, and have expected every instant the tent would be dashed to pieces. The hospital, which stands directly opposite our present abode, when a *bouran* has arisen, has been completely hidden from view. These winds carry everything before them, bricks or anything that comes in their way: the safest plan, when one arises, is to throw yourself flat on the ground."[9]

Lucy relates that all the women at Kopal advised her to swaddle Alatau, as was customary with Russian children at the time. But the child would not allow it and the project was abandoned. She says that he only awoke at bathing time and for another hour or so a day for the first month of his life. "Even the second month I scarcely had him in my arms,

---

9. *Recollections, op. cit.*, p. 108.

and, until he was nine months old, he never had a tear in his eyes. I have seen him restless and uneasy, and it was very remarkable that this always took place before a storm: he was as good as a barometer on the road."

There was one other incident that Thomas certainly had good cause to remember. It happened during the Christmas holidays, when Captain Abakumov suggested that he and Thomas should take an evening drive in his sledge. The "sledge", it turned out, was little more than a wicker basket on runners with straw in the bottom covered by wolf skins. This unusual contraption was to be drawn by three fierce Kazakh stallions. Thomas stepped in, but before Abakumov could get in the horses bolted, throwing the *yemshick* (driver) from his seat. Thomas describes his terrifying experience: "They dashed off at full speed, going straight towards the ravine. I understood my position in an instant – to attempt to leap from the sledge would have been certain death and I decided to take my chance in the gorge, believing this to be the least dangerous. The horses rushed madly on and I felt that a few minutes would decide the fate of all of us, the ravine being sixty feet deep at this part."[10]

Just short of the ravine, the horses turned, throwing the sledge almost over the edge. They raced away, increasing in speed, with the basket almost turning over and trapping Thomas' hand at one point. It was not until almost five miles from the fort that one of the horses fell and the other two drew to a halt. Soon there were artillerymen everywhere, gripping the reins and helping Thomas from the basket. He realised that he had broken a finger and had a long chip of wood driven far up beneath one of his nails. That he drew out with pliers, and Captain Abakumov set the broken finger with splints. The next day, says Thomas, he was unable to stand, but following a sauna he felt much better. It was several weeks before the finger bone healed.

With the coming of spring, political developments in the steppe were beginning to take shape. The Kazakh tribes in this part of Semirecheye had been split over whether or not to accept Russian rule. In 1846 the revolt led by Kenisary Kasimov had come to an end with his capture and decapitation by one of the Kirghiz tribes. The arrival of the Russians

---

10. *Amoor, op. cit.*, pp. 164-5.

and the establishment of their forts along the border with China clearly had a substantial effect on the tribes and most now were in favour of accepting Russian rule, not least to protect them from the depredations of the Khans of Khokand and Bokhara, who regularly raided into their territories, seizing livestock, women and children.

In March 1849 a large gathering was held in Kopal, bringing together the leaders of the Great and Middle Hordes to discuss the boundary between their tribes, which had been the subject of dispute. Senior Russian officials arrived from Ayaguz, and Captain Abakumov was encouraged to put on an artillery display, not least to show the truculent tribes what to expect if they failed to accept Russian rule. "During this operation many of the Kazakhs rushed forward to get a better view. Before they had gone half the distance the first gun belched forth its flame, smoke and thunder, instantly checking their ardour and causing a rapid retreat. As one gun after another echoed in the mountains, they gazed with perfect horror and were evidently greatly relieved when the salute was ended," wrote Thomas.[11]

Sultan Souk – more correctly Sjuk – as one of the most senior leaders of the Great Horde, was prominent in the proceedings. He listened as the Russian officials explained that Prince Gorchakov wished for the two hordes to accept a boundary and to stop their mutual raids. Sultan Souk said he would consent to a boundary along the line of the Ak-Su river, a position supported by his followers. In response, one of the Russian officials insisted that the boundary should be along the line of the River Bean and that the prince would not consent to any other boundary. A chief from the Middle Horde now spoke out in favour of the River Bean as a boundary. It was a stalemate and despite several more days of discussion, no decision was reached.

Souk was clearly a great favourite of Thomas and Lucy and they learned much about his background. In his first book, Thomas is rather dismissive of Souk and portrays him as vain, asking Thomas not to draw his crooked nose. In the frontispiece of the book he depicts him wearing a gold medal presented to him by Tsar Alexander I, but implies

---

11. *Ibid*, p. 175.

he had sold his birthright to gain such a bauble. But by the second book, he is more sympathetic, and Lucy certainly has been won over.

In fact, Thomas devotes two whole chapters to the story of Souk's tragic elopement with a Kyrgyz princess. Thomas starts with the history of Souk's father, Sultan Timour, who at the beginning of the 19th century was head of the Great Horde. A direct descendant of Genghis Khan, his territory included almost all of what is today known as Djungaria or Semirecheye. To the south, the ruler in the territory that is now Kyrgyzstan, was Sultan Djan-gir Khan. Sultan Timour and Djan-gir Khan lived in uneasy proximity to each other, sometimes uniting for raids, at other times at loggerheads following a depredation by one group or the other.

As Sultan Timour's eldest son, Sultan Souk established a reputation as a brave fighter for himself while still in his early 20s it was clear that one day he would inherit his father's mantle as chief of the Great Horde. When he indicated that he would like to marry one of Djan-gir Khan's daughters, his father did not object and sent messengers to the latter to conclude an agreement. The khan gave his consent to the marriage and all that remained to be settled was the *kalym* – the bride price paid by the groom's family.

Thomas' story follows the exploits of Sultan Souk as he attempts to visit his bride-to-be, in the process outwitting and outrunning one of the many robber bands that infested parts of the region. After a dangerous journey of almost 20 days he returned to his father's *aoul*, having met his betrothed. Later that year, during winter when their *aouls* were only three days apart from each other, Sultan Timour decided to send another deputation to Djan-gir Khan to pay the *kalym*. The price demanded – 200 camels, 3,000 horses, 5,000 oxen and 10,000 sheep – was thought too high by Sultan Timour's retainers, who decided, reluctantly, to return empty-handed. They had intended to offer about a third of what was being asked and realised it would be seen as insulting even to make the offer.

When Sultan Timour heard the price being demanded he was enraged, saying it was an insult against his family and vowing revenge. However, better counsel prevailed and the following spring Souk decided to return back to the mountains to see Ai Khanym, his intended wife, carrying with him a present and a message to the khan from his father. He was received warmly enough, but Ai Khanym let Souk know that her father had already promised her to the Khan of Badakhshan in northern Afghanistan and that the marriage was scheduled for the summer. She was not happy and told Souk she would happily go wherever he chose to take her. He returned home to plan his next step.

The following May Souk returned again to the *aoul* of Djan-gir Khan, during which time he made arrangements with Ai Khanym, telling her he would return for her in June, before she was married off to the Afghan khan. He returned, only to run off with her into the mountains, travelling in the high pastures at the head of the Terek river (itself the subject of a beautiful watercolour by Thomas, which now hangs in the dining room of the Royal Geographical Society in London) far to the east of the Lepsou and then down towards the Ili and the safety of the Great Horde. Despite eluding their pursuers, Souk's bride was killed by a tiger and the young man returned to his father's *aoul* empty-handed.

Time was now pressing on. Thomas and Lucy had left Moscow in February 1848 and had barely stayed beneath a conventional roof since then. Their child Alatau, lucky enough to survive a winter in which all the other newly-born children had died, was now nearly nine months old. Summer was approaching fast and would offer the best chance of returning north to Barnaul in the Altai region of Siberia. Thus it was that on 24 May 1849, after eight months in Kopal, Thomas, Lucy and Alatau set off back towards the north. Accompanied by a large group of Cossack officers on horseback and their wives in a horse-drawn *char-à-banc*, they rode out past the Byan-ja-Rouk Mountain and across the steppe towards Arasan.

At Arasan, famous even then for its thermal waters, there was singing, dancing and a feast before everyone turned in for the night. The following day Captain Abakumov travelled on further with them, over the Hasford Pass, together with their Cossack guides. From the top they could see the rivers Sarcand, Bascan and the Ak-Su far below them rushing onwards from the mountains towards distant Lake Balkhash. That is where they would spend the next few months, exploring the remarkable river valleys in the Djungar Alatau.

Soon after leaving their friends at Arasan, Thomas and Lucy, together with Alatau, headed on horseback for the remote valley of the Ak-Su River, about 20 miles away across the vast steppe dotted with dozens of *kurgans* – signs that this area had been frequented for thousands of years. The Ak-Su is one of the seven rivers of the Zhetysu/Semirecheye region and it appears that Thomas's aim was to visit as many of these beautiful river valleys as possible.[12] All flow out from the massive glaciers and snowfields of the Djungar Alatau towards Lake Balkhash across the steppe.

In fact, following the course of the Ak-Su into the mountains is almost impossible. In the summer of 2014, I tried myself to ascend the Ak-Su, but after a long hike was defeated as the mountains closed in and the path disappeared. The only way to get any higher towards the source is to climb the mountains flanking this very steep-sided gorge.

Somewhere in the mountains close to the source of the Bascan – there are Big and Little Bascan rivers – Lucy says that they saw a place that appeared to be a vast crater surrounded by large masses of granite, with a cone-like shape in the centre. There were two circles of rocks around the centre of this place, which they dubbed Granite Crater. From this high point, Lucy reports that they saw a sunset over the steppe: "The steppe was spread out like a map, the rivers looking like threads of silver, whilst towards the Balkhash lay a boundless dreary waste, where at this time of the year it would be frightful to travel; then the golden tints of the sky I try in vain to find language to describe. Those who have not visited these regions can form no conception of the splendour of an evening scene over the steppe." Nearby, there were nomad encampments, with their thousands of animals.

High above the Bascan are some of the biggest mountains in the Djungar Alatau. The gorge of the Little Baskan river begins from just beneath the Zhambyl glacier, one of the largest glaciers in the region. The three highest peaks of the Djungar Alatau are on the eastern side of Zhambyl glacier: Semenov Tien-Shansky peak (4,622 m), Shumskoi (4,442 m) and the peak of Abay (4,460 m); Zhambyl peak (4,249 m)

---

12. The Ili, Karatal, Bean, Ak-Su, Sarcan, Bascan and Lepsou. Thomas visited them all.

is found above the western part of Zhambyl glacier. The tallest peak, named after the Russian explorer Per Petrovich Semenov Tien-Shansky, straddles the border between Kazakhstan and China. To the west of the peak is the Amanbokter pass (3,933 m) which leads from the Little Baskan gorge in Kazakhstan to the valley of the Boro-Tala river in China.

From here above the Bascan, writes Lucy, they decided to descend to the Lepsou, down dangerous paths of almost impossible steepness. At every turn they saw Kazakhs in their high summer pastures with their animals. At one point, far below them, they spotted a lake of extraordinary green colour, which they tried to reach. Finding the way impossible, they retraced their tracks back to the Lepsou via an easier route with the intention of heading back up the mountain to try and locate the lake they had glimpsed.

On 2 June they reached Sarcand, where they pitched tent. They had to cross the river on a narrow, frail bridge made of little more than a few trees laid across the stream from a large stone in the centre. "The crossing was not agreeable," wrote Lucy, "seeing the raging torrent under our horses' feet. One false step, and all would have been finished. The noise of the stones being brought down, and the roar of the torrent, was so deafening, that we were obliged to go close up to each other to hear a word that was spoken. At last it became really painful; the head appeared full to bursting. I walked away some distance to try and get a little relief, but it was useless; a *verst* from the river the roar was still painfully heard. This din, coupled with the thunder, was awful; the latter we had almost daily – indeed, when it did not take place, there seemed to be a want in our life – and in these stupendous mountain masses it was fearfully grand, there being a short heavy growl in the distance, as if the spirits of the storm were crushing huge mountains together, and grinding them to powder; and the lightning descended in thick streams."[13]

From Sarcand, where they spent a few days exploring the area, on 8 June they headed back into the mountains. As they advanced up the

13. *Recollections, op. cit.*, pp. 149-50.

river valley, they met many of the large groups of Kazakhs they had first seen a year before travelling across the steppes from their winter quarters on Lake Balkhash on the way to their summer pastures – *jailau* – in the Djungar Alatau Mountains.

Many of them were charmed by the baby Alatau, often asking if they could keep him. Some even argued that Alatau belonged to them, as he was born in their territory, had been fed by their sheep and other animals, ridden their horses and received their name. Leave him with us, they said, and he will become a great chief. They brought him presents, including pieces of silk, ikats from Bokhara, young lambs and goats to ride upon. One sultan told Lucy that if she would leave him behind he would be given a stud of horses and attendants.

Lucy says that some of the tribes had never seen a European woman, with the strangest of consequences: "These believed I was not a woman, and that, I being a man, we were curiosities of nature; that Allah was to be praised for his wonderful works – two men to have a baby! One of our Cossacks I thought would have dropped from his horse with laughter. I was obliged to doff my hat, unfasten my hair, and let it stream around me, to try and convince them; but this did not at first satisfy them, still I believe at last I left them under a conviction that I was not the wonderful being they had first imagined me to be. My stays were objects of much speculation; they imagined they were never taken off. When told they were usually worn with steel, and that we took them off nightly, they were astounded; their exclamations were many and various."[14]

Lucy was particularly struck by the position of women in traditional Kazakh society, noting the difficulties they faced. "Do fancy, for a moment, what a position a woman fills. A dog is even considered her superior. When a favourite one is going to have pups, carpets and cushions are given her to lie upon; it is stroked, caressed, and fed upon the best of everything. Woman alone must toil, and they do so very patiently. One Kazakh, seeing me busy sewing (indeed I was occupied in making a coat for my husband), became so enamoured of my fingers that he asked Mr. Atkinson whether he would be willing to sell me; he

14. *Ibid*, pp. 153-4.

decidedly did not know the animal, or he would not have attempted to make the bargain. With me amongst them, there would shortly have been a rebellion in the camp." Of that, we can have little doubt.

On one occasion, when Thomas wanted to sketch, Lucy invited a group of women for tea. They came attired in their best costumes, including a bride wearing her tall, conical *saukele* hat. The samovar was brought in and tea given out, except to the men present: "This was the crowning point," wrote Lucy. "The 'lords of the creation' could no longer stand this slight, so arose and made their exit, and I saw no more of them that night. The women appeared to enjoy the fun of the thing."

Thomas and Lucy's descendants still have the samovar the couple took with them throughout their journeys in Siberia and the Kazakh Steppes. They also have a small fruit knife carried by Lucy during her travels.

Having left a Cossack in charge of their baggage they took the other two with them, along with the supplies they would need for an extended stay in the mountains, borne on camels, horses and bulls. Alatau was passed between Thomas and Lucy, depending on the difficulty of the terrain.

After their first overnight camp they awoke to find six inches of snow on the ground in the morning. Later that morning one of the camels fell and was killed. A few hours later some Kazakhs came into their camp to say they had just lost eight horses that had fallen down the mountain, three of them in foal. After a day's delay, during which they decided to switch their baggage to bulls instead of camels, they moved off on horseback to find the elusive verdigris-coloured lake. Once again, they moved high into the mountains, where they found an *aoul* of eight yurts. Sitting on the edge of a steep precipice, far below Lucy could see the beautiful lake. Thomas placed his shotgun besides Lucy and walked off to choose a spot to pitch the tent.

Suddenly, and without apparent explanation, events took a dangerous turn. Lucy looked round to see that one of the Cossacks had been surrounded by men holding sticks. Thomas ran over to help him, only to be confronted by more men carrying sticks – actually yurt poles. Several women too joined in and very quickly a dangerous situation had developed. Not that Lucy could hear anything; all sound was drowned out by a nearby waterfall. She knew that none of the others were armed. Her first thought was to put down the child and run over with the double-barrelled shotgun, but concerned that Alatau might roll off the cliff in her absence, abandoned the idea. She decided to sit still and see what would happen.

At this point, a second Cossack, who had been with the bulls, came into view. He immediately rode forward, just as a man and two women launched an attack on the first Cossack, who struck one of them. Two men tried to pinion Thomas' arms, but he was too strong for them and broke away. As he did so the second Cossack levelled a rifle. One of the Atkinsons' Kazakh guides now also appeared and drew two pistols from his holsters, cocked and pointed them. No sooner had this happened that everything changed. The men dropped their sticks, doffed their caps and moved back. Lucy, a double-barrelled shotgun over one arm and a baby in the other, walked forward.

By this time, the Cossacks had been able to bind one person from the group, the leader of the *aoul*, who had led the attack. He had urged his confederates to knock the brains from the strangers and seize their goods, thinking that they were a party of Russians. Thomas asked the Cossacks to release him, but they declined, saying he was still dangerous. After some time, when things had calmed down, Thomas persuaded him to allow two men from the *aoul* to accompany him and a Cossack in a descent to the lake far below. Lucy and Alatau were to stay at the camp, from where she watched Thomas descend through her opera glasses. The leader of the *aoul* saw the glasses and came over to take a closer look. Lucy was not prepared to take any risks: "I arose from my seat, determined to show no fear, and stood perfectly still, merely placing my hand in my pocket and grasping my pistol, but without drawing it forth."

The incident seems to have left a strong impression with Lucy. She noted that they had been just three against 20 or so. "Amongst this grand mountain scenery I seemed to conceive a more vivid idea of the power and presence of the Deity; and then I felt that the beneficent Being who had called all I saw around me into existence, did not neglect to watch and guard even the least of His creatures, if they trusted in Him. What care had been bestowed upon us this very day!" Just as quickly as the atmosphere had changed earlier, so it changed again. Soon one of the women came over from the *aoul*, bringing with her a Chinese silk handkerchief with mother-of-pearl decoration, which she presented to the baby Alatau. Lucy, in turn, presented a little red hat she had made for Alatau, to one of the children from the *aoul*. "Had I offered a bar of gold it would not have given half the pleasure that this hat did," she wrote.

The leader of the attack, now remorseful, killed a sheep with which to honour his guests and when Thomas returned, went forward to shake his hand. He took tea with the Atkinsons and from then on there was no further trouble.

The next day Thomas wanted to go back and sketch the green lake from another angle. Lucy added: "The cause of the peculiar colour of the water we could not ascertain. The lake was about three quarters of a verst wide, and two to two and a half long; and the Kazakhs said it was as deep as the mountain was high, but that we could not believe, though evidently the depth was great. They called it the Jassel-kool, which, translated, means young lake; perhaps a lake newly formed by an earthquake, as the rocks appeared tossed about in great confusion."

Today the lake is known as Zhassyl Kol, which, contrary to Lucy's interpretation, means Green Lake. Even now it is not easy to reach, as I found out on my first visit in the summer of 2015, when I was able to stand on its shore after a difficult ride on horseback of almost 20 km. Located at an altitude of 1,630 m, the lake is a beautiful green colour and is fed by mountain streams and a higher lake. In all likelihood it was formed by rocks being jammed into the narrow mountain valley. It is one of the great sights of the Djungar Alatau National Park.

For much of this journey through the river valleys of the Djungar Alatau, Thomas and Lucy's guide was a local man, who told them he had once ridden with the great warrior "Kinsara". He was referring to Kenesary Kasimov (1802-47), a Khan of the Middle Horde who is today regarded as a Kazakh national hero for his resistance to Russian rule.[15]

---

15. Known today in Kazakhstan as Kenesary Kasymuly Kasimov.

Kenesary had refused to accept the Russian decision to abolish the title of khan and at one point in the early 1840s had as many as 20,000 horsemen under his command. As previously mentioned, he was murdered in 1847 by Ormon Khan, a leader of the Kirghiz, who decapitated him and sent his mummified head to Russia.

The Atkinsons' guide was proud of his association with Kenesary and entertained them with stories of his bold raids and *barimtas*.[16] These mountains had often provided protection to Kenesary, as no-one was brave or foolhardy enough to follow him into the trackless valleys and forests. At one point the old guide came across one of the former campgrounds of Kenesary: "He pointed to a place on the north-west side of the valley, near some high precipices, as the locality of the Sultan's yurts. Farther to the west, he indicated the position of the aoul of his band and directed my attention right across the valley to a point near the bank of a torrent, as the spot where the party had always been stationed to guard the pass."[17]

Not far from this spot, said the guide, the river was swallowed up by a cavern. This in all likelihood refers to the River Lepsou, which disappears underground for a short distance, not far from its source. By darkness Thomas' party was in the exact spot of Kenesary's old encampment. "My guide told me that no one of the band ever dared to disobey his orders, as doing so would have been certain death. He had acquired unbounded power over the minds of his followers by his indomitable courage. If a desperate attack had to be made against fearful odds, he led the van and was ever first in the fight – shouting his war-cry with uplifted battle-axe and plunging his fiery steed into the thickest of the battle. This gave confidence to his men, and was the secret of his success."[18]

Later, the guide led Thomas to the exact spot where Kenesary had pitched his yurt: "There were the black ashes of his own hearth; he looked at these for a few minutes and then led the way to the eastwards. As he strode along he often looked back evidently lingering affectionately over a locality that had called up many pleasant recollections." At the

---

16. Atkinson usually uses the term *baranta*, an aural transcription.

17. *Amoor, op. cit.*, p. 221.

18 *Ibid*, p. 223.

end of several days travelling with the guide Thomas presented him with his fee: two pounds of gunpowder, 50 rifle balls and a small piece of lead, with which the old man was more than delighted.

Thomas describes some remarkable sights in the mountain gorges and valleys, although I have not yet been able to identify all of them. This is still a remote and barely explored region. Vast forests of apples can be found and scientists estimate that this region is the world's most important place for wild apple biodiversity. The cultivated apple (*Malus domestica*) arose in the Tien Shan from the wild apple (*Malus sieversii*) and was spread by bears and other wild ungulates. In the Lepsinsk Valley alone – which I visited in the summer of 2015 – there are 14,000 hectares of wild apple trees of more than 40 varieties. And besides the trees and wild flowers, the Djungar Alatau remains a wildlife refuge; bears, lynx, wolves, snow leopard, wild boar, Maral deer, ibex, wild sheep and many other animals and birds can be found. And until the 1950s this was also the hunting ground for the tiger, tracks of which Thomas and Lucy came across regularly.

Seven days after leaving their Cossack on the banks of the Lepsou, Thomas and Lucy returned to the camp. The Cossack had almost given up hope, believing they were lost forever in the mountains. It was now 2 July and they decided to follow the Lepsou down to the steppe, visiting an old Kalmyk fortress *en route*. As they made their way to the plains they found many Kazakh *aouls*, including that of Sultan Boulania, whom they had often met in Kopal and who was one of the most senior chieftains on the steppes.

Lucy found the Lepsou river valley to be beautiful and termed it Happy Valley, despite the heat and the swarms of mosquitoes. The heat at this time of the year can reach between 40 and 50°C. Thomas put his rifle down on the sand at one point and received a nasty blister when he tried to pick it up a few minutes later. The mosquitoes were particularly troublesome for Alatau, wrote Lucy: "He was one mass of bites. No one could have recognised him. I myself was not much better. I placed the little fellow in bed, perfectly naked, and covered with a piece of muslin, which we contrived to prop up; but still the brutes succeeded in getting in, and it was impossible to sit by and watch the whole time."

In the steppes at the foot of the Alatau Mountains, Thomas and Lucy came across more large groups of Kazakhs moving up into the summer pastures. They stayed in one *aoul* consisting of 13 yurts and more than 30 adults, along with thousands of animals. Thomas describes in detail a visit to the *aoul* of his host Djani-bek by his future son-in-law, who arrived to show off in front of his bride-to-be. At another *aoul* he was entertained by an old chieftain, one of whose retainers recited epic poetry to entertain them. "Homer was never listened to with more attention than was this shepherd poet, while singing the traditions of the ancestors of his tribe," wrote Thomas. "Whatever power the old Greek possessed over the minds of his audience, was equalled by that of the bard in front of me."[19]

Thomas was now in his element. One of his main ambitions before reaching the Kazakh steppes had been to travel with the nomads as they moved up to their summer pastures. His descriptions of camp scenes, including the contents of the yurts, the particularities of dress and the methods of animal husbandry are some of the finest ever written to describe this way of life. He describes this vast mass of animals entering a pass on the way up to the summer pastures: "The mouth of the pass was about 300 yards wide, between grassy slopes up which it was impossible for either man or animal to climb. The whole width, and as far as I could see, was filled with camels, horses and oxen; Kazakhs were riding among them, shouting and using their whips on any refractory brute that came within their reach. At length we plunged into a herd of horses, with camels in front and bulls and oxen in our rear. We presently passed the grassy slopes to where the gorge narrowed to about 100 yards in width, with precipices rising up on each side to the height of 600 or 700 feet. From this mob of quadrupeds there was no escape on either side and to turn back was utterly impossible, as we were now wedged in among wild horses. These brutes showed every disposition to kick, but fortunately for us, without the power, the space for each animal being too limited. This did not, however, prevent them from using their teeth and it required great vigilance and constant use of the whip to pass unscathed."[20]

---

19. *Ibid*, p. 252.

20. *Ibid*, p. 256.

Finally, after many weeks exploring the river valleys and glaciers in the mountains Thomas and Lucy made it to the shores of Ala Kol lake, which lies just to the north of this part of the Djungar Alatau and marks one of the main entry points into China at the place known as the Djungarian Gate. It was through this region – and the adjoining territory of what is now northern Xinjiang or Chinese Djungaria – that the great armies of Genghis Khan moved first into Central Asia before their onward marches to Russia, the Middle East and large parts of Europe.

Thomas and Lucy pitched their tents at the foot of the mountains about an hour or so's ride south of the lake's southern shore. Today, little has changed in the area, except for a few beach huts and the first signs of tourism. You cannot see from one side of the lake to the other – a distance of 90 km – although Piski Island, which has a flock of flamingos, and which was mentioned by Lucy, can easily be seen. The Kazakhs, she writes, used to take their animals over to the island during the winter, when they could cross the ice. She adds that the great geographer Alexander von Humboldt told Thomas in Berlin that he thought there had originally been a volcano in the lake, although Thomas says he found no trace of volcanoes anywhere in Central Asia. The lake has a surface area of over 2,650 sq km and is salty, although it receives water from streams flowing out of the Tarbagatai Mountains.

The stay near the lake was eventful, not least when they were disturbed by intruders in the middle of the night. Lucy was certainly not one to miss out on any action and her account is riveting: "I always at night placed everything where I could lay my hands upon it at a moment's notice. Placing my husband's pistols and gun into his hands, he started, bidding me lie down and keep quiet, but such was not my nature. If we were to be captured I was determined to see how it was managed, so put on my dressing gown and slippers, and out I went, with my single pistol in my hand; the other had been stolen. It appeared there were about six or eight men; they had come within fifty yards of our tent, but, observing the sentinels, had retreated across a little glen, and rode under the dark shade of a small mountain in front of us. Our Cossacks, Kirghis, and Mr. Atkinson, mounted their horses and rode over the ground, but they were gone; the place afforded many ways of escape, even quite near to us. What appears a vast plain, as level as the hand, when we come to ride over it we find undulating ground, intersected by gullies, where horse and rider may soon be lost to view. It was undoubtedly the intention of these men to have stolen our horses; had they succeeded in doing so, we should have been an easy prey, as without them to have ascended the deep ravine would have been impossible, and the sultry sun and burning sand across the steppe would soon have killed us, to say nothing of the want of water."[21]

At the same time, Lucy seems to have found the place enchanting, describing how she and Thomas sat watching the sun go down over the lake: "On such nights as these one feels as though living in a land of spirits, everything calm and serene around, not a whisper of any kind. Sometimes a feeling of sadness creeps over one, on thinking that we must once more return to the busy world, with all its ceremonies, cares, and troubles; and one would almost wish to be a Kazakh, wandering, like them, amongst all that is beautiful in nature – but then comes the thought that this would be but an idle life." They found many ancient tombs on the shores of the lake made from sunburnt brick, many of which still remain.

Thomas and Lucy used the camp on the shores of Ala Kol as a base for their further treks into the mountains. Lucy took part in these journeys and became adept at crossing streams on horseback, including some, she wrote "where we had all to ride in together, the one to bear the other up. The Kazakhs, invariably placing me in the centre, and clutching my dress, seemed determined to take care of me. Some of the streams were broad and deep. When it was so, I used to retire behind the reeds or rocks, as the case might be, and, stripping, put on my bathing gown, with my belt round my waist; and tying my clothing into a bundle, boots and all, I jumped on to my horse – merely holding tight on to him with my legs, there being no saddle – and swam him across in the company of a Kazakh, he gallantly carrying my bundle for me; when I would again retire with my bundle, to re-equip myself."[22] As she noted, "I am vastly altered since leaving Petersburg."

---

21. *Recollections, op. cit.*, pp. 183-4.

22. *Ibid*, p. 190.

It was not until 26 July that they returned to Ala Kol for the last time, where once again they faced intruders near the camp, this time four men on horses. A brief skirmish resulted in George, one of the Cossacks, capturing a lance and the pursuit party also found a tethered camel which had been stolen from a neighbouring *aoul*. Soon they were on the move again, camping close to Sasyk Kol, Ala Kol's neighbouring lake, where they were tormented by mosquitoes.

On 9 August, having travelled through the Tarbagatai Mountains to the north of Ala Kol, Thomas and Lucy arrived at a picquet close to the Chinese border town of Chougachac, between Ala Kol and Zaisan lakes and about 700 km from Semipalatinsk. Now known as Tacheng, the town has long been a crossing point between the Kazakh Steppes and Chinese Djungaria and is close to the present border crossing at Bakti. The Atkinsons had made the journey despite advice from the Cossacks that they would face imprisonment.

From the picquet they could see the town in the distance and their intention was to apply for permission to enter. Lucy was struck by the costumes of the officials they met, the first Chinese she had seen on this journey. "There was no mistaking them and their peculiar costume; their boots were principally of black satin, with very high heels and thick soles; their jackets pleased me amazingly, and were really pretty. Those of the servants were of blue cotton, but their superiors wore silk or satin. The latter is called *kanfa*, and can be washed exactly like a piece of cotton."

An inquiring Chinese border official asked why they wanted to visit the Celestial Empire and Thomas replied that being so near, he merely wanted to pay his respects to the governor and see the town. They were asked to wait for a reply, which would arrive in the evening. Nothing happened that evening, but the following morning they saw the official party of three officers approaching, together with a military retinue. The border guard insisted that they take Alatau to a meeting with the officials, which took place on a carpet spread beneath some nearby trees. After handshakes and greetings, tea and sweetmeats arrived and, before anything else, the *kalki*, the most senior official, took great delight in picking up Alatau and smothering him with kisses. The officials were very cordial and the scene is portrayed affectionately in a woodcut of Thomas's sketch that appears in Lucy's book.

Conversation was not easy. The Chinese spoke to a Tatar, who then translated their words into Russian to a Cossack, who in turn translated into English. When Thomas asked if they could enter the town, the official said they were the first English people ever to have visited the region and that the governor would have to obtain special permission from the emperor. This would have meant days, if not weeks, of delay and Thomas declined the offer.

Lucy then asked if she could go alone, but the official told her he was likely to lose his head for allowing such a visit. But if Thomas was willing to shave his head and dress as a Tatar, perhaps he would be able to gain entry. Thomas replied that if he could not enter as an Englishman, he would not visit the place at all. Nonetheless, they agreed to share a meal that the officials had brought with them consisting of rice, meat and soup followed by sweetmeats and then tea. Lucy tried to use chopsticks, while the Chinese struggled with spoons and forks. When the time came to depart, Alatau was passed down a long line of soldiers, each of whom embraced him.

With that, Thomas and Lucy decided to press on northwards and made their parting farewells. One of the officials presented Alatau with a large cucumber, which Thomas eyed hungrily, having not tasted vegetables for nearly a year. The following day was hard, ten hours riding over burning sand, which affected their eyes and made Lucy very dizzy, but after a night's sleep she was fine again. She emphasises how systematic they all were in seeing to their duties once they arrived at a new camp. By now she was a seasoned traveller and even with a small baby, she knew exactly what to do and in which order.

For food they relied on flour given to them by the Chinese which they mixed with milk from a Kazakh *aoul* if they were near one and then fried. Lucy says she was never quite satisfied with food on the steppes: "From the hour of our entering the steppe until we left it, I never knew what it was to have a sufficiency of food; without bread or vegetables it was impossible, at least for me, to feel quite satisfied. Fancy only meat and nothing but meat, then tea without sugar or cream. I was the worst off, having two to nourish; and I can assure you the keen air of the mountains sharpened the little fellow's appetite. One good thing, he had learned to eat meat: he began before he was three months old; at first he ate morsels the size of a pin's head, but bread he did not even know the flavour of." She mentions the pleasure of eating apples ("we lived a good deal on them") in those areas where they found them in the mountains.

Somewhere between Chougachac and Ayaguz the Atkinsons came across the *aoul* of the wealthy Sultan Beck, where Lucy was struck by the beauty of his two daughters. "The youngest was more to my taste, being very pretty; her hair hung in a multitude of braids around her face, and just on the crown of her head she wore quite a coquettish-looking cap. She was slim, and exceedingly graceful in all her movements. Her elder sister was a perfect Amazon." Thomas completed a beautiful portrait of the sultan and his daughters, which appears in his first book. He was to visit their *aoul* again four years later as he travelled south from Djungaria back towards Kopal.

Now Thomas and Lucy were almost on the last leg of their journey. In Ayaguz they exchanged horses for their carriage, which had survived their absence for a year. They bade farewell to their Cossack companions with many a tear and headed north to Zmeinogorsk, where they arrived on 3 September. Not surprisingly, their friends barely recognised them. As Lucy noted: "Mr. Atkinson was in a terrible plight, his boots had been patched and mended with the bark of trees, till they would scarcely hold together. The first person in request was a bootmaker, whose ingenuity you would find a difficulty in matching. We gave the order for the boots and supplied the man with leather. He looked at Mr. Atkinson's foot, and was going away, when I stopped him, to say he must at once take the measure, as they were required immediately. 'Oh, I never measure,' he replied, and went away: we felt sure the leather would be wasted. In two days they arrived, when my husband declared he had never had a pair of boots fit him so well."

It was then back to a round of evening parties and cards, which Lucy found intensely boring until she had a go at fortune telling, which proved very popular – and in at least one case, very accurate. And then, after a month's rest, they were off again, heading for Barnaul in the Altai region of Siberia where Thomas intended to spend the winter painting and Lucy in catching up on her reading.

That, of course, was not quite the end of this episode of their adventures. On the first night back in Barnaul, having dined with their old friend Colonel Sokolovsky, they returned to their rooms, which had been heated in their absence due to the freezing conditions outside. In the night Lucy was disturbed by Alatau's laboured breathing and as she attempted to light a candle and get up, found herself almost unable to move and suffering a severe headache. She woke Thomas, who realised what was happening and stumbled towards the door which he pushed open before crashing to the floor where he lay without moving for ten minutes. The oxygen flooded in and they escaped suffocating to death. As soon as they could, they woke all the other residents and then opened the stove, to find it was still burning and consuming all the oxygen in the room. "Had the child not fortunately awakened me, I make no doubt that it would have been our last sleep", wrote Lucy.

It was the end of an extraordinary 18 months of Lucy's life. From a governess in an aristocratic family in cosmopolitan St Petersburg, she had married, become pregnant, travelled thousands of miles with her new husband, nearly died of thirst and of cold, delivered a baby under the most extreme of circumstances, ridden on horseback into some of the most remote mountain valleys in the world up to altitudes of over 3,000 m, faced robbers intent on murdering them in their beds and become friends with some of the great characters and leaders of the Kazakh hordes. Nothing like this had ever been achieved by a woman traveller before. And this was only the start. Another four years would go by before Lucy and Thomas returned to St Petersburg. Their adventure had barely begun.

In conclusion, we have seen that during the 18 months or so the Atkinsons spent living in the Kazakh Steppes, they probably got closer than any outsider before or since to nomadic inhabitants of the region. They explored thoroughly all the river valleys in the Zhetysu, as well as climbing high into the mountains to heights of more than 3,500 m. Thomas achieved his ambition of experiencing the excitement of the annual migration of the nomads and their great herds up into the summer pastures of the Djungar Alatau. It is doubtful that anyone else ever had the same experience. Certainly, I can find no other written account.

The Atkinsons arrived in Kopal only a year or so after it had been founded and were the first visitors. They shared the privations of the Cossacks and enjoyed the hospitality of their officers. They also experienced the hospitality of the nomads, particularly Sultan Souk, and always regarded this region as somewhere special. When travelling in remote parts of Siberia they would compare the most beautiful scenes with those they had witnessed in the Djungar Alatau.

What is more, all this was achieved while looking after a new-born baby. As soon as they thought he was strong enough, they set off without a second thought back to Barnaul on a 1,000-km horseback journey that must have been exceedingly tough. Their achievement puts them in the ranks of the greatest explorers of all time, a fact that will one day be more widely recognised.

—ɯ—

Minarets and madrassa
in Khiva old town,
Uzbekistan.

5
THE RACE TO KHIVA
The Travels of Vassili Mikhailov,
Nikolai Muraviev, Eugene Schuyler,
Januarius MacGahan, David Ker,
Fred Burnaby and Robert L Jefferson

—ɯ—

MANY OF THE ACCOUNTS OF LIFE IN THE GREAT STEPPE come from travellers making their way from southern Russia to the ancient city of Khiva, which lies surrounded by deserts to the southeast of the Aral Sea. Although it is not a Kazakh city, it was always an important place for the nomads, particularly after Orenburg came under the control of the Russians. By the beginning of the 19th century there was growing concern in St Petersburg about the slave trade that provided much of Khiva's financial dynamism. Tens of thousands of Persians, often captured from boats sailing on the Caspian, and hundreds of Russians seized from the southern edge of the empire, were known to be in the city, sold into slavery by Turkoman and other raiders. It became a priority for the Russians to break the power of the Khivan khans and stop the trade that was a barrier to Russian expansion into the steppe.

To give an idea of what the slave trade meant to Russians in the late 18th and early 19th centuries in Central Asia, it is worth reading the remarkable story of Vassili Mikhailov, whose recollections were first published in German in 1804 before being published in England in

1820.[1] The story of Mikhailov was one of many narratives of captivity on the steppe, most of which served to contrast the so-called barbarism of the nomads with the "civilised" values of the urban Russians.[2]

Although Mikhailov had a Russian name, he started his life in a small Persian village to the south of the Caspian Sea in 1741. His life story reads like something out of *1001 Nights* or *Haji Baba of Isfahan*, with a never-ending series of calamities that would have destroyed a lesser person.

In 1747, when our hero – then known by his Persian name of Buy – was just six, the circumstances of his family were not good. The death of Nader Shah, war with the Turks and a poor harvest had led to a famine in Persia and many people began to die. His parents decided the family's best chance of survival was to make for the coastal town of Rasht. But soon they were hit by their first calamity; on the road his brother was stolen from their camp by Caucasian robbers and was never seen again. In Rasht his parents sought work as day labourers, but there was little money. Soon after, his sister was married off to an Armenian merchant, leaving just the six-year-old boy with his parents.

With little work or food, an uncle advised Buy's father to either sell the boy or give him away. He rejected the advice at first, but as their desperation increased, the boy's parents finally agreed to go ahead and set off for the central market. As they approached the house of the Russian Consul in Rasht, Ivan Bakunin, his Armenian groom happened to ask where they were going. When he heard they were taking the boy

---

1. *Adventures of Michailow, A Russian captive amongst the Kalmucs, Kirghiz and Kiwenses*, Sir Richard Phillips & Co, London 1822. In fact, Mikhailov's account was actually written by Benjamin Bergman, a Lutheran pastor born in Livonia. In 1802 Bergman was sent on a scientific expedition to the Kalmyk Steppe by the commission of the Imperial Academy of Sciences. Over the course of two years he learned Kalmyk and collected many Kalmyk stories, including the Oirat epic Jangar. He also met Mikhailov and recorded his experience of captivity. In 1803 he handed his notes to Tsar Alexander I, who approved their publication in German in Riga. Later this account was translated into English. For a review of Russian accounts of captivity in the steppe, see Yuan Gao, *Captivity and Empire: Russian Captivity Narratives in Fact and Fiction*, Thesis submitted to the School of Humanities and Society Sciences of Nazarbayev University, Astana, Kazakhstan, 2016. See https://nur.nu.edu.kz/bitstream/handle/123456789/1672/Captivity+and+empire.pdf?sequence=1

2. For a detailed history and assessment of the slave trade in Central Asia, see Jeffrey Eric Eden, *Slavery and Empire in Central Asia*, Doctoral dissertation, Harvard University Graduate School of Arts and Sciences, 2016. http://nrs.harvard.edu/urn-3:HUL.InstRepos:33493418

to town to sell him, he offered to buy him. "I received a buttered churek-cake and my father half a rouble and three churek-cakes. I ate my cake with cries and tears and my father left me forever," writes Mikhailov.

That same night, Ivan Afanasitch, a Russian Orthodox priest staying at the consul's house, offered to buy the boy from the groom and this was speedily agreed. In Astrakhan he baptised the boy as a Christian and named him Vassili Mikhailov. Later, he also taught him to read and write. Many more adventures followed, but after some months Vassili was taken to Tsaritsyn – now Volgograd. Five years later, when Vassili was 11, the priest died. As a result, Vassili became the property of the priest's widow, who took him to Saratov, an important shipping port further up the Volga.

Nor was this the end of the transactions concerning Mikhailov. The priest's widow decided to move to a nearby town to be closer to her daughter, herself the widow of a Kalmyk interpreter called Kirilli Makaritch Veselov. When both women died a few years later, Vassili Mikhailov was taken on by Lieutenant Ssava Spiridonitch Veselov, half-brother of the translator, who served with a company of Kalmyk dragoons, who always lived close to their nomadic brethren on the steppes. "I served my master in two Kalmyk campaigns and was at the great battle of the Kalaus, where about 5,000 of the enemy was slain," he writes.[3]

In December 1770, aged 29, Mikhailov enlisted into the Astrakhan Cossack Host, where he received an annual pay of 80 roubles, plus a 30-rouble bonus, although he still remained the property of his master. At this time great events were taking place in southern Russia. The great horde of Kalmyks who had settled in southern Russia and who acted as a barrier between the Russian homelands and the marauders of the Kazakh Steppe, decided to return to their homelands in China. This was truly an extraordinary event, a great mass movement in which more than 200,000 nomads and six million animals undertook a terrible 2,000-mile journey eastwards, harried all the way by Kazakhs and Cossacks who were under orders from St Petersburg to stop them at any

---

3. This was during the Russian-Turkish war of 1769-70.

cost. Only about 70,000 of them reached their final destination.[4] This mass migration was later famously described by Thomas de Quincey in his superb novella, *The Revolt of the Tartars*.[5]

Mikhailov says that the Kalmyk leader Ubashi Khan at first tried to lull the Russian commander into believing that there were signs of an uprising among the Kazakhs on the steppe and that he wished to suppress them, hence his mobilisation. The Russian commander, Kishinsky, immediately sent a small group of Cossacks to assist the khan – more likely, to keep an eye on them. Included amongst them was Mikhailov. He says he was then falsely accused of stealing a cow, for which he received a flogging with a cat-o'-nine-tails, although the intervention of his master's wife meant he only received two stripes.

A few days later, on 2 January 1771, in the freezing cold, Mikhailov embarked with his fellow Cossacks on a barge to the east bank of the Volga, marching onwards to the swollen River Aktobe which they crossed on the backs of their horses, continuing the next morning on towards the camp of the Kalmyk khan. As they were on this journey, the khan and his close kinsmen made known to the horde that they were to make secret preparations for their journey back to China. All the Kalmyks the Cossacks met on the road held to the story about the insurrection of the Kazakhs.

That night it became clear that something strange was afoot. The Cossacks were not allowed into the main camp, but put up in a group of yurts some distance away. A Kalmyk Buddhist priest they met made a number of odd comments that turned out to be a warning, a fact that they recognised only belatedly. In the night Vassili and two of his comrades were awoken by shouts and cries. When they tried to leave the yurt to find out what was happening, a group of Kalmyks prevented them from leaving. Now they were surrounded and drew their knives to protect themselves. They called for the priest to return to see them. He did so and told them he had tried to warn them, but that they had not

---

4. The Kalmyks had arrived in the lower Volga in 1636 seeking protection from attacks by the Djungars in Western China. After the Chinese defeated the Djungars in 1756 the Kalmyks began to think about returning to China.

5. Thomas de Quincey, *Revolt of the Tartars*, American Book Company, New York, 1895.

believed him. He now told them that the entire horde of the Kalmyks was returning to China and that the Cossacks' captain had already been made a prisoner. A worse fate had befallen some of the others.

Faced with such circumstances Vassili and his friends had no choice but to surrender and beg for protection. The priest tried to intervene on their behalf, offering sheep in exchange for their custody. At first the Kalmyks present refused, saying that their khan had ordered them to kill anyone who tried to return to Russia, even if he was Russian. But they then relented and departed. Vassili and his friends were able to procure horses and so mounted up and rode alongside the priest in whose custody they now found themselves. Close by the yurt in which they had stayed they saw the body of a Cossack with his head cloven, which they buried before moving on.

Now they were moving with the main group of Kalmyks, staying close to the priest. A second attempt to remove them failed and the priest asked for a message to be taken to the Kalmyk khan to settle the matter once and for all. Six days passed and already the group had reached the River Ural (known until 1775 as the River Jaik). Yet another attempt, this time by seven Kalmyks, was made to take the men prisoner, but was repulsed by the priest. A messenger arrived the following day to say that the khan had now agreed to see them, but by diligent questioning the men found that this was a ruse to take them away and murder them.

But while this attempt failed, a few days later three Kalmyks seized their horses and took them into the desert, away from the marching column of Kalmyks. Vassili was separated from the others, but was soon brought to a spot where he recognised his two Cossack companions, one of whom was being cut to pieces as he approached. The other was tied to the tail of a horse and dragged around until he expired, when he too was cut to pieces. It was clear that this was also to be the fate of poor Mikhailov, but at that moment a *saissang* (commander) and his *tushimell* (interpreter) rode up and told the assailants to hand over Vassili and his interpreter, at the command of the khan. Eventually they agreed to do so. Vassili mounted up behind the interpreter and they rode off. Later he learned that the murdered Cossacks had been heard planning to kill their hosts and steal their horses and were hence butchered. This Kalmyk interpreter agreed to look after Vassili and left him with his brother and wife who were part of the column moving eastwards.

Another month passed, by which time the Kalmyks had reached the Irtysh river. Some of them now thought that there would be a negotiation with the Russians and that the horde would return to Russia. Then a rumour began to spread that the Kalmyks on the west bank of the Volga had crossed to the east and intended to join with the main group. They had burnt cities behind them and there could be no going back. "I was now too intimidated to make an attempt to escape, being fearful of falling into the hands of the Kalmyks who were approaching us in the rear. I therefore remained with my host," wrote Mikhailov.[6]

Winter passed into spring and still Mikhailov was a prisoner of the Kalmyks. He came across two Cossacks he knew who were now slaves, one of them having lost an eye. And he suffered daily abuse to such an extent that he decided to try to escape. By the beginning of April the horde had reached a desert region and were now subject to increasingly frequent attacks from Kazakh marauders. Vassili decided to take his chances on an escape. He managed to steal some flour, mutton, a fat sheep's tail and a field kettle, which he put into a bundle, along with some silver buttons and 17 silver roubles. Grabbing a musket from one of the tents he mounted a brown mare and rode away from the camp. He found another horse and tied that behind him as he tried to put as much distance as possible between himself and the horde.

The following day Vassili saw a group of horsemen riding towards him. Realising that escape was impossible, he waited until the seven horsemen had ridden up to him. From their dress he knew that they were Kazakhs. They motioned him to throw down his gun and get off his horse. They now dismounted too and stripped him of everything he had, including his clothing, offering him only a dirty rag that had been thrown away by the Kalmyks. Next they ordered him to follow them to a nearby hill on the top of which was a Kazakh encampment. Here Vassili was told they would take him to Orenburg, but they offered him no food. His legs were put in irons and his hands fastened to his

---

6. *Adventures of Mikhailow, op. cit.*, p. 14.

neck with ropes. A large piece of felt was placed over him so that only his head was showing. The seven Kazakhs then arranged themselves around the edge of the encampment in such a way that it would be impossible for him to escape.

In the morning he was untied and the group then divided up his belongings amongst themselves. Vassili himself became the property of the group's leader, Isbossar, who had never seen a flintlock weapon before; he promptly took the lock off and put it in his pocket. Once again, Vassili went through the endless cycle: ill-treatment, an attempt to escape, discovery followed by punishment. But delivery came when he was able to offer a cure for a child sick with asthma. He told the boy's father not to give him any milk and to make him some mutton broth. The child improved soon after but was then given cream by his parents. Once again, he became ill. Soon after, the poor child died and, in the process, seemed to have established, more by luck than judgement, Vassili's credibility as a healer.

A year went by, in which Vassili remained in the custody of the Kazakhs but was better treated. He survived reasonably well, fearing only that he would be sold to another group and that he would have to start the process of ingratiation all over again. The inevitable eventually happened and he then became the property of a Kazakh hunter, who immediately began preparing for a long journey. They rode south for ten days until they reached the shores of the Aral Sea, eating only dried sheep cheese on the way. Here he once again tried to escape but failed when he was caught in the act of trying to slit the hunter's throat. Needless to say, he received a severe beating that almost killed him.

Vassili was now taken to Khiva for sale, but this time he was forced to walk. At Khiva he was exchanged for a Persian slave and two Bokharan dresses. His new master turned out to be humane. He was only required to do light domestic work and sometime to work in the fields cultivating the family's plot. Still, he dreamed of returning to Russia. A further escape attempt ended in failure – although he managed to convince his new owner that he had been captured against his will and taken away from the city. Even after he fell in with another Russian captive he was no luckier; his fellow-Russian failed to turn up at their first appointed meeting place prior to mounting their escape and when he did eventually appear, he was more trouble than he was worth, complaining about the lack of food and constantly delaying their travel by requesting time to sleep.

After two days they were discovered and put in chains in the town of Kipchak. Their masters soon turned up to collect them. Back again in Khiva, Vassili was chained in leg-irons, although after a day his master relented once again, mainly due to pressure from the women in the house, who said it was natural for a man to try to escape to his own country. The following spring he had another chance, when his master sent him out to the fields on a horse. He tied up another slave, an Uzbek, and set off towards the Amu Darya river. There he stole a boat to cross the river and then floated downstream towards the Aral Sea, which he quickly reached. Here he landed, along with the provisions he had brought with him and then set off on foot northwards. He stole a horse from a Karakalpak settlement and then two more before setting off in a northwesterly direction. After 19 days during which he nearly starved to death he came across some Kazakh yurts, telling the inhabitants he was an escaped Persian slave. They immediately stripped him and divided all his belongings between them, providing him only with a piece of cloth to hide his nakedness. He was put to work gathering dung for fuel from the steppe and fetching water and was tied up each night.

Vassili found out from another slave in the encampment that he was due to be sold that night to the younger brother of Ablai Khan, who was on the point of marrying. Not surprisingly, he began to regret ever leaving his master in Khiva, who had treated him well even after he had tried to escape. Now he thought it likely that he would never see Russia again. In desperation he jumped onto a horse tied to one of the yurts, even though he was wearing nothing but a skin, and made off as fast as he could. After about three days he made it to the Jaik (Ural), closely followed by three riders. These got close to him, but he lost them in the reed beds. He saw some people in a boat on the river, but they could not hear his calls. Travelling on further he eventually saw a *stanitza* (village) and church on the other side of the river.

Finally he found a fisherman who, once he had got over the surprise of seeing a near-naked man speaking to him in Russian, took him across the river where he was taken to the *ataman* (chief), who asked him to identify himself. Bread and sour milk were brought in and Vassili was given a place to sleep. The next morning, after he had been given clothes, he found out he was in the village of Kalmykowsk. From there he was driven to the Chancellor's office in the town of Jaik where a letter describing his strange arrival in the village was given to the commanding officer. Incredibly, this officer remembered that he had previously been with Sawwa Spiridonitch Veselov in the Cossack platoon. Vassili then remembered meeting him previously. The officer, a major, gave him money and soon he had amassed the best part of 15 silver roubles from the kind gifts of the soldiers in the town. He spent a month there and eventually sold his horse for another 17 roubles before leaving for Astrakhan.

In Astrakhan he was told that he could return to the town of Jenatajewsk, from where he had left several years before. He entered into service with a relative of his previous master, Michailo Sawwich Veselov, who was *pristan* (superintendent) of the Darbat Kalmyk hordes, and stayed with him for the next 30 years.

Whether this story is true in every detail is not really the point. Undoubtedly the ups and downs of Mikhailov's life mirrored to some degree the kind of things that could easily happen to Russian travellers in the southern parts of the Russian Empire. And it undoubtedly provided part of the justification for the Russians to complete their subjugation of the Central Asian khanates and tribal federations, a process that had been started by Peter the Great at the beginning of the 18th century.

TRAVELLING TO KHIVA

The Western Steppes – the land between the Caspian and the Aral Seas – attracted travellers from the earliest times. Travelling from Europe to Moscow and then down the Volga to the Caspian and onwards had numerous advantages over the route from Eastern Turkey. And the fabled city of Khiva always had about it an air of mystique.

As already mentioned, Khiva was a large slave market, where Turkoman and Kazakh raiders sold captive Persians – and a smaller number of Russians – into a life of servitude. Three times the Russians had failed to capture this remote oasis town, several hundred miles south of the Aral Sea. Around 1602, a group of free Yaik Cossacks made three raids on Khiva. Then in 1717, Prince Alexander Bekovich-Cherkassky attacked Khiva and was also soundly defeated, with only a few men escaping to tell the tale. The ultimately unsuccessful Russo–Khivan War of 1839-40 was the final failed Russian attempt to conquer the khanate, when Count Vasily Perovsky, military governor of the Orenburg region, set out from that city with 5,000 men during a particularly freezing winter. After losing most of his camels and horses, and more than 1,000 casualties among his soldiers, he was forced to turn back after reaching only halfway.

These attempts to capture Khiva were stimulated in part by a desire to protect Russian citizens from capture and a life of servitude and in part by the Russian desire to find a way to capitalise on the trade with India. Russian merchants wanted to expand their trade with the East, but the trade via northern branches of the Silk Road was firmly in the hands of the Khivans. Silk, tea and porcelain from China, tobacco and black lambskins from Bokhara and many other valuable items came across the desert on huge camel trains, to be traded for Russian linen, metal goods, silver, glass, paper and sugar. The Khivan merchants who controlled much of the trade were reluctant to let it fall into the hands of the Russians.

By the beginning of the 19th century relations between Khiva and Russia were at their worst ever. The khan warned that any Russian envoy who crossed the borders of the khanate would be executed or sold into slavery. At the same time, Russian sailors on the Caspian and settlers in the northern steppes were still being traded into slavery. But the Russians were not going to give up easily. In the long run the only answer was to bring the unruly Central Asian khanates under Russian control. From the time of Peter the Great the Russian strategy was to build long lines of military bases, first across the northern edge of the Central Asian steppelands, then down the eastern shore of the Caspian and then, finally, south along the eastern border with China.

The forts built along the eastern Caspian shore would allow the Russians to deal with the ferocious Turkoman tribes that lived in the area and whose main trade was capturing Persians and Russians to sell into slavery at Khiva. At the same time, the Russians wanted to commence negotiations with the Khivan khan, Mohamed Ragim Khan, and persuade him that opening up trading relations would be better for everyone. The person selected to try to build a relationship with the khan was a young Russian Army officer called Nikolai Nikolaevich Muraviev (1794-1860), from a prominent military and diplomatic family. His brothers were all military men; one of them, Mikhail, as well as being one of the founders of the Russian Geographical Society, was also the employer of Lucy Finley, who in 1848 married the English explorer Thomas Witlam Atkinson. Nikolai's elder brother Alexander was involved in the unsuccessful Decembrist Uprising against Tsar Nicholas I in 1825 and several of his close relatives were arrested, including one who was executed. Nikolai was in the Caucasus at the time of the Uprising, so was not involved.

Nikolai Muraviev began his journey to Mahomed Ragim Khan on 18 June 1819, leaving from the Georgian capital of Tiflis, where his commander, General Yermolov, was stationed. His task was to survey the eastern coast of the Caspian and then to proceed alone to Khiva to negotiate an alliance with the khan and compile a detailed description of the region and its inhabitants.

Once on the eastern shore of the Caspian, he dressed as a Turkoman and went by the name of Murad Beg, travelling by camel: "During the whole journey I suffered less from the unpleasant jolting and the unaccustomed ride on camel-back than from the terrible *ennui*, for I found myself alone without a soul to talk to," he wrote.[7] Once, when they met a large group of Igdur Chodor Turkomans and it seemed that his disguise would be uncovered, his travelling companions told them that Muraviev was a Russian captive being taken to Khiva to sell as a slave. "'Well done', cried the Igdurs with wild, mocking laughter; 'Off with them, the accursed infidels. We sold three Russians in Khiva this very trip and got a good sum for them'."

---

7   Nikolay Murav'yov, *Journey to Khiva through the Turkoman Country*, Oguz Press, London, 1977, p. 32.

Muraviev eventually arrived in Khiva at the beginning of October, where he found there were around 3,000 Russian slaves along with 30,000 Persians. He heard the plaintive cries of the Russians as he passed them in the street, begging him to help them return to Russia. On one occasion he found a note in the barrel of a gun he had sent for repair: "We venture to inform your Honour that there are over 3,000 Russian slaves in this place, who have to suffer unheard-of misery from labour, cold, hunger, etc. Have pity on our unhappy situation and reveal it to the Emperor. In gratitude we shall pray to God for your Honour's welfare."[8]

Muraviev spent the next 48 days confined to a small room in a fortress called Yal Kaldi about 30 miles from Khiva itself. He was a prisoner in all but name. There was no lock on the door, but he was followed at all times and not allowed to leave the fortress. Finally, on 20 November, he was invited to meet the khan, who received him in a yurt set up in a courtyard in his palace. The khan was courteous and agreed to send an emissary back to the Russians to discuss in more detail the possibilities of trade. On 27 November, Muraviev set out on his return journey, on 15 December reaching the Caspian shore, where a Russian corvette was waiting to take him to Baku.

In the end, nothing came of Muraviev's visit to the Khan of Khiva. He returned to army life, serving in the Caucasus, in Persia and in Turkey. He took part in the Polish war in 1831 but was later dismissed from service for trying to protect exiled Decembrists and for criticising the army's administrators. However, he was allowed to re-join the Grenadiers and by 1854 was appointed Governor General of the Caucasus and Commander-in-Chief of the Caucasus Army. His defeat of the Turkish forces at Kars led the tsar to give him the honorific name of Muraviev-Karsky.[9]

*

---

8. *Ibid*, p. 77.

9. His brother Mikhail received the honorific name of Muraviev-Vilensky for crushing the Polish insurrection of 1860, while his cousin Nikolai was given the name of Muraviev-Amursky for his role when Governor of Eastern Siberia in exploring the River Amur.

It was several years before any other foreigners tried to reach Khiva. The Russian expedition of 1839 under General Perovsky was a terrible failure, with more than 20 per cent casualties among the 5,000 troops and the loss of more than 10,000 camels and 8,000 horses. A British Army officer sent from Herat in Afghanistan, to try and forestall the Russian invasion, Captain James Abbott, had little success and ended up being captured by Turkoman slavers – although when they realised he held a letter from the Khivan khan to the Russian tsar, they immediately released him.[10]

A second British officer sent to find out what had happened to Abbott had more luck. Embarrassingly, for the Russians at least, Richmond Shakespear managed to make his way to the city, also from Herat, arriving not long after the debacle of the Perovsky Expedition. Shakespear convinced the khan that unless he yielded up the Russian slaves in his city, the Russians would attempt another invasion. Incredibly, the khan agreed with him and released into his custody 416 Russian slaves, whom he marched across the desert to Orenburg, to the amazement of the whole town. Shakespear's extraordinary achievement led to an audience with Tsar Nicholas I and a knighthood from Queen Victoria on his return to London in 1841.[11]

After that, however, there were few if any outsiders brave enough to risk visiting Khiva and Transcaspia. Not until the next Russian attempt to capture the city did anyone feel confident enough to make the journey.

SCHUYLER, CRITIC OF RUSSIA'S CENTRAL ASIAN ADMINISTRATION

Eugene Schuyler states in the preface to his magnificent two-volume account of his travels through Central Asia in 1873 that his chief aim "was to study the political and social condition of the regions which had recently been annexed by Russia, as well as to compare the state of the inhabitants under Russian rule with that of those still living under

---

10. See James Abbott, *Narrative of a Journey from Heraut to Khiva, Moscow and St Petersburg, during the late Russian invasion of Khiva*, W H Allen & Co, London, 1843.

11. For more detail of this incredible event, see Sir Richard Shakespear, "A Personal Narrative of a Journey from Herat to Orenburg, on the Caspian, in 1840", *Blackwood's Magazine*, June 1842.

the despotism of the Khans".[12] It was an ambitious task that was to have significant repercussions for the American diplomat.

Schuyler set off on his journey in the wake of a large Russian military force that had been assembled to deal with the Khivan khanate once and for all. By the time he left in the early spring of 1873 much of Central Asia had already been conquered by the Russians. Only a few years before Schuyler's journey, in 1868, Russian forces under General Konstantin Petrovich von Kaufmann had captured the Central Asian cities of Tashkent, Bokhara and Samarkand and had also gained control over the Khanate of Kokand in the east. The Kazakhs had already mostly come to terms with the Russians and the Kyrgyz too had been neutralised. Suddenly a vast new territory, barely known even to the Russians, opened up, ripe for exploitation. Kaufmann went to considerable lengths to find out about the massive new territory he had conquered, bringing in scientists, artists and educationalists to evaluate the region.

Now Schuyler, who was a remarkably "hands on" diplomat – he was secretary of the United States Legation in St Petersburg – wanted to see for himself just what the Russians had achieved in their new dominions. In his findings he did not mince his words. For mingled in with the descriptions of the places he visited during his eight-month journey, was sharp criticism of the Russian officials who were now administering this vast new conquered territory. "I hope that my readers will believe that the criticism made upon certain acts of the Russian administration in Central Asia are not made in a spirit of fault-finding," he wrote in his introduction. "It is evidently for the interest of Russia that the mistakes and faults of the Russian policy should be known and should be remedied as soon as possible." We shall come back to these points later.

Schuyler was no ordinary diplomat. He was born in Ithaca, New York, in February 1840 and began his studies at Yale University when aged only 15, before graduating in 1859. He became one of the first three graduates to gain a Ph.D. from an American university. He then turned his attention to gaining a law degree and it was while practising

---

12. Eugene Schuyler, *Turkistan: Notes of a Journey in Russian Turkistan, Khokand, Bukhara and Kuldja*, Sampson Low, Marston, Searle & Rivington, London, 1876, 2 vols.

in New York that he decided to learn Russian. Two years later, in 1865, he joined the staff of the newly-launched weekly news magazine, *The Nation*, which is still in print today, highly regarded for its progressive and liberal editorial line.

The following year he joined the US Consular Service and was sent to Russia because of his language skills – none of his colleagues there could speak Russian. He met the great writer Ivan Turgenev at Baden-Baden while on his way to Moscow, who in turn introduced him to leading literary figures, including Leo Tolstoy – Schuyler later translated Tolstoy's work, *The Cossacks*, into English. Schuyler also became the translator of Turgenev's *Fathers and Sons* and soon joined the literary salon of Prince Vladimir Odoyevsky. By 1868 he was travelling extensively, taking a steamer down the Volga to Orenburg and crossing into what is now northwestern Kazakhstan. He spent a week at Tolstoy's estate at Yasnaya Polyana in October that year, helping to reorganise the great writer's library.

In July 1870 he was promoted to secretary of the US Legation in St Petersburg and during the following six years travelled extensively across Russia and parts of Central Asia, writing for the National Geographic Society and completing his major work, *Turkistan*. Later he also wrote a biography of Peter the Great.

Schuyler set out from Moscow by train on the first leg of the journey that would form the basis for *Turkistan* on 23 March 1873, heading for the southern Russian town of Saratov, built on the ruins of the Golden Horde city of Uvek that was destroyed by Tamerlane in 1395. The spring thaw had not yet set in and snow still lay deep on the ground. Far to the south, Russian forces under General von Kaufmann were cautiously heading across the desert towards Khiva, divided into five separate armies to ensure they would finally be successful. Schuyler had been officially invited to tour the newly-conquered areas of Central Asia by the Russian government and was given special permission to visit places that were out-of-bounds to most civilians – excluding Khiva itself.

His companion, for the first part of the journey at least, was fellow American, Januarius Aloysius MacGahan, a renowned journalist and correspondent of the *New York Herald*, who was determined – despite Russian objections – to reach Khiva to witness the Russian military operation to seize the city. He was ultimately successful, and his despatches later became the substance of his book *Campaigning on the Oxus and the Fall of Khiva*.[13]

Schuyler's intention was to travel in a long arc from west to east, passing from Orenburg south to Khiva, Bokhara, Samarkand and then to travel on to the Semirecheye region of what is now eastern Kazakhstan, Kokand and then northwards back to Siberia, before returning to St Petersburg.

Schuyler mentions in his book that he and MacGahan were joined by another person on their 930-mile rail journey from Moscow to Saratov; it was Prince Tchinguiz, described by Schuyler as "a lineal descendant of the famous Genghis Khan, and son of the last Khan of the Bukeief Horde of Kirghiz", who had just returned from the Haj and was on his way to spend the summer on his estates in Samara.[14] In common with most writers at this time, Schuyler often referred to the present-day Kazakhs as Kirghiz.[15]

Having left the train behind and transferred into a far less comfortable *tarantass* or horse-drawn carriage, Schuyler and MacGahan headed east and then south. Schuyler's first sight of Kazakhs on this journey came in the Cossack town of Uralsk – now known as Oral and located in northwestern Kazakhstan, close to the Russian border: "The streets were full of Kazakhs, most of them mounted on camels, which at once

---

13. MacGahan pulled off the scoop of the century by following the Russian forces across the deserts to Khiva, despite their best efforts to stop him. The two men were to remain friends and in 1876 Schuyler, who was by then US Consul-General in Constantinople, invited MacGahan to investigate reports of large-scale atrocities committed by the Turkish Army following the failure of an attempted uprising by Bulgarian nationalists in April that year. MacGahan's reports for the London *Daily News* created a sensation and even today he is fondly remembered in Bulgaria, as is Schuyler.

14. Schuyler notes that the Bukeief, or Inner Horde, was living in Europe, between the Ural and the Volga, and numbered around 150,000. This horde, he says, was formed in the early years of the 19th century by about 7,000 of the Lesser Horde, led by Bukeief, a grandson of Abul-Khair, who crossed the Ural river to occupy the land left vacant by the Kalmyks following their return to China in 1771. In 1812 Bukeief was confirmed khan. He was the ancestor of Prince Tchinghiz, mentioned above.

15. The Kazakhs were often called Kirghiz during the Imperial Russian period, or Kirghiz-Kazakhs, as distinct from the Kirghiz who today inhabit Kyrgyzstan. During the 19th century the Kirghiz were usually known as the Kara-Kirghiz or Dikokamenny. In this book I have changed Kirghiz to Kazakh wherever it makes sense to do so.

gave the town an Oriental aspect and altogether it seemed far more Kazakh than Cossack." He says this was a result of the new Russian regulations issued in 1869 which placed the town under the same government as the Ural Cossacks. Before this, the Kazakhs were rarely seen on the Russian side of the Ural. Orenburg too, had an Eastern flavour, having become an *entrepôt* for the trade carried on between Tashkent and Central Asia and Russia.

After Orenburg, and then Orsk, the next stop of any significance was at Kazaly, on the Syr Darya river, reached after an 11-day journey and an important crossroads for trade from Central Asia to Russia. It was also the site of Russia's Fort No.1. From here on southwards, Schuyler was in territory that few outsiders had ever seen, although Russia had been gradually encroaching on the vast steppelands for more than a century. In the 17th and 18th centuries Russia had built a chain of forts across its southern domains as protection against the marauding nomads, both Turkomans and Kazakhs, who inhabited these distant lands. Guryev on the Caspian, Uralsk, Orenburg, Orsk, Troitsk, Petropavlovsk, Omsk, Pavlodar, Semipalatinsk and Ust-Kamenogorsk had all become Russian military encampments that stretched eastwards from the Caspian to the borders of China close to the Altai Mountains.

Many were located along the banks of the River Irtysh that flowed westwards from the Altai before heading north into Siberia. Even further south, along the line of the great Syr Darya river – the Jaxartes of old, which flows from the Tian Shan Mountains on the border with China to the Aral Sea – another 200-mile-long defensive line of forts was built during the 1850s.

By the time Schuyler travelled post-houses had been hastily constructed across much of these steppelands, even if they were occasionally somewhat primitive, often consisting of little more than a few yurts and stabling for horses. Once he had reached Kazaly, on the fringes of the Kara-Kum desert, he began to see many Kazakhs. "All through the Kara-Kum we met numbers of Kazakh families, who were going from their winter to their summer quarters, seeking pasturage for their cattle and flocks in the Steppe south of Orenburg – long caravans of horses and camels laden with piles of felt, tent-frames, and household utensils, on top of which sat a woman, perhaps with an infant in a cradle before her." Schuyler adds:

"The Kazakhs speak a language which is one of the purest dialects of Tartar, though as a race they contain many foreign elements. They originated from several Turkish tribes and families, which in the second half of the fifteenth century followed Sultans Girei and Jani Bek in their flight from the tyranny of their rulers to the neighbourhood of Lake Balkash. They were soon joined by others and rapidly became a flourishing community, known by their neighbours as Kazakhs. The kernel of the race is evidently Turkish and many of the tribes and families have the same names as Uzbek tribes in Khokand and Bokhara. Gaining more and more strength and importance, they soon numbered a million of men, with over 300,000 warriors and in 1598 their Khan, Tevvekal (Tawwakul-ed), conquered the cities of Taskhent and Turkistan, which were the seat of the Kazakh dynasty till 1723. It was in this flourishing period of their sway that the Kazakhs became divided into three parts – the provinces of Tashkent and Turkistan forming the Middle Horde, the Great Horde going to the east and the Lesser Horde to the west and north."

Schuyler had done his research and provides one of the earliest and most accurate histories of the Kazakhs in Western literature, explaining the history of the negotiations between Khan Abul Khayir and the tsars during the early 18th century, the Russian policy of relying on tribal leaders who had little backing amongst their own people and the eventual abolition of the Kazakh khanate in 1824. Bearing in mind the meagre written sources available at the time, he makes a reasonable job of it, relying to some extent of the writings of Captain Shokan Walikhanov, the celebrated Kazakh ethnologist who had joined the Russian Army and wrote with great authority on his people.

Schuyler says that at the time of his writing the Kazakhs numbered around 1.5 million, although he acknowledges that it was difficult to be certain. "In the Greater Horde, in the district of Alatau, there are about 100,000 of both sexes; in the Middle Horde, occupying the whole of Southern Siberia and country north of Tashkent, there are 406,000; and in the Lesser Horde, between Fort Perovsky, the Ural and the Caspian, there are 800,000." He adds that the Bukeief (Inner) Horde, mentioned above, living between the Volga and Ural, added another 150,000 to the total numbers.

The economic importance of the Kazakhs to the Russian Empire can be gauged from the fact that according to the Russian statistics for 1869, they sold the following numbers of animals at the bazaars in Orenburg and Troitsk:

Camels:	1,150
Horses:	1,001
Herding cattle:	16,031
Sheep:	273,823[16]

The total value of these transactions, says Schuyler, was 1.5 million roubles or £200,000 at the then exchange rate. At Petropavlovsk on the border with Siberia, cattle sales from 1856 to 1863 amounted to over 2.5 million roubles (£340,000) a year. In addition, the sale of leather and hides added another 400,000 roubles (£55,000) a year.

Schuyler went on to describe the internal arrangements in Kazakhs' yurts, their clothing and, most important of all, their horse trappings: "Their greatest adornments are their belts, saddles and bridles, which are often so covered with silver, gold and precious stones as to be almost solid."

He says that even though the Kazakhs were nomadic, "they do not wander indiscriminately over the vast expanse, but have their settled winter and summer quarters, each *volost* – as they are now divided by the Russians – keeping its own limits." Only in the area around Aulie-Ata and the Alexandrovsky Mountain range in what is now southern Kazakhstan, where there was good money to be made from growing wheat, did he find Kazakhs engaged in agriculture.

He remarks that they wore their religion – almost entirely Islam – comparatively lightly, having few mosques or Islamic preachers. Islam, he says, was introduced into the steppe "by the mistaken efforts of the Russian Government. At first but a few of their sultans and chiefs had

---

16. Schuyler reproduces in his book *Turkistan* many sets of detailed statistics that he culled from official Russian government reports, aided by his excellent Russian language skills.

any idea of the doctrines of Islam and there was not a mosque nor a mullah in the Steppe, but the Russians (just as they insisted on using the Tartar language in intercourse with them) insisted on treating them as though they were Mohammedans, built mosques and sent mullahs, until the whole people became outwardly Musselman, although the farther from the Russian lines, and the nearer to the settled populations of Central Asia, the weaker was the faith."[17]

Schuyler and MacGahan parted company at Fort Perovsky – Fort No.2 – the second Russian military encampment on the Syr Darya, as the journalist struck out alone to link up with the Russian forces far to the south. We shall hear more of him later. After passing through Samarkand and Bokhara, both of which he described in great and fascinating detail, Schuyler's journey took him through Aulie Ata towards Aksu, a distance of 150 miles that he accomplished in 24 hours. At Merke, a small military post, he admits he was worried about the presence of a venomous spider, known in Kazakh as a *kara kurt* ("black worm"), but more commonly known as the Steppe Spider (*Latrodectus lugubris*) and closely related to the European Black Widow: "It is said that its poison will kill a man, although I have never known of authenticated instances; here I was told that the Kazakhs who live on the small streams coming down from the Alexandrovsky range, especially in the neighbourhood of Merke, annually lose many animals through the bite of this spider. It lives in the grass, and there is a belief that it is unable to walk over a woollen substance, for which reason the Kazakhs, as well as the Cossacks and the soldiers, always spread down large pieces of felt, on which to sit."

Schuyler also had to put up with occasional encounters with a tarantula (*Lycosa singoriensis*), often called the Wolf Spider and now critically endangered, and large Camel Spiders (*Solpuga araneoides* and *S. intrepida*). The latter were first described by Pallas in 1772 during his journeys throughout southern Russia. The Camel Spider, says Schuyler, "is of a yellowish or reddish brown, also with long hair, and when walking seems as large as one's two fists. They frequent the steppes and

---

17. *Ibid*, p. 38.

live in the sand, but are rarely found in gardens or villages."

Schuyler made a short visit to Lake Issyk Kul in present-day Kyrgyzstan, and also describes some of the Kyrgyz tribes and the ways they administered their territories, particularly concerning the role of the *Bis* or traditional judges. When he returned to Tokmak on the Chu river, he found that an extraordinary session of the *Bis* of two of the large districts of that town and Issyk Kul was taking places. He describes the scene:

"The Bis, who were all big, stout, well-to-do looking men, were seated on the ground in a circle in a large kibitka. In the centre was a small table, at which sat the Prefect of the district, while the interpreter with his bundles of papers, had a chair nearby. The proceedings were marked by regularity and good order. Plaintiff and defendant told their stories, which were supported, if necessary, by witnesses. The interpreter related the gist of the case to the Prefect, and made a short note of it in his book, and after a consultation of the Bis of each district, first separately and then together, the decision was entered in the book and they affixed their seals."[18]

From Tokmak Schuyler set off north again via Konstaninovskaya toward Uzun-Agatch in present-day Kazakhstan. It was here that in October 1860 that Russia's Lieutenant-Colonel Kolpakovsky had defeated a large force of around 20,000 Kokandians under Khanayat Shah who had attempted to drive the Russians out of Semirecheye, having first won over the Kyrgyz and gained the passive cooperation of the Great Horde of the Kazakhs. The Khokandians had intended to blockade the Russian garrison at Kastek and then move on to Vierney (Almaty), but instead decided to attack Uzun-Agatch. The garrison held out and managed to despatch a messenger to Kolpakovsky at Kastek, who led a small force of around 800 Cossacks to relieve the garrison. Their field guns terrified the Khokandians, who retreated in disorder back over the mountains.

In Vierney, Schuyler quickly made the acquaintance of General Rossitzky, who was acting governor of the province, and spent time talking to Chinese merchants who exported jade and the horns of

---

18. *Ibid.*

the Maral deer back to China. He noted the agricultural riches of the region, particularly of the river valleys. The Seven Rivers that give the Russian name to the province of Semirecheye[19] he names as follows: the Lepsa, the Baskan, the Sarkan, the Aksu, the Karatal, the Koksu, and the Ili. (There does not seem to be any agreement over this; other authors include the Chu, for example.)

Schuyler also took an interest in the Russian colonies that were beginning to sprout up across Semirecheye. "I passed through many of these colonies on the road, and I stopped at some of them and entered into conversation with the farmers, by far the greater number of whom were peasants from the provinces of Voronezh, Tambof, and Saratof. They seemed quite satisfied with their lot; indeed, so far as mere physical well-being and immunity from taxes is concerned, they are far better off than they were in European Russia. They are given their lands either gratis or at a low price, the payments extending over a long period, and they are freed from taxes and duties for a term of years. They make the journey at their own risk, and usually with their own horses and oxen. The fertility of the soil and the personal independence possible on this remote frontier more and more attract immigration, and during the last two or three years the number of colonists has considerably increased."

He notes that the Cossack settlements and Russian colonies were very different, the former being set up by order, both to settle the land and also to defend it against marauding Kyrgyz and Khokandians. The Cossacks were taken by quota from the various armies of the Ural, Orenburg and Siberia. Peasants were also drafted in from Russia, given land, tools and weapons and told to regard themselves as Cossacks. They became known as the Cossack army of Semiretch. Later the peasant settlers arrived, travelling *en masse* from their villages in southern Russian in search of land and a new life – and a generous tax-free allowance.

Schuyler travelled on from Vierney, heading northeast until he reached the River Ili, which he crossed on a large barge filled with Kazakhs and their horses. Even at this time, coal from Kuldja in Chinese Turkestan was brought down the river to the Ili station and taken on to Vierney by cart,

---

19. In the Kazakh language today this region is known as Zhetysu, which also means Seven Rivers.

where a *pud* (36 lb) could be bought for 11½ d. The distance on the river was around 280 miles and navigation was open almost all year. Attempts to bring goods up the Ili from Lake Balkash – a distance of around 240 miles – by towing barges were abandoned early on because of the cost.

After an excursion to Kuldja, which he reached through the Altyn Emel pass, the next point on Schuyler's itinerary was Kopal,[20] the town founded in 1847 at the foot of the Djungar Alatau Mountains and where the Atkinsons lived for nine months in 1848-49. On the road he says he came across two *balbals* – the stone humanoid figures found across the Eurasian steppes and as far east as Mongolia. In the 19th century they were believed to date back to Scythian times, but today are generally thought to have been carved by early Turkic invaders. Kopal was thriving when Schuyler visited in 1873 and had around 5,000 inhabitants. "It is well built, with spacious wooden houses, and maintains two schools, two churches, and a mosque. It formerly did a very thriving business in the steppe; but as this has now been chiefly transferred to Vierney, the importance of the town has diminished," he wrote.

Two hours on from Kopal, Schuyler reached Arasan, where the famous hot springs – also noted by Thomas Atkinson – were becoming increasingly popular. By this time bathing houses had been erected in a pretty garden and close by there was a hotel. As early as 1886 a health resort opened at the site – the first in what is now Kazakhstan. During the Soviet period it became an important medical treatment sanatorium. The Kopal-Arasan mineral springs are classified as weakly radioactive and weakly sulphate-chloride-natrium thermal springs. The temperature of the majority of springs is 35-37°C. The springs have been used to treat medical conditions such as rheumatism, metabolic and blood disorders and also for treating people suffering from copper and lead poisoning.

In the 1870s the annual spring migration of Kazakhs from their wintering ground on the shores of Lake Balkhash up into the Djungar Alatau Mountains was still a spectacular sight. Schuyler describes

20. Sometimes written as Kapal.

coming across large groups on the road "… sometimes changing their camp and travelling across the steppe with long files of horses and camels laden with their kibitkas and household goods, and sometimes in small parties, apparently out hunting, for they carried on perches fixed to their saddle-bows falcons and *burkuts*, large golden eagles which will bring down deer, foxes, and wolves."

From Arasan, Schuyler crossed the Gasfort – sometimes Hasford – Pass towards Sarcand and not long after got his first view of Lake Balkhash, the fifteenth largest lake in the world. He notes that most Kazakhs call the huge lake *Ak Tenghis* (White Sea) or *Ala-Tenghis* (Striped Lake, on account of its islands). Most simply called it Tenghis: the Sea. Before long he had reached Sergiopol (now Ayaguz) and then on to Semipalatinsk (Semey) before turning back west to reach Omsk. He arrived back in St Petersburg on 15 November 1873, after an absence of around eight months.

Schuyler had not originally intended to publish a book on his travels through Central Asia. His manuscript was originally written as an official report, published by the US Department of State. It was here that he made clear his attitude towards the corrupt Russian officials then administering the vast newly-conquered territories of Central Asia. It was a devastating critique, based on detailed information and on-the-spot observations, including Russian military reports and many discussions with officials.

He explained how the rivalry between military officers and state administrators led to an impasse. Drunkenness, insubordination and lack of training – particularly among the Cossacks – weakened the morale of the troops, while their officers were starved of funds and a clear strategy. However, Schuyler praised the decision not to allow missionaries to work in the newly-conquered territories and favourably contrasted the open attitude of Russian Army officers towards locals with Anglo-Saxon attitudes towards "natives" in India and elsewhere.

But he is scathing about Russian tax laws, the arbitrariness of officials and the ubiquitous corruption. "It is not only the fact that cases of glaring corruption and venality have occurred, but that these cases when brought to the notice of the Governor-General have frequently been condoned, and the guilty officials allowed to go unpunished, which has exerted a very bad influence on the minds of the natives," he writes.[21]

Nor is Schuyler afraid of naming names: "Since 1865 a tax of 20 kopeks on each kibitka had been collected from the nomads of Semiretch, to be devoted to the general needs and to the demands of the local Kirghiz, especially for making loans to them. This fund, with the interest, amounted in 1871 to more than 23,000 roubles. Up to 1873 not a single Kirghiz had received any of this money on loan or as a grant and out of this Kazakhs capital more than 18,000 roubles had been applied for other purposes – 10,000 for loans, 5,000 of which were not to be repaid. In this sum were included the journeys of different officials and their extraordinary expenses, searches for coalmines, the expenses of completing and repairing the house of a former assistant-prefect and loans were even to be made to Russian merchants, one for 8,000 roubles, for completing a distillery. The conduct of the Prefect of the district of Preovsky was investigated and he was removed for extortion and bribery. Instead of being punished he was appointed to the district of Aulie-Ata, where his conduct again called for investigation and he was removed for exacting an illegal contribution from the natives on the occasion of a demand for camels for the Khivan expedition."[22]

In another case a Russian official called Eman claimed he had been robbed of a considerable amount of government funds. Twelve local Kazakhs were arrested and put on trial and, after admitting their guilt, found guilty. However, during the trial Eman committed suicide and left a letter in which he admitted he had taken and spent the money himself. Only then was it discovered that the Kazakhs had all been tortured. The officer responsible was removed from his post but given another similar job in a different district.

Schuyler also mentions an incident where an unpopular district prefect at Kopal was robbed and badly beaten. Sixty local Kazakhs, including Sultan Tezak, who held the rank of a major in the Russian service and was the most aristocratic and respected of the Kazakh chiefs

---

21. Schuyler, *op. cit.*, vol. 2, p. 247.

22. *Ibid*, p. 249.

– and a good and loyal friend of Russia – were blamed for the robbery. Some of the property was found in Sultan Tezak's yurt. Only later did a Cossack confess he had placed the articles in the yurt, under direct orders of the judge in the case. The judge was said to have done this because the sultan was close to General Kolpakovsky, of whom another group of officers, including the judge, were jealous. Sultan Tezak was eventually acquitted in 1875 by the Senate at St Petersburg.

Schuyler describes many similar examples, using his excellent language skills to learn first-hand about such scandals. He notes that anyone openly trying to highlight these issues was punished. Correspondence with newspapers was strictly forbidden. He gives examples of official graft, where no accounts were kept, money was given out without receipts and extravagant lifestyles were funded from the public purse or from extortion of the local population.

Schuyler quotes extensively from official reports to make his points, thus ensuring that he could not be criticised for bias or inaccuracy. He found ghost armies of non-existent soldiers on full pay, hospitals for populations of 150,000 with only four beds, construction of grand houses for officials, the quadrupling of heating bills in a year, employment of "inspectors" who actually served as cooks and gardeners – in short, all the scams that can be imagined.

This section of Schuyler's book is a *tour de force*, seldom equalled by other writers before or since. It was irrefutable and clearly hurt the Russian authorities. In a 1968 article on the controversy that resulted from the publication of Schuyler's report, author Frank G Siscoe notes that the Berlin correspondent of *The Times* published a fascinating report on the impact of the affair: "Mr Schuyler's remarkable despatch on Central Asia has naturally created a great sensation here. The public are so unaccustomed to the free criticism of official acts and to expressions of blame against individuals occupying official positions, that a document arraigning the conduct of several officers still forming part of the Administration of Turkistan necessarily produced a startling effect."[23]

---

23. Frank G Siscoe, "Eugene Schuyler, General Kaufman and Central Asia", *Slavic Review*, vol. 27, no. 1, March 1968.

Not surprisingly, the pro-government Russian newspapers were less kind, suggesting that Schuyler should look towards home and criticise the American policy towards the "North American Indians".

In publishing his book two years later – and knowing the uproar it was likely to create – Schuyler was careful to ensure he could be certain of his facts. In the preface he writes: "In endeavouring to give a true picture of the condition of affairs, I have sometimes felt obliged to speak at length of subjects upon which it has given me little pleasure to dwell. I think, however, that my friends in Russia will not mistake my object in speaking. I have lived too long in Russia, and have made too many friends there, to have other than kind feelings for the country and the people. I hope, then, that my readers will believe that the criticisms made upon certain acts of the Russian administration in Central Asia are not made in a spirit of fault-finding."

When Schuyler's book was republished in 1966, its editor, Geoffrey Wheeler, said it was "by far the best account of contemporary conditions – cultural, political, military and economic – that has ever been published in any language... Indeed, although the life of the people has undergone great changes since Schuyler's visit, study of his book is still essential for anyone wishing to understand the basic characteristics of the people of Central Asia and the significance of the Russian presence there."[24]

MACGAHAN AND THE FALL OF KHIVA

Eugene Schuyler's companion for the first part of his journey, fellow-American Januarius MacGahan, experienced many adventures before he finally made it back to St Petersburg. His book on the fall of Khiva contains a detailed account of his travels across the Kyzyl-Kum desert to Khiva and his interactions with the Russian military and the many Kazakhs he met on the road.

It starts with a description of the wearisome *tarantass* journey that he and Eugene Schuyler shared across the steppe: "Four weeks of travel,

---

24. Eugene Schuyler, *Turkistan: Notes of a Journey in Russian Turkistan, Khokand, Bukhara and Kuldja*, ed. Geoffrey Wheeler, Routledge and Kegan Paul, London, 1966, pp. xi-xii.

day and night, across the level frozen steppes of Russia and the broad snowy plains of Asia, with the thermometer ranging from 30 degrees to 50 degrees below zero; of struggle with exasperating perversity of Russian *yamstchiks*, the wearing, patience-trying stolidity of Kazakh *djigits*, the weakness of enfeebled, half-starved horses that were scarcely able to drag themselves along; the obstinacy of refractory camels, that tortured us for hours at a time with their dismal half-human howls, had reduced us to this dejected state of apathetic resignation."[25]

He describes passing through the tidy German settlements on the Volga, established by the Empress Catherine II in 1769, then on to Nikolaevsk and the Cossack town of Uralsk. Here there were no regular post-houses, only simple Russian peasant dwellings, where little food was available and the horses were thin and tired, having not yet fattened up on the new grass of spring. Once out onto the steppe proper, the post-horses were all Kazakh, again very weak at this time of the year (April) and thus on occasion up to 20 of them would be attached to the *tarantass*.

Sometimes they could only obtain camels. "Day after day, night after night, week after week, finds us on the road, gliding silently forward; changing horses at stations so much alike, that we seem to be arriving at the same place over and over again; the same endless plain, the same ever-receding horizon, until the steppe becomes to our benumbed imaginations a kind of monstrous treadmill on which, no matter how fast we travel, we always remain in exactly the same place."[26]

Gradually the weather warmed and MacGahan mentioned seeing the first large groups of Kazakh nomads heading towards their summer pastures to the north. Then the first glimpse of the Aral Sea's northern shore: "Darkly calm and silent it lies in the midst of the sandy desolation that surrounds it. Here its banks are rolling hillocks covered with brushwood, but far away can be seen rising, abrupt and precipitous, the western shore, in a serrated mountainous range, and standing out in the evening sunshine bare and bleak, like mountains of rugged brass. It is a

---

25. Januarius MacGahan, *Campaigning on the Oxus, and the fall of Khiva*, Harper & Brothers, New York, 1874.

26. *Ibid*, p. 12.

picture of strange and weird loneliness, according well with the sinister desolation of the surrounding waste."[27] Finally they arrived at Kazala, on the banks of the Syr Darya.

Kazala itself was built in 1847 by General Perovsky and called Fort No.1. A small earthwork about 200 m square defended by a ditch and a few artillery pieces, the Fort was home to around 1,000 men. Almost all the town's 5,000 inhabitants were Central Asians, a mixture of Kazakhs, Karakalpaks, Tatars, Tadjiks and Bokhariots. On the nearby river was the Aral Flotilla, made up of three side-wheel steamers, two stern-wheelers, a steam launch and many barges. Most of the vessels had been built in Liverpool or London and were brought to Central Asia in pieces of the backs of camels.

From here, the steamers, full of munitions and supplies, would sail down the Aral to the mouth of the Amu Darya (Oxus) and then follow the river upstream to get as close to Khiva as possible to link up with General von Kaufmann's expedition, which had started out from Tashkent.

MacGahan was expecting to find the Kazala column of the Khiva Expedition still in the town, but it had left on 21 March, and was already 300 miles to the south, where they were waiting to meet up with General von Kaufmann's column. He decided he would attempt to join up with them, believing he could complete the journey with a small group on swift horses in about eight days, despite the presence of irregular units of Khivan cavalry and the harsh conditions of the Kyzyl-Kum desert. "I had already spent so much of the *New York Herald*'s money that I felt morally obliged to push forward; and I was very certain that anything less than my entry into Khiva would not be a satisfactory conclusion of my undertaking," he wrote.[28]

However, the Russian military officers in Kazala opposed MacGahan's plan, telling him it was too dangerous. Instead, in a subterfuge, he decided to set out upstream on the Syr Darya to Fort No.2 – Fort Perovsky – and attempt the journey from there. He convinced the Russians he was aiming for Tashkent, to which they had no objection. So together with

---

27. *Ibid*, p. 13.

28. *Ibid*, p. 21.

Schuyler, he headed on to Fort Perovsky, which they reached after four days. After engaging a Karakalpak guide and six horses, and with the blessing of the district governor, Colonel Rodionoff, who was clearly out of touch with his fellow officers, MacGahan set off, although he would later regret the decision not to use camels instead of horses.

He bade farewell to Schuyler on 30 April, crossing the Syr Darya and heading south, his party now consisting of his Tatar servant Ak-Mamatoff, the Karakalpak guide Mustruf and a young Kazakh called Tangerberkhen. His "light and unpretentious" weapons consisted of a double-barrelled English hunting rifle, a double-barrelled shotgun, an 18-shot Winchester, three heavy revolvers and a muzzle-loading shotgun, besides knives and sabres. "I only encumbered myself with these things in order to be able to discuss with becoming dignity questions relating to the rights of way and of property with inhabitants of the desert, whose opinions on these subjects are sometimes peculiar," he wrote, somewhat tongue-in-cheek.[29]

At the end of his first day out of Fort Perovsky, MacGahan stopped for the night at a Kazakh *aoul*: "I was now for the first time in the midst of the Kazakhs of the Kyzyl-Kum, and beyond the protection of the Russians. These people, as I have already said, have the reputation of being robbers and murderers; and I had sufficient property to make a rich prize for even the richest amongst them. When starting into the desert I knew I must adopt one of two systems in dealing with such people. Either fight them or throw myself entirely upon their hospitality and generosity; I chose the latter system." It was the right choice. He was treated courteously by his new-found hosts.

Before long MacGahan was in the Kyzyl-Kum itself. He noted the strong smell of a bush that turned out to be absinthe and saw numerous saiga antelope, that primitive creature with huge nostrils that make it look very ugly. Today their numbers are much reduced, but Kazakhstan remains one of their strongholds. At one point he came across a Karakalpak *aoul*, where the chief, called Dowlat, fed and accommodated the journalist and told him that he was responsible for 2,000 yurts, each of which paid three roubles a year in tax to the Russians.

29. *Ibid*, p. 30.

MacGahan remarks on the hospitality of the Kazakhs with whom he stayed during his journey across the desert: "I have always found them kind, hospitable and honest. I spent a whole month amongst them; travelling with them, eating with them and sleeping in their tents. And I had along with me all this time horses, arms and equipments, which would be to them a prize of considerable value. Yet never did I meet anything but kindness; I never lost a pin's worth; and often a Kazakh has galloped four or five miles after me to restore some little thing I had left behind."[30]

Five days into his journey southwards MacGahan came across a completely ruined and abandoned city, around a mile in circumference, with the remains of a substantial wall and watch towers, all built of sun-dried bricks. It appeared to have been abandoned after the river – the Yani Darya – had changed course. Soon after he met two Russian soldiers, who told him that there was a Russian military encampment not far away. He soon came upon the main camp, where the Russians at first thought he was part of the Khivan ambassador's caravan, which had travelled to Kazala to try to meet General von Kaufmann to sue for peace. Unfortunately for them, the general had long since departed and the ambassador only reached him two days after Khiva fell.

As the main Kazala column had moved out two weeks previously, MacGahan decided to press on, freshly supplied by the Russian soldiers. His trail, in the wake of the Kazala column, was marked with numerous camel carcasses. He was now in the deep desert, where water was scarce: "Once lost in this desert ocean, without guide or water, you may wander for days, until you and your horse sink exhausted to die of thirst, with the noxious weed for bed, winding sheet and grave."[31] The first well was 60 miles away and the five men and eight horses in MacGahan's party had between them only eight gallons of water.

Another day and the party reached the remote Bukantau Mountains, 50-60 km north of Uchkuduk in what is now the Navoi region of northern Uzbekistan. Here they found good water. A party of Kazakhs

---

30. *Ibid*, p. 63.

31. *Ibid*, p. 78.

they met here turned out to be guides who had escorted the Kazala column south and was now returning north. It eventually took 17 days and a journey of 500 miles for MacGahan to find an outlier of von Kaufmann's column, at a place called Khala-ata, about 100 miles west of Bokhara. The general himself had marched out five days previously, heading to cross the Amu Darya, before moving on to Khiva. Here the commandant, Colonel Weimarn, refused to allow MacGahan to proceed, but nonetheless he managed to get away, avoiding both Cossacks and the many roaming bands of Turkoman raiders who were in the service of the Khan of Khiva.

At Alty-Kuduk MacGahan was given a warm reception by the small group of Russian soldiers, who watered and fed him and his companions. Then, on 27 May, he left hoping to reach the Amu Darya, which he did, two days later. "Broad and placid it lay, sweeping far away to the north and south, through the far stretching yellow sand, like a silver zone bordered with green and sparkling in the morning sunlight like a river of diamonds. I forgot Kaufmann, the Turkomans, the object of my expedition, everything, in the one delight of looking on its swiftly rushing waters."[32]

But of von Kaufmann there was no sign. His army had certainly been there but had already moved on. MacGahan had now been chasing him for 29 days. After following along the banks of the river for another 24 hours he heard a sound that made him stop in his tracks – cannon fire. Soon they come across the main Russian camp, close to a place called Sheikh-Arik. On the other side of the river, Khivan riders were galloping back and forth as cannonballs tore up the ground around them. In the distance the gardens of Khiva could clearly be seen.

Before long MacGahan was taken to see General von Kaufmann, whom he found wrapped in a Bokharan *khalat*. The general congratulated the journalist on his remarkable journey and told him he had no objection to him accompanying the army into Khiva itself. From this moment onwards until the end of the campaign against Khiva he stayed with the Russian Army whose personnel treated him with

---

32. *Ibid*, p. 142

kindness and courtesy. Now that the various sections of the Russian Army were surrounding Khiva, it was only a matter of time before the city fell. It did so on 9 June. MacGahan witnessed the surrender of the city and also the appalling Russian massacre of Yomud Turkomans just outside the city a week later.[33]

His ride through the dreaded Kyzyl-Kum desert has rightly entered the annals as one of the greatest journalistic coups of all time. He was the only journalist to witness the fall of Khiva and his despatches were sensational. Having already witnessed the fall of the Paris Commune in 1871 he went on to cover the Third Carlist War in Spain in 1874, and the following year joined British explorer Sir Allan William Young on the steam yacht HMS *Pandora* in an unsuccessful effort to find the Northwest Passage from the Atlantic to the Pacific.[34]

After leaving the *New York Herald* he joined the *London Daily News* in 1876 and was invited by Schuyler to investigate reports of large-scale massacres by Turkish troops in Bulgaria. His reports caused a sensation, forcing the pro-Turkish British Prime Minister Benjamin Disraeli to reverse his support for the Ottoman sultan. When Russia declared war on Turkey in April 1877 Disraeli could not back the Turks because of the strength of public opinion. MacGahan covered all the main battles of this war and was present at the signing of the Treaty of San Stefano, which brought it to an end. MacGahan is remembered by public events and a statue in Belgrade, where he is known as the Liberator of the Bulgarians.

In June 1878 MacGahan, only 33 years old, died at the British Hospital in Galata, Constantinople, from typhoid. He was initially buried there, until six years later his Russian-born wife repatriated his body to America, to be buried in New Lexington.

---

33. For a detailed account of the preparations for the military campaign that led to the fall of Khiva, it is worth reading the account of Lieut. Hugo Stumm, a German Army officer who was invited by the Russians to observe the campaign. See C E Howard Vincent, *Russia's Advance Eastwards: Based on the Official Reports of Lieutenant Hugo Stumm*, Henry S King & Co, London, 1874.

34. For more detail on MacGahan's reporting, see Dale L Walker, *Januarius MacGahan: The Life and Campaigns of an American War Correspondent*, Ohio University Press, 1988.

"FAKE NEWS" AND THE FALL OF KHIVA: THE STRANGE CASE OF DAVID KER

Russia's decision to take on the Khan of Khiva in 1873 was well known in St Petersburg's government circles for months before the troops set out across the desert. The news also excited a number of journalists, some of whom tried to cover this important advance into Central Asia, not least those working for the British press, who were already fixated on developments in what came to be known as the "Great Game". War reporting was in its infancy, but already William Howard Russell of *The Times* had made his name during the Crimean War of 1854-56 and the First Indian War of Independence in 1857 with his remarkably honest (and sometimes brutal) reports.

In addition to the American MacGahan, another of those who tried to get close to the action was a British writer called David Ker. Ker was born in Bowden Vale in Cheshire in 1842, the son of a Scottish merchant who had a business in Rio de Janeiro in Brazil. He was educated at Rugby School and at Wadham College, Oxford, from where he graduated in Easter 1865 before becoming a journalist.

Ker was a prolific writer, penning features for a wide range of magazines as well as newspapers, often travel pieces containing plenty of colour. He had already visited South America and Turkey and the Hejaz, before ending up St Petersburg, working for *The Morning Post*, a British paper. He had worked there for three years, when, according to one contemporary report, "His letters became, in fact, the subject of grave comment and inquiry at St Petersburg and the Government and police began to ask who could be the correspondent of the London newspaper who was finding out so much that it was very desirable should not be disclosed. Inquiries were made; Mr Ker (who seemed to know everything that was going on) satisfied himself that his identity was discovered and made his escape from St Petersburg, returning by way of the Crimea and getting away but a few hours before a warrant had been issued for his arrest and transmission to Siberia."[35]

---

35. *The Belfast Newsletter*, 3 June 1873.

On his return to England, Ker approached the *Daily Telegraph* with a suggestion that he should make his way to Khiva as a special correspondent to follow the Russian campaign to capture the city. Knowing that the Russians had expressly forbidden any English reporters from the region and that he himself was *persona non grata*, he chose to represent himself as an American and to carry a false passport, hoping that this deception would get him through the Russian lines. He started off from London on 8 March 1873 with several hundred pounds' worth of gold in his baggage, courtesy of the newspaper. His journey took him to Moscow and then south to Saratov, where he seems to have decided that he would not be able to get through to Central Asia. Instead, he headed for the Crimea and thence across the Black Sea to Tblisi, the capital of Georgia, which he reached by the first week in May.

It was in Tblisi that things began to go wrong. The clock was now ticking and as he languished in this remote city in the Caucasus, he became increasingly frustrated. And then he made a number of serious miscalculations. First, Ker filed an incorrect report that Khiva had fallen. He later claimed he had heard this from four independent sources, but it was wrong. That should have set alarm bells ringing, but worse was to come. On 7 May the *Telegraph* published a despatch from Ker, datelined Tiflis (Tblisi), in which he described the following scene: "Here, cross-legged on the doorsill of his father's shop, sits Aladdin, as he may have sat on the memorable evening when the African sorcerer invited him to that expedition of which we all know the result. There, with his axe stuck in his belt, trudges our old friend Ali Baba, behind his laden asses, a shade of anxiety upon his weather-beaten countenance, as if pondering whether he may not have forgotten the cabalistic 'Open Sesame!' or whether that brute Cassim may not ferret out the secret of his newly-acquired wealth…"

Something about this description raised suspicions at Ker's old paper, the *Globe*, and it was soon revealed – with much glee – that a similar description had appeared a fortnight previously in the magazine *All The Year Round*, but this one described a scene in Turkey. And then further embarrassment; a third version of the story had also appeared *Chamber's Journal* two years previously, on 21 October 1871, but datelined Jiddah, Arabia. That version read as follows:

"Here sits Aladdin at the door of his father's shop, just as he may have been sitting on that memorable evening when the African magician invited him to that expedition of which we all know the result. There, plodding methodically behind his laden donkey, comes Ali Baba, with an anxious expression on his weather-beaten countenance, as if doubting whether he may not have forgotten the cabalistic 'Open Sesame!' or wondering whether that brute Cassim will ferret out the secret of his newly-acquired wealth...". Even worse, the same description had also appeared previously in *Cassell's Magazine*.

The story was taken up by *The Times*, which demanded an explanation. At first the *Telegraph* tried to bluff its way through the scandal, but when the revelations of the *Chamber's Journal* article appeared it had no choice but to act. Its correspondent appeared to have been filing completely false reports and filing the same reports to different publications anonymously, in breach of an agreement to work exclusively for the *Telegraph*. As one paper commented at the time: "Now, nothing in the world delights your true newspaper people so much as discovering that a little piece of rascality has been perpetrated by a brother of the pen, and consequently Mr. Ker and the *Daily Telegraph* received but scant consideration, indeed, from writers connected with other journals. Nearly all the home papers, little and big, seemed to unite in one joyous shout to herald to the ends of the earth the news of the delinquency of the unhappy Ker."

Faced with the overwhelming evidence of Ker's behaviour, the *Telegraph* had no choice but to capitulate: "Our correspondent has committed an offence against the public, against the morality of composition, and against ourselves – an offence which he must answer for. Meantime we rely no longer upon anything which he may send us, and, as the immediate result of this second exposure of his conduct, we shall discontinue the publication of his letters." Without telephones to communicate the news from London to Tblisi, it would be some time before Ker became aware of his erstwhile employer's considerable dissatisfaction.

Even Charles Dickens became involved in the controversy, as he was editor of *All the Year Round* at the time, which had published the description of "Aladdin at the door of his father's shop". In a letter to

The Times Dickens wrote: "It is hardly necessary for me to say that when I accepted the article in question I had no idea that its author had entered into an arrangement to write exclusively for the *Daily Telegraph* and no reason to expect that he would commit the 'irregularity' of making 'his irreclaimable old savage' do double duty."

After his exposure, which took place before the fall of Khiva and about which at this point he knew nothing, Ker decided to try to get to Central Asia. Now without a sponsor, but oblivious to this fact, he headed to Astrakhan and then by carriage to Russia's Fort No.1 at Kazalinsk (Kazala), to the east of the Volga. Here he was detained by the Russians, who did not believe that he was a legitimate American journalist. He arrived on 17 June – Khiva had fallen on the 9th – but was not allowed to leave until 7 August, upon which he headed for Tashkent and then Samarkand. By then, of course, all military action had ceased.

Ker later published a book on his alleged adventures in Central Asia called *On the Road to Khiva* – now very rare, presumably because not too many people thought it worth buying.[36] Its most interesting section is the unusual introduction, entitled "A few words, personal and prefatory". Here he outlines the charges against him: concocting letters at a distance from the action; wilfully sending false news of the fall of Khiva; writing magazine articles subsequent to his engagement with the *Daily Telegraph* in direct violation of his own written contract; and having filled his reports with extracts from former articles.

Ker had little defence against the most serious charges, although he says that he was not the only person to wrongly report the fall of Khiva. He maintains that the strain of sustaining a number of false identities, together with his poor health, "made the task of constant writing (when as yet there was little to write about) so intolerable, that I was glad to lessen the strain by using familiar words, even while conscious that I must have used them before." He says the only reason he did not reach Khiva was that the Russians had got wind of the fact that his name had appeared in the English press in connection with his falsehoods. "In the

36. David Ker, *On the Road to Khiva*, Henry S King, London, 1874. In fact, Ker never made it to Khiva.

meantime," he wrote, "all that I wish to do is to tell my own story fairly and to leave among my own countrymen, from whom I have been parted so many years, some better reputation that that of a liar and imposter."

Needless to say, Ker never again worked as a journalist. However, this "fake news" scandal did not stop him writing, though he chose to express himself in a different way, eventually becoming one of the most prolific and successful of those Victorian writers who wrote "imperial" fiction for boys. His titles include: *Ilderim the Afghan: a Tale of the India Border* (1903); *Into Unknown Seas, or the Cruise of Two sailor-boys* (1886); *Prisoner Among Pirates* (1895); *The Rajah's Legacy* (1904); *O'er Tartar Deserts, or, The English and Russians in Central Asia* (1898); *In Quest of the Upas: a Tale of Adventure in New Guinea* (1934); *Among the Dark Mountains, or, Cast Away in Sumatra* (1907); *The Lost City, or, The Boy Explorers in Central Asia* (1885); *Swept out to Sea* (1897), and so on. All stirring stuff.

On his death in 1914, one obituary noted: "Mr. Ker was a man of many gifts and remarkable ability. His memory was prodigious. Homer, Aristophanes, Horace, Livy, Walter Scott, Gibbon, and many other great writers were at his command. It is said that be used to visit a blind man, to whom he recited almost the whole of *Ivanhoe*, the man supposing the book was being read to him. When he settled at Haslemere he paid a visit every week to the hospital, where he delighted the convalescent patients with stories of his travels and thrilling tales from his favourite writers."

Clearly David Ker never lost his ability to conjure up a good tale.

SEND FOR THE CAVALRY: CAPTAIN BURNABY'S RIDE TO KHIVA

Remarkably, David Ker's doomed effort to get to Khiva proved to be the inspiration for the most famous journey by an Englishman to that fabled city – that of Captain Fred Burnaby of the Royal Horse Guards whose book *A Ride to Khiva* is widely regarded as a travel classic.[37]

Burnaby's story starts in Khartoum, where the six foot four-inch cavalryman was lodged, having just returned from interviewing Colonel –

---

37. Captain Fred Burnaby, *A Ride to Khiva: Travels and Adventures in Central Asia*, Cassell, Petter & Galpin, London, 1876.

later General – Gordon for *The Times*. As he notes in his Introduction: "It may seem strange thus to commence the narrative of a journey to Central Asia in Central Africa, and yet, had it not been for a remark made by one of the men in the low square room to which I have just referred, in all probability I should never have gone to Khiva... At that moment my eye fell upon a paragraph in the paper. It was to the effect that the Government at St Petersburg had given an order that no foreigner was to be allowed to travel in Russian Asia, and that an Englishman who had recently attempted a journey in that direction had been turned back by the authorities."

Burnaby explained that his "contradictoriousness" meant he saw the arrest of David Ker – the purveyor of fake news – as a challenge and decided there and then to try to reach the fabled city. He had tried several years before to get to the city from the south but had been prevented by a bout of typhoid. He found the Russian ambassador to London friendly but non-committal about the idea of a British Army officer travelling to the heart of his country's newly-conquered lands in Central Asia. He also met Januarius MacGahan, who said to him, "You will get on very well as far as Kazala, but then you will have to pull yourself together and make your rush."[38]

Burnaby left London on 30 November 1875 *en route* for St Petersburg, where he also met Eugene Schuyler, the US Secretary of Legation, who offered him seasoned advice. A letter to General Milutin, the Russian defence minister, was received favourably and he was told that Russian military commanders in Central Asia had been sent orders to help him. He was soon on his way, wrapped up against the bitter winter weather.

Soon after leaving Karabootak (Qarabutaq) in present-day northwest Kazakhstan Burnaby made the serious error of forgetting to pull on his gloves, with the temperature at -40°C. He fell asleep in his open carriage and awoke with serious frostbite. "I looked at my finger-nails; they were blue, the fingers and back part of my hands were of the same colour, whilst my wrists and the lower part of the arm were of a waxen hue. There was no doubt about it, I was frostbitten and that in no slight degree."[39]

---

38. Thomas Wright, *The Life of Colonel Fred Burnaby*, Everett & Co, London, 1908, p. 89.

39. Burnaby, *op. cit.*, p. 139.

His servant's attempt to restore circulation by rubbing them with snow was unsuccessful. Seven miles on, at a post-station, three Cossacks plunged Burnaby's arms up to the shoulder into a tub of ice and water. Still he felt no sensation. They told him he would likely lose his hands. Still they continued by rubbing his arms with naphtha. Little by little he felt a faint sensation at his elbow joints. Further rubbing and steeping in the ice bucket brought intense pain and a return of circulation. He was immensely grateful to the Cossacks who had saved his hands.

He arrived on the Orthodox Christmas at Fort No. 1 at Kazala, where he hired a Kazakh guide, a Turkoman camel driver, three camels and two horses. He stayed in the Russian commandant's rooms, where he learned that the previous summer the British Army officer, Major Herbert Wood, had stayed while attached to a Russian scientific expedition exploring the Aral Sea and the Syr Darya.[40] The local governor, Colonel Goloff, then invited Burnaby to stay with him, and he was royally entertained as the officers continued with their Christmas festivities.

Several days later he set off again, moving mostly at night and covering about 40 miles a day. The weather was still bitterly cold. "The sentries posted outside the Governor's and Commandant's houses were obliged to wear the thickest of galoshes stuffed with hay, and to keep running backwards and forwards the whole time they were on duty, to prevent their feet freezing. The instant any man left the house his moustache was frozen into a solid block of ice. If his nose were exposed to the wind for a minute or so it turned first blue and then white, whilst, as to touching anything in the shape of metal with the bare hand, you might as well have taken hold of a red-hot iron."[41]

Burnaby chose to travel via what was known as the winter march road to Khiva, much shorter than the usual route via Irkibai, but lacking any decent wells. With plenty of snow on the ground this was not a worry. He had arranged for cabbage soup with large pieces of meat cut into it to be poured into two large iron buckets which quickly froze and

---

40. Wood subsequently wrote *The Shores of Lake Aral*, Smith, Elder & Co, London, 1876, about his experiences. He later told Burnaby that he had not been permitted to go within 60 miles of Khiva on the express orders of General von Kaufmann. See Chapter 8.

41. Burnaby, *op. cit.*, p. 195.

Anthony Jenkinson's remarkable map of Central Asia.

2. Portrait of Jonas Hanway by James Northcote.

3. John Castle's portrait of Khan Abul Khayir.

4. Detail of woodcut from Castle's book showing the interior of a yurt.

A Kazakh of the Middle Horde
 Johan Peter Falck.

A Kazakh 'woman of the common people'
 Johan Peter Falck.

illustrations showing local dress, from Johan Peter Falck's travel journal.
sandrovskaya, O.A., Shirokova, V. et al., Альбом-исследование «М. В.
оносов и академические экспедиции XVIII века», Moscow 2014
es 233 & 235).

7. Peter Simon Pallas by Ambroise Tardieu.

8. Peter Petrovich Semenov by Alexandre Quinet

© BNF Alexandre Quinet.

9. Nikolai Przhevalsky

0. Iakinf Bichurin (Hyacinth)
Nikolai Bestuzhev

11. Shokan Walikhanov

2. Adolph Schlagintweit (centre) and his brothers Robert and Hermann.

13. Capt. Fred Burnaby by James Jacques Tissot.

14. American journalist, Januarius MacGaha

15. US Diplomat Eugene Schuyler.

16. Robert Louis Jefferson.

7. Lithograph by Thomas Witlam Atkinson: *A group of Kazakhs with two brides.*

8. Lithograph by Thomas Witlam Atkinson: *Sultan Souk and family.*

19. Lithograph by Thomas Witlam Atkinson: *Sultan Beck and family.*

20. Woodcut by Thomas Witlam Atkinson: *A group of Mohammed's Kazakhs.*

. Woodcut by Thomas Witlam Atkinson: *Lucy Atkinson in a Kazakh yurt.*

. Woodcut by Thomas Witlam Atkinson: *Discussing the journey to Nor-Zaisan.*

23. Relatives of the Atkinsons at the Tamchiboulac Spring in Kapal, Eastern Kazakhstan, July 201
© David O'Neill

4. Commercial advertising picture cards illustrating the travels of Gabriel Bonvalot.

25. Xavier Hommaire de Hell.

26. Adèle Hommaire de Hell.

27. Interior of a yurt from Hommaire de Hell's book on the Caspian.

28. A Kalmyk lama from Hommaire de Hell's book on the Caspian.

29. Mme Marie de Ujfalvy-Bourdon in her very fashionable travel clothes.

30. Swiss traveller and collector, Henri Moser.

31. Cambridge scientist, William Bateson.

32. Bateson's photograph of a Kazakh tribesman

33. Bateson's photograph of a Kazakh bride

. Portrait of Rev. Henry Lansdell in
kharan armour.

35. Lansdell dressed in Turkoman costume.

36. A pair of leather embroidered trousers
(tchimbar) Lansdell brought back from
Central Asia.

37. Industrialist E Nelson Fell.

38. Butter merchant and mountain climber Samuel Turner.

39. Idealist and aid worker Ralph Fox.

40. Mining engineer John Wilford Wardell.

were suspended on either side of a camel. A hatchet was needed to cut up the meat and break the frozen soup. He had to cover his stirrups with felt to prevent his feet freezing to the steel.

On their approach to Khiva, Burnaby was told that he would not be able to enter the city without having first obtained the khan's permission. Even though the khan had been overthrown by the Russians, he had been allowed to return to his palace, having accepted that he was now a Russian vassal. A passing mullah wrote the document for him and it was duly despatched. Meanwhile he continued on, reaching the Amu Darya, which was frozen. Khivans in their long red robes and tall black lambskin hats could now be seen everywhere.

As he rode through the gardens on the outskirts of the city, he met the messenger he had sent with a letter to the khan, accompanied by two Khivan nobles who had been sent to greet him and conduct him to his lodgings. He was beguiled by the city, writing that it was the most beautiful place he had ever seen. A day after arriving he went to meet the khan who questioned him on the geography of India and Europe and complained about being obliged to pay tribute to Russia.

Burnaby was very struck by the manner of the khan: "He was very kind in his manner and shook hands warmly when I took my leave; the impression being left on my mind that the Khan of Khiva is the least bigoted of all the Mohammedans whose acquaintance I have made in the course of my travels, and that the stories of his cruelties to Russian prisoners, previous to the capture of his city, are pure inventions which have been disseminated by the Russian press in order to try and justify the annexation of his territory."[42]

Bokhara was intended to be Burnaby's next destination, but a letter arrived from the local Russian commandant requiring him to report to his headquarters at Petro-Alexandrovsk around 50 miles outside the city. There he found a telegram had arrived from Prince George, the Duke of Cambridge, the British Army's commander-in-chief, requiring him to return immediately to European Russia. In fact, had he called at Petro-Alexandrovsk *en route* to Khiva, he would never have been

---

42. *Ibid*, p. 323.

allowed to enter the city. He had specifically avoided the fort on his journey down to Khiva, knowing that in all likelihood, even if he was allowed to enter the city, it would have been with a military escort.

Two days later Burnaby started back across the frozen desert, hoping even at this late stage to be allowed to return to Europe via Tashkent and Western Siberia. He arrived back at Kazala, after a journey of 371 miles, on 12 February 1876, which took just over nine days. Before long he was back in England where he was regarded as a hero. When his book was published a few months later it went into 11 editions within a year. His caricature appeared in *Vanity Fair* and before long he was attracting further headlines with his ballooning exploits from Crystal Palace.

Nor was that the end of his adventures. The following year he left for Turkey, determined to show that the Turks, who had received terrible publicity over their massacres in Bulgaria (as reported by MacGahan and Schuyler), were not as bad as made out. Together with his servant George Radford he set off on horseback from Constantinople, heading for Lake Van in Eastern Turkey. He may have intended to visit Armenia and the Caucasus, to demonstrate that it was Russian provocation, rather than Turkish reaction, that was behind the massacre of Christians in Bulgaria. The Russians warned their border troops and in the end Burnaby headed to the Black Sea and returned to Constantinople, his views of both the Turks (positive) and the Russians (negative) confirmed.

Soon after his return to England Burnaby set off again for Turkey, this time to witness the Turkish-Russian war of 1877-78. He was pro-Turkish, believing that Russian needed to be humiliated militarily in order to guarantee the safety of India. However, as explained above, MacGahan's reports of Turkish atrocities against Bulgarian Christians made it impossible for the British government to support the Ottomans. On his return to England in February 1878 Radford, his batman, died of typhus in Dover. "A brave soldier, a faithful servant and as true as steel" is how Burnaby described him on his epitaph.[43]

Further air balloon adventures followed. He crossed the English Channel in March 1882 and then travelled to the Sudan in 1884, where

43. Wright, *op cit.*, p. 143.

he was wounded at the battle of El Teb when acting as an intelligence officer for his friend General Valentine Baker. Soon after, in January 1885, he was killed by a spear through the neck in hand-to-hand fighting at the Battle of Abu Klea against the forces of the Mahdi, thus cementing his reputation as one of the great Victorian war heroes.

ON TWO WHEELS TO KHIVA

In the 18th century the wealthy elite had travelled around Europe on the Grand Tour as a rite of passage, bringing home art collections to decorate their country houses and stories to entertain their friends. Merchants and military officers had made forays to distant lands looking for information or trading opportunities. By the late-1800s the advent of steam power – in the form of railways and steamships – had democratised travel. Now young men and women seeking adventure could make their way around the world with little danger and at little expense. By the end of the century the idea of foreign travel as a leisure activity had taken a firm hold in Europe.

Amongst those new adventurers was Robert Louis Jefferson. Just as Ker had been inspired by MacGahan to try to reach Khiva and Burnaby was in turn inspired by Ker's failure, so Jefferson was inspired by Burnaby to try to reach Khiva – on a bicycle. As he explained in the foreword to his book describing the journey: "That there was a certain amount of fascination in the idea I admit, for I have always been a keen admirer of the stalwart guardsman whose horseback ride across the desert of Kyzyl-Kum will be remembered long after his brave exploits in Egypt have been forgotten. My object was to emulate Captain Burnaby's ride to Khiva, but as a sportsman only."[44]

Only a generation before, Khiva had been renowned for its alleged barbarism and slavery, but now it was safe enough for cyclists!

There is a mystery surrounding Jefferson's background. He claimed he was born in St Joseph, Missouri, in 1866, but had been taken to England soon after, never having lived in America. His English father

---

44. Robert L Jefferson, *A New Ride to Khiva*, Methuen & Co, London 1899.

may have fought in the Crimea and then in the American Civil War. As a young man Jefferson trained as a journalist and then worked for the Press Association wire service for 13 years, where he ended up as a parliamentary sketch writer. In 1885 he began cycling and won numerous prizes, including several for speed racing. This was the era of extreme cycling adventures, typified by Americans William Sachtleben and Thomas G Allen's ride across Asia in 1890[45] and Scotsman John Foster Fraser's two-year ride around the world that began in July 1896.[46]

In 1894 Jefferson made the first of his five epic bike journeys when he cycled from London to Constantinople. The following year he rode to Moscow and back, covering the 4,300 miles in under 50 days. In 1896 he cycled 16,000 km across Siberia to Irkutsk and back – a world distance record at the time – and then made a journey across Mongolia. Then in 1899 came his trip to Khiva.

Jefferson found plenty of fellow cycling enthusiasts on his journey, recording that the Governor General of Samara was a fan, as was Prince Boris Golitsyn. On leaving Samara for Orenburg he was accompanied for the first 60 miles by Nikolai Dmitrivich Batyushkov, a local industrialist. Everywhere along his journey he excited considerable interest. At Orenburg he was met by a local committee of cyclists, who tossed him into the air three times for luck while a band played "God Save the Queen". Spectators looked on, many of them never having seen a bicycle before.

In common with many Victorian travelogues, Jefferson exhibits what today would be regarded as racism towards the peoples of the East: "Here the civilisation of the West holds out its hand to the barbarism of the East," he writes. "Here from the burning sands of the Kara Kum come the black and forbidding-looking denizens of the desert to barter their wool and camel hair for tea, tobacco, and other simple luxuries." However, by the end of his book he was at least able to express his appreciation for the kindness he had been shown on innumerable occasions by Kazakh nomads.

---

45. See Thomas G Allen & William L Sachtleben, *Across Asia on a Bicycle*, The Century Co, New York, 1894.

46. John Foster Fraser, *Round the World on a Wheel*, Methuen & Co., London 1899.

At Orsk on the northern borders of the Kazakh steppes, the local *natchalnik* (headman) told him that for the 12-day journey across the Kara-Kum desert to Fort No.1 at Kazala he would need to be accompanied by a *tarantass* and three horses to carry provisions – as none would be available on his journey. And from the fort onwards to Khiva itself he would have to have an armed escort to protect him from robbers. Even so, his bicycle caused uproar at some of the places he stopped: "My bicycle was looked upon with alarm and dismay, and when I approached the encampment, the Kazakhs, mounting their horses, made for me with a rush, rending the air with their screams and shouts and cracking their long whips in fury. Fearing that they intended to ride me down I dismounted. Along came the Kazakhs like a whirlwind, then circled around me, shouting and jabbering in a most furious manner. I threw up my hands to show that I meant them no harm, but I was not quite certain as to the better course – to draw my revolver or to submit."[47]

After this incident, once the Kazakhs had had a chance to examine his machine, they became friendly and entertained Jefferson in their yurt. "Disgusting in their manners though they were, still I could not forget that they had given me all they had – mutton and *koumiss* – which constitutes practically the only food the Kazakh has ever known."

Jefferson says that sometimes he was able to make around 30 miles a day, although the very soft sand often forced him to push his bike for 10 or 15 miles. His feet became so blistered that he could not take off his top-boots without dragging away the skin. By the end of August he reached Kazala and Fort No.1, where the commandant offered him his hospitality and told him that conditions while crossing the Kyzyl-Kum would be even more difficult, with no good wells and no food. He bought six camels and hired two Kazakhs as guides, while the commandant provided him with three *djiggits* (Kazakh soldiers), three armed Cossacks and a dragoman to act as interpreter. Jefferson himself was armed with a Winchester repeating carbine.

Besides Captain Burnaby only one other outsider – a Russian geographer, who had made the journey in 16 days – had crossed the

---

47. Jefferson, *op. cit.*, p. 178.

Kyzyl-Kum from north to south prior to Jefferson. Nonetheless, all the officials Jefferson met were courteous, delighted to help this unusual two-wheeled traveller. Since the completion of the trans-Caspian railroad in 1898, few people now passed by the fort, except for the few remaining camel caravans that still travelled up from Bokhara. The first 30 miles along the banks of the Syr Darya were likely to be the most difficult due to swamps and the deep sand. At these points the bike was strapped to the side of a camel and Jefferson had to make do with a pony instead.

From the beginning, therefore, the journey was exhausting. Jefferson rode where he could or mounted one of the camels when the sand was too deep for the bike wheels. His journey became even more difficult after just four days when he became ill: "I became feverish and hysterical and only by liberal doses of quinine could I that night compose myself to sleep." The bread began to rot and the water to smell bad. One day, when the caravan failed to keep pace, Jefferson backtracked to find his Cossacks and guides sitting down to a hearty meal of their scarce provisions and drinking the remaining bottle of brandy. "Jumping from my machine, I was amongst them in a moment, the bottle of brandy was snatched from the hands of one of the Cossacks, a piece of melon was knocked out of the fist of another fellow and a hearty kick given to one of the lazy guides before a word had been uttered on either side."

After eight days they reached the halfway point at the wells of Bia-Murat, where they were able to replenish their water skins and to buy a few more sheep from the Kazakhs who lived close to the wells. The guides now returned to Kazalinsk and Khalibi Bekel, while a Bokhariot working for the Russians, along with four Kazakhs, took over guiding duties. The road was no easier and Jefferson says he was forced time and again to take to the camels. He became despondent, particularly when the desert sand dunes increased in height to more than 30 feet. There was barely a shrub or bush to be seen and even the guides had difficulty finding their way through this difficult terrain. A bite under his eye from a large spider that left him in excruciating pain only added to his woes.

Four days on from the wells Jefferson was so weak "that bicycling was completely out of the question, especially as we were passing over sand so deep and hot that to venture the foot upon it meant raising blisters all over the skin." The following day, having gone ahead of the camels with Bekel, the two men got lost. Still feeling the pain from the spider bite and having not eaten for 24 hours, Jefferson was in serious difficulty, only ameliorated when late into the night they heard the jangling of camel bells and fell in once more with the rest of their party. Even so, he had a fever and soon became delirious. The fever lasted until they reached the Russian fort at Petro-Alexandrovsk after two weeks of travelling across the desert. "I have no clear recollection of what happened. I was in a high state of fever, my clothing in rags, and so far as my memory goes, I must have been delirious," he wrote.[48] The ground being firmer, at least he was able to ride his bike into the fort.

Jefferson remarks that he was astonished by the gentle nature of the Kazakhs he met and could not understand why they were so castigated by the Russians. "Everything that was bad was attributed to the Kazakhs. They were dirty, they were cut-throats, they were thieves of the meanest character, they were people whose words were absolutely unreliable, and so on and so forth. My Siberian experiences were the contrary and as a matter of fact I frequently placed myself at their entire disposal when absolutely alone and hundreds of miles from the nearest centre."

He had particularly warm comments for those Kazakhs from the Middle Horde, whom he found to be reliable and honest: "Journeying as I did through the Middle Horde practically alone, that is to say with only one attendant in the shape of the *yemshik* of a *tarantass*, I was in very little more protected state that when I journeyed through Siberia, and though my nights had frequently to be spent in the neighbourhood or the company of these wanderers of the steppe and desert, in place of being subjected to annoyance or being placed in jeopardy, I was received by the Kazakhs with every demonstration of welcome and speedily found that my life was as safe or safer in their hands than might be the case with the somewhat mixed Slav people forming the population of Siberia."[49]

At the Russian fort of Petro-Alexandrovsk Jefferson was received by the Russian administrator of the province, Mr Galkin, who was very

---

48. *Ibid*, p. 235.

49. *Ibid*, p. 241.

hospitable. Jefferson stayed for three days in order to recover from the rigours of the desert crossing. He was astonished at the Russian-ness of the town, with its Orthodox church, Russian architecture and wooden houses. Even in the desert heat the Russian civilians wore top boots, baggy trousers, a red shirt and belt and a white hat – the same as worn by almost every male Russian from St Petersburg to Vladivostok. In the market, much to his surprise, he found canned lobster.

When a few days later Jefferson eventually got inside the walls of Khiva he found the city to be in a state of severe decline: "Ruin and disorder spread in every direction. The great walls, seventy to eighty feet high and proportionately thick, were broken and lay in great heaps of sun-baked clay on all hands. Huge gaps appear here and there. The roadway which we had to traverse was simply a chaos of dismantled wall."[50]

He entered the house of Mohamed Mat Murat, the prime minister of Khiva, but to mixed emotions. "Gratified as I was at having completed my cycle ride to Khiva, I yet felt a strange, unaccountable desire to get out of it as speedily as possible. The gloom, the wretchedness, the utter decay on every hand filled me with anything but inspiring feelings... The suggestion of the doctor in Petro-Alexandrovsk that the Russians were simply waiting for Khiva to die out had here ample corroboration and during the three days I remained in the city, it became patent to me that Khiva is absolutely doomed to obliteration within a few short years."

He found the prime minister to be well-informed; he could not remember Burnaby's visit, but remembered Henry Lansdell perfectly, as well as the Swiss traveller, Henri Moser.[51] The prime minister told him about the German colony that had recently been founded just outside the city, and he was later introduced to Emile Reeson, its headman, who acted as a translator for him. Reeson was wearing a collar and tie when Jefferson met him. "I lay back and gasped," Jefferson wrote.

Jefferson was very disappointed by Khiva. The great city he had read about, the city of the khans, was now a wretched, decaying place, full

---

50. *Ibid*, p. 264

51. See Chapter 9 for more on Lansdell. Moser wrote the beautifully illustrated *A Travers L'Asie Centrale*, (Librairie Plon, Paris, 1885) about his experiences travelling in Central Asia. See Chapter 7.

of sadness. It must once have been a great place, when the caravans from China and the Afghan border stopped there on their way to the Russian border. The railways which now stretched all the way to Merv, Bokhara, Samarkand and Tashkent, and the steamers that now plied the Caspian and Aral seas had ended the old trade. Now it had little point in existence. The khan had lost his powers and for the past 25 years had been forced to pay reparations to the Russians. The landscape was dominated by Russian fortresses bristling with cannon and trigger-happy Cossacks, and the population – stripped of its thousands of slaves – was in decline, falling from around 110,000 in 1880 down to 80,000 in 1899. The only industry still flourishing was the production of Khiva's famous silk carpets, where techniques had not changed in generations.

After a brief audience with the Khan of Khiva, Jefferson made a visit to the German colony eight miles outside the city where Reeson's wife offered him a cutlet, white bread and butter and asparagus, at which Jefferson marvelled. The men were mostly skilled artisans – glassmakers, blacksmiths, carpenters and coachbuilders. Reeson told him that he remembered Moser's visit to the village and that the traveller had sent him copies of his book. He added that every German family had one main intention – to send family members to America as soon as possible.

The next day Jefferson quit Khiva to head back to the fort at Petro-Alexandrovsk. "Khiva held out no charms whatever. Instead, I had a feeling of gladness permeating me when a bend in the lane hid its walls from me. I saw even with gladness the disappearance of its round stunted tower on the horizon." His objective now was to reach Bokhara where he could take the railway to Merv and then Krasnovodsk on the Caspian shore. The first part of the journey, by *tarantass* along the Amu Darya to Bokhara, would take five days. Then at Krasnovodsk he took the ferry to Baku on the western side of the Caspian, travelled across the Caucasus into Georgia and then to Batumi on the Black Sea coast. A five-day voyage brought him to Constantinople, from where he boarded a steamer to Marseille and then a train to London. It was the end of his journey.

His bike parked for good, Jefferson later turned to the Rover motorcar for his next adventure in 1905, which was a repeat of the cycle ride to Constantinople. Further drives promoting Rover ventured to India (1906) and South Africa (1907). He then drove coast to coast across Canada (1909) and New Zealand (1911). In 1914, while driving for the Wolsey Motor Company, Robert travelled to Australia and it was in Melbourne that he succumbed to a stroke. He was 46 with a wife and three children.

And with that the Western preoccupation with reaching the fabled desert city of Khiva came to an end. The First World War followed by the Russian Revolution in 1917 prevented travellers reaching the city for almost three generations, until it slowly re-introduced itself to the world in the 1990s.

Januarius MacGahan
the correspondent.

Peter Simon Pallas

6

THE RUSSIANS IN CENTRAL ASIA
Opening up the New Empire

—⁂—

THE GEOGRAPHICAL RELATIONSHIP BETWEEN THE RUSSIAN EMPIRE AND CENTRAL ASIA, not to mention the geopolitical relationship between the tsars and the Chinese emperors – and later, the tsars and the British Crown – were the immediate stimuli for serious interest in the largely unknown regions in Central Asia that separated these great powers.

Chinese records indicate that as far back as the 13th century Russian prisoners were taken to China via Mongolia to serve in the Russian regiment of guards at the Yuan court in Beijing. Later, under Ivan the Terrible (1530-84), Russia began its great expansion eastward, rapidly conquering the khanates of Kazan, Siberia and Astrakhan. The tsar sent two Cossack *atamans*, Ivan Petrov and Burnash Yalyshev, to China in 1567, and further delegations followed later as Peter the Great explored the possibility of expanding Russian trade with India.

As early as 1618 an unofficial envoy, the Cossack Ivan Petlin, had reached Beijing by travelling south to the River Ob, crossing the Abakan Range into Tuva and then around Lake Uvs (now in northern Mongolia) to the court of the Altyn khan. From there he travelled east across Mongolia to the Great Wall and reached Beijing in late August the same year. He was not allowed to see the Wanli emperor because he did not bring proper tribute and thus returned empty-handed to Russia. Even the letter Petlin had brought back with him in Chinese inviting the Russians to begin trading, could not be read until 1675, over 50 years later.

Tea was to play an important role in building the relationship between the two empires. In 1638 another Russian envoy to China,

Vasily Starkov, brought tea back to Russia as a gift from the Mongolian khan, the first time the beverage had been seen in Russia. Starkov had at first refused to accept the large boxes of dead leaves as a gift. In 1654-58 Fedor Isakovitch Baykov, an envoy of Tsar Aleksey Mikhailovich, travelled past Lake Zaisan – now in northwest Kazakhstan – and along the upper course of the Black Irtysh river, then through Djungaria to the Great Wall at Kalgan and on to Beijing. His was the earliest official diplomatic mission from Russia to China.

Not long after, the Treaty of Nerchinsk, signed in August 1689, was the first agreement signed between the two empires. Under its terms the Russians relinquished control over the area north of the River Amur in Russia's far eastern regions, as far as the Stanovoy Range, while keeping the land between the Argun river and Lake Baikal.

This agreement, which opened the market for Russian goods into Manchu China and allowed Chinese goods – mostly brick tea – in the other direction, was to last until the Amur Acquisition in 1858 and 1860. The Chinese insisted in the treaty that all trade should be confined to a single place on the frontier. They decided on Kiakhta, a desolate spot south of Lake Baikal in the middle of nowhere, more than 1,000 miles across the Mongolian Gobi from Beijing and over 4,000 miles from St Petersburg. Russian caravans laden with furs would cross the Russian border here, travelling a few hundred yards to the south to exchange with Chinese traders in Kiakhta's equivalent, Mai-mai-cheng – "Buy-Sell City".[1]

The transport of tea into Russia by the caravan trade road was not easy, with the trip of around 11,000 miles often taking over 16 months to complete. Caravans of several hundred camels would start from Kashgar, in Western China – often known later as Little Bokhara – where tea grown in South China was concentrated and processed. Here agents from the Russian trading companies purchased the tea and sent the caravans northward across the Gobi Desert towards Urga – now Ulaan Bator – in Mongolia. From there they travelled on to Kiakhta,

---

1. For a more detailed history of the trade relations between Russia and China, see Martha Avery's *The Tea Road: China and Russia Meet across the Steppe*, China International Press, Beijing, 2003.

where boxes of tea were sewn into raw bull hides called *tsybics*. Bales containing the expensive black tea were more carefully packed using paper and foil wrappings to retard mould. Bundles of the paper and foil packed tea were then placed in bamboo boxes. The *tsybics* were loaded on carts or sledges – depending on the season – and sent on to Irkutsk in Eastern Siberia and then to the tea trade fairs to the west.

Trade was the immediate reason for Russian expansion eastwards but by the time of Peter the Great at the turn of the 17th century there was already a political project in the making. Peter wanted to Europeanise Russia, to turn it into a kind of northern Hapsburg Empire with its own colonies, even if they were largely contiguous with the mother country itself. The mountain chain of the Urals, running almost north-south, became the dividing line between the homeland and its exotic colonies in Siberia and Central Asia. And with that geographical boundary came a psychological one: the question of whether Russia faced east or west. The division between European and Asiatic domains would remain not just a geographical boundary, but one that that lay at the heart of the debate about who the Russians were for generations to come.

Russian travellers in Central Asia were now not just traders, but colonial administrators in the making. The same process was happening at almost the same time in North America and in India under the British. Mapmakers, ethnographers and adventurers were often the first to arrive, to be followed later by the military and then, finally, the settlers and functionaries.[2] A spate of travellers from Russia began to make the long and dangerous journeys into Central Asia, including Florio Beneveni (Bokhara and Khiva, 1724-25), Karl Miller (Tashkent, 1738-39), Dmitriy Gladyshev and Ivan Muravin (Khiva, 1740-41), Shubai Arslanov (Tashkent, 1741-42), Danila Rukavkin, Pyotr Chuchalov and Yakov Gulyaev (Khiva, 1753-54), Mendiar Bekchurin (Bokhara, 1781), Yegor Blankennagel (Khiva, 1793-94), Timofei Burnashov (Bokhara, with Alexei Beznosikov, 1795, and Tashkent, with Mikhail Pospelov, 1800), Dmitriy Telyatnikov and Alexei Beznosikov (Tashkent, 1796-97).

---

2. For a detailed discussion of this subject, see Mark Bassin, "Geographies of Imperial identity", in *The Cambridge History of Russia*, vol. II, 2015, pp. 45ff.

The first Russian known to have reached Kashgar and Yarkand in what was then Chinese Turkestan was Filipp Sergeyevich Efremov (1750-1811). His was a remarkable story. In 1774 he was captured in the Orenburg Steppes, taken to Bokhara, and sold into slavery. After escaping, he disguised himself as a merchant and journeyed through the almost completely unknown regions of Central Asia including Kashgar, the Karakorum Mountains and Ladakh, before arriving in India. In 1782 he returned to Russia by sea via Africa and England. Four years later, in 1786, he published his book *Nine Years of Wandering (1774-1782)*[3] in St Petersburg. The book contains valuable geographical, ethnological, and historical information on the countries and peoples of Central Asia, Tibet and India.

Johann August Carl Sievers (1762-95), a German pharmacist and botanist, also travelled into Central Asia. A member of Peter Simon Pallas' expedition to the southern mountains of Siberia in 1790-95, he was particularly interested in rhubarb (*Rheum palmatum*) and places where it could be grown. During his five years of travel, he collected hundreds of botanical specimens, including the wild apples of southeast Kazakhstan – one variety of which was named after him – and the first example of Schrenk's Spruce (*Picea schrenkiana*). Sievers also travelled in the Yablonoi Mountains to the south of Lake Baikal in Eastern Siberia, as well as the Altai and the Tarbagatai Mountains, reaching Lake Ala Kol in 1794.

Serious scientific study of Central Asia in Russia began with the work of a priest, Nikita Yakovlevich Bichurin, usually known as Hyacinth or Father Iakinf (1777-1853). He was sent as a missionary to Beijing in 1807 and spent the next 14 years in the city. Although Iakinf's main interest was China, he believed that the country could not be understood without studying its border regions. "It was the order of things that Tibet, Turkestan and Mongolia should be dealt with first, as those countries have long maintained contacts with China and given China itself access to India, Middle Asia and Russia. It seemed appropriate

---

3. Filipp Sergeevich Efremov, *Stranstvovanie nadvornago sovietnika Efremova v Bukharii, Khivie, Persii i Indii*, i vozvrashchenie ottuda chrez Angliiu v Rossiiu (Pech. na izhd. P.B. i prod. po Nevsk. perspektivie u Anichk. mostu v domie Grafa D.A. Zubova: V Sanktpeterburgie, 1794).

to begin by surveying the geographical location and political structure of the aforementioned countries and then go on to describe China's political views on those."[4]

Iakinf went on to publish books on Tibet (1828), Mongolia (1829), Eastern Turkestan and Djungaria (1829). In 1848 he also published a detailed history of the peoples of Central Asia. All of these works, and the expansionist ideas encouraged during the reign of Tsar Nicholas I, led in 1845 to the formation of the Russian Geographical Society, which was established by royal decree in order to collect information about Russia and the territories on its borders. Two German geographers, the great Alexander von Humboldt and his collaborator Carl Ritter, were to provide further impetus with the publication of their works (*Asie-Centrale* and *Die Erdkunde von Asien*, respectively) which examined in more detail the geographical processes that had led to the formation of the Central Asian mountains and plateaus.

Further details of Russians who managed to penetrate the steppelands and some of the outliers of the Tian-Shan Mountains are given by the celebrated Russian geographer Per Petrovich Semenov, better known as Semenov-Tianshanksy, in the preface to the second volume of his Russian translation of Ritter's *Erdkunde von Asien*.[5]

Semenov claims that for 40 years following Sievers' journeys in Central Asia, no scientific explorer travelled as far as he did. He mentions a number of names of non-scientific travellers: K A Mayer, who reached the Arkat Mountains in northern Kazakahstan; C Snegiref who reached the Altai and the Chinese border post of Chuguchak while searching for gold; the noble Madatov who reached India via Semipalatinsk; the interpreter Putinsev who visited Kuldja and Chuguchak in 1811; and the merchant Bubeninov who reached Kashgar in 1821. The astronomer Vasili Fedorovich Fedorov (1802-55) reached the southern shore of Lake Zaisan as well as the mouth of the River Lepsa in the Zhetysu. He also made trigonometrical measurements in the Tarbagatai Mountains.

---

4. Quoted in I F Popova, *Russian Expeditions to Central Asia at the turn of the 20th Century*, Institute of Oriental Manuscripts of the Russian Academy of Sciences, St Petersburg, 2008, p. 13.

5. See P P Semenof, "Djungaria and the Celestial Mountains", *Journal of the Royal Geographical Society*, vol. 35 (1865), pp. 213-31. Retrieved from http://www.jstor.org/stable.3698091.

Only after the acceptance of Russian rule by the Kazakh tribes of the Middle Horde and Great Horde did Russian explorers feel safe enough to travel into the mountains of the Djungar Alatau. Naturalist Gregory Silych Karelin (1801-72), who was exiled to Orenburg in southern Russia in 1822 after writing some mocking verses about the minister of war, Count Arakcheev, spent the rest of his life collecting minerals, plants and animal specimens from Central Asia, with which he supplied Russian and foreign museums. By the late 1820s he had made his first expedition onto the steppe, visiting the lands of the Bukiev Horde of Kazakhs in what is now western Kazakhstan and making maps of the region. He became renowned for his ability to negotiate with the independent khans of the steppes and in 1831 was offered employment by the Asiatic section of the Russian State Department.

Little of his written work survives, although two diaries written when Karelin was exploring the eastern coast of the Caspian Sea in 1832 and 1836 have survived and have been translated.[6] On the first of these voyages in 1832 Karelin, who headed a flotilla of four ships and a complement of 170 Ural Cossacks, visited the northeastern coast and the Gulf of Mertvyi Kultuk. In 1836 he visited the Gulfs of Astrabad, Krasnovodsk and Kara-Bugaz, and also penetrated inland, making excursions into Astrabad province and to the great Balkhan Mountains, where he met with local Turkomans. Karelin's diaries provide invaluable general descriptions and lists of the flora and fauna of the Caspian shore. His remarks on the old bed of the Amu-Darya, which he visited and mapped in 1836 as far as 37° E. long., his descriptions of the nature and inhabitants of the province of Astrabad and of the Turkoman coast, and his remarks on the falling levels of the Caspian, remain as valuable today as when they were written.

Thousands of Karelin's plant specimens can still be found in the Herbarium of Vascular Plants of the Komarov Botanical Institute in St Petersburg, one of the largest collections in the world and the main herbarium in Russia.[7] The collection includes specimens from the

---

6. See "Voyages of G S Karelin on the Caspian Sea", *Nature*, vol. 28, issue 730, 1883, pp. 611.

7. See http://www.mobot.org/MOBOT/Research/LEguide/collections/48/index.html

journeys to the Caspian, as well as from two expeditions with Ivan Petrovich Kirilov (1821-42) into the Djungar Alatau Mountains in the early 1840s, when the two men visited the headwaters of the Lepsa, Sarkan, Bascan and Aksu rivers – also visited at the end of the same decade by British explorer Thomas Witlam Atkinson and his wife Lucy.

Karelin lived in Semipalatinsk from 1840 to 1845, travelling every summer along the steppe borderlands from Omsk in the north to the western foothills of the Djungar Alatau in the south. He was particularly interested in the River Irtysh where it passed through the Altai Mountains, in the mountains of the Southern Altai, and in Lake Zaisan and the Tarbagatai Mountains. Twice he sailed along the Irtysh, rafting downstream from the Ust-Bukhtarma fortress – now gone – to Ust-Kamenogorsk. From here he made deep forays into the Altai Mountains, the upper reaches of the Chui, the Narym and Kurchum ranges and the beautiful Lake Markakol. In 1840-41 he worked closely with the Baltic German botanist Alexander Gustav von Schrenk, who "discovered" Lake Ala Kol, as well as 76 new species of plants and 33 new insect species while working as a plant collector for the St Petersburg Botanic Garden.[8] He crossed the Alatau Mountains to the Chinese side and also penetrated to the upper reaches of the Tentek river.

Karelin's main collaborator, the young botanist Ivan Kirilov, had studied in Tobolsk and Irkutsk under the renowned botanist Nikolai Stepanovich Turczaninov (1796-1863), who took him on collecting trips to the coast of Lake Baikal and the western Baikal Mountains. So impressed was Turczaninov with Kirilov's aptitude for botany that he took him to St Petersburg to enrol him at the university. Soon after, Kirilov met Karelin, who unofficially adopted him into his family.

In 1839 Karelin was asked to organise a scientific expedition to the Altai and Tarbagatai Mountains and chose to take his protégé Kirilov, with him. They set off in March 1840, with Kirilov in charge of botanical collecting. He also made most of the identifications and completed the

---

8. Schrenk wrote two papers on his travels in the *Djungarian Alatau: Bericht über eine im jahre 1840 in die östliche Dsungarische Kirgisensteppe unternommene Reise* (Report on a trip undertaken in the eastern Dzungarian Kirghiz Steppe in the year 1840), St Petersburg, 1840; and *Reise nach dem Balchasch und auf dem Tarbagatai*, 1841 (Journey to the Balkhash and the Tarbagatai).

plant enumerations under the supervision of Karelin and Turczaninov. On the expedition, Kirilov left Karelin in order to independently explore Lake Zaisan and the northern slopes of the Tarbagatai range. In this first year, some 38,000 botanical – as well as zoological and geological – specimens were shipped to Moscow.

In 1841 the party moved on to the Altai and Semirecheye regions. Despite having to fend off attacks by hostile Kazakhs – they were protected by 50 Cossacks[9] – the party managed to gather another 55,000 botanical specimens that year. In the autumn Kirilov was sent to Krasnoyarsk, where he worked on classifying some of the collections under Turczaninov's supervision. The latter contributed significantly to the important *Ennumeratio plantarum*, with its list of nearly 1,900 species (220 of them new, plus eight new genera).

Sadly, tragedy struck in September the following year when Kirilov contracted cholera and died suddenly at Arzamas in Nizhny Novgorod province while travelling from Siberia to Moscow. Karelin was devastated at the news and remained depressed for many months. His daughter later said that he was put on suicide watch by his companions. He never published another botanical paper during his lifetime and the identification and description of the expedition's specimens from 1842-44 fell to S S Shchegleev. Karelin continued with his expedition for another three years. Files on the expedition were subsequently lost from the Moscow Society of Naturalists, though Karelin's family preserved other papers relating to it. As V C Asmous says of the relationship between Karelin and Kirilov: "Their joint contributions to science are great and their famous expedition of 1840-45 into the Altai, Djungaria, and Semirechensk regions is justly considered one of the most fruitful and important of the nineteenth century. Without exaggeration it may be said that they discovered and explored an enormous region for science."[10]

---

9. One of whom turned out to be Captain S M Abakumov, who by September 1848 was in command of the Cossack detachment at Kopal when Thomas and Lucy Atkinson arrived at that remote settlement. Abakumov had been trained by Karelin as a very proficient plant and bird collector. Later, a town in Zhetysu was named Abakumovsky (now Zhansugarov) after him.

10. For further information, see V C Asmous, "Karelin (1801-1872) and Kirilov (1821-1842),

Strangely, and for reasons that have never been clear, Karelin's explorations in the eastern steppes came to an abrupt halt in June 1845, when a police detachment escorted him back to Russia. It seems that the Finance Ministry wrote to Prince Alexander Mikhailovich Gorchakov, the Governor of Western Siberia, asking him to ensure that Karelin returned to St Petersburg. Gorchakov, who disliked Karelin, was only too willing to oblige.

For the last 20 years of his life, having left his family near Moscow, Karelin retired to the distant province of Guryev in the southwest of present-day Kazakhstan where he lived as a hermit and continued to write up his many trips and his scientific research, although he was debilitated by rheumatism. Eventually he produced in manuscript 11 volumes of descriptions of his travels. But in a second terrible tragedy, all his work was consumed in a fire that destroyed his house in the summer of 1872. Heartbroken, the 70-year-old Karelin died in December that year, unable to bear the loss of the results of his whole life's work. It was a tremendous loss for Russian science.

With the destruction of his writings, most of his routes remained unknown, although in the early 20th century Ukrainian scientist Vladimir Ippolitovich Lipsky, chief botanist at St Petersburg, tried to retrace Karelin's routes in eastern Kazakhstan by carefully analysing the botanical specimens he had collected and which were stored in the St Petersburg Botanical Gardens. He also collected every scrap of information he could: notebooks, letters, memoirs of relatives and colleagues, entries in the books of registration of postal stations, etc. In 1905 he was able to publish a detailed biographical essay on what he had found out.[11]

There was at least one other Russian traveller who visited eastern Kazakhstan and the Djungar Alatau at this time. Aleksandr Georgievich Vlangali (1823-1908) was a geologist who, after service in the army, had taught young engineers how to find silver ores at the mining department

---

Explorers of Siberia and Middle Asia", *Journal of the Arnold Arboretum*, 1943, vol. 24(1), pp. 107-17.

11. V Lipsky, "Karelin, Grigorij Silych, his life and travels", *Flora Asiae Mediae*, pt.3, Trudy Tiflissk, Bot. Sad. vol. 7 (3), pp. 589-789.

in Barnaul, southern Siberia. In 1849-51 he travelled to the Djungar Alatau, where he compiled a brief physical and geographical sketch of the Seven Rivers and the mountains themselves. He also collected detailed information about the nature of the valleys of the seven rivers – Ayaguz, Lepsy, Karatal, Ili, Aksu, Bien and Koksu – although not everyone agrees on the same seven rivers. When describing the expedition, the term "Semirecheye" – "seven rivers" in Russian – was first introduced into scientific circulation. By 1852 Vlangali had a post at the Main Physical Observatory in St Petersburg. By the time he died he had retired as a major-general having fought in the Crimea, been the Russian Ambassador to Italy and China, a member of the State Council, a privy councillor, and a close adviser to the tsar. His book describing his expedition was published in St Petersburg, in German, in 1856.[12] He was travelling into the Djungar Alatau at almost the same time as the Atkinsons were slowly moving out of the region, visiting, like Vlangali, each of the river valleys. Did they ever meet? If so, neither recorded the event.

The further exploration of the Djungar Alatau region was now dependent on Russian military might. Ever since the days of Peter the Great Russia had dreamed of expanding into Central Asia as a precursor to making inroads into India. Fear of this eventuality was the underlying reason for the emergence of the Great Game as a British preoccupation during the latter part of the 19th century. But events in far-off Semirecheye barely registered in the minds of British administrators in India. They were more concerned about events in Afghanistan and Persia. In these northern areas, Russia's aim was to secure a clear border with China and pen in the troublesome steppe nomads, with a view to moving against the Central Asian khanates at Bokhara, Samarkand, Khiva and Kashgar at a later date. Only after the fall of the khanates did Britain become seriously concerned about Russian intentions in Central Asia.[13]

---

12. Aleksandr Georgievich Vlangali, *Reisen nach der östlichen Kirgisen-Steppe*, Kaiserlichen Academie der Wissenschaften, St Petersburg, 1856. See https://archive.org/details/ reisenachderstl00vlangoog/page/n8

13. A good example of the lack of concern felt by British geographers about Russian expansion into the steppes can be found in an article by Robert Michell, a Russian speaker, who followed closely the Russian expansion southwards. His paper on the Syr-Daria river, published in 1868, is clear: "Those who form a correct estimate of the power of the Russians to affect us in any way on the

Yet it was not a Russian, but a man descended from Kazakh nobles, who made the greatest contribution to Russian knowledge about these northern and eastern steppes, their peoples and politics. Shokan Shynghysuly Walikhanov was born in November 1835 in the Aman-Karagai district of what is now the Kostanay Province of northern Kazakhstan. His great grandfather was Ablai Khan, a leader of the Middle *zhuz*, while his father was senior Sultan of Kushmurun *okrug* – a position equivalent to chief Kazakh adviser to the Russian frontier board. Although brought up in a yurt, at the age of six Walikhanov started a secular education and learnt to read and write Arabic script, as well as Russian, Chagatai, Turkic, Arabic and Persian. He also learnt to sketch from some of the many artists and topographers who stayed with his family, including exiled Decembrists, who awoke in him a strong interest in science, literature and art.

Soon after he moved to his paternal grandmother Aiganym's home at Syrymbet, and was enrolled by her into the prestigious Siberian Cadet Corps. The house, on an estate granted to her husband Vali, was said to be the first European-style home built for and inhabited by Kazakhs. Aiganym herself had developed extensive connections with Russian officials throughout her life, corresponding regularly with the Asian Department of the Ministry of Foreign Affairs and with the Siberian Committee in St Petersburg.

In 1847 Walikhanov entered the Russian military institute at Omsk, where he was taught a very varied curriculum including Russian and English literature, calligraphy and yet more languages. As a Russian-educated Kazakh he was a rarity at this time and his skills were much in demand by the Russian military who were desperate to know more about the structure and organisation of the Kazakh tribes that lived to the south.

Despite being one of the most talented scholars at the institute, Walikhanov was not allowed to graduate and carry out the final year's

North-West frontier of India, and who know the footing on which they stand in relations to the Khivans, Bokharians, Kokandians and nomads, entertain only a feeling of pleasure at the prospect of comparative well-being now opening before the degraded fanatics of those regions, and they rejoice to see that a large tract of the earth's surface is being cleared of the dark shadows which tyranny and barbarism have so long cast over it." See Robert Michell, "The Jaxartes or Syr-Daria, from Russian Sources", *Journal of the Royal Geographical Society*, vol. 38 (1868), pp. 429-59.

coursework, on the grounds that as a Muslim he was *inorodets* – a non-Russian, not Orthodox, an outsider. Instead, in 1853 he was appointed adjutant to Gustav Khristianovich Gasfort, Governor-General of Western Siberia, and during his years in Omsk met members of the Russian intelligentsia, including the geographer Per Petrovich Semenov, the poet Sergei Durov and Fyodor Dostoyevsky, who had been exiled to this remote outpost. The two men were to form a close, life-long friendship.

In 1854 Walikhanov accompanied the Russian military officer, K K Gutkovsky to Kopal in the foothills of the Djungar Alatau and in May 1856 he joined his first military mission, through central Kazakhstan, the Tarbagatai Mountains, the Djungar Alatau region and then on to Lake Issyk Kul in present-day Kyrgyzstan. The aim of the expedition was to obtain an oath of loyalty from the Kyrgyz Bugus clan and to collect topographical information about the Issyk Kul area.

Throughout the journey he collected samples of local folklore and the historical legends of the Kazakhs and Kyrgyz. It was on this trip, for example, that he was able to note down verbatim excerpts from the great Kyrgyz poem, the *Epic of Manas*. Before the end of the year he embarked on a further expedition, this time to the city of Kuldja, lying just on the southern flanks of the Tian Shan Mountains in Chinese Turkestan. It was on the completion of this expedition that in February 1857 he was asked to go to St Petersburg to make a full report to the Russian Geographical Society and while there was elected to membership, having been proposed by Semenov.

In June 1858 Walikhanov set out on the expedition that would cement his reputation. Disguised as a Tashkent merchant, he joined a camel caravan made up of 43 men, 101 camels and 65 horses heading for Kashgar, a city in Chinese Turkestan on the other side of the Tian Shan Mountains that was almost unknown to outsiders. Russian officials were increasingly concerned about reports of ongoing insurrection in Chinese Turkestan and were actively considering whether or not China's weakness in putting it down could be an opportunity for Russian expansion. Many thousands of Kazakhs regularly migrated with their herds along the Ili river valley into the Chinese-controlled regions and back again and the Russians wanted to know more about their opinions.

It was Semenov who was first to recognise the unique skills possessed by Walikhanov and the fact that he could be utilised to gather vital information on the Kazakh tribes and other inhabitants of the steppelands. He wrote the following about the young Kazakh and his trip to Kashgar: "Walikhanov was the single most capable officer at that time, in the staff of the general-governor, who, being sent in a Kazakh costume to Kashgar, had the possibility, because of his maturity and talent, to collect precious (for Russia) pieces of information about the contemporary situation of not only Kashgar, but also all of the Alti-Shahr and elucidate the causes of the disturbances that were occurring in Chinese Turkestan at that time."[14]

That, then, was the basis for the journey, which was backed by the Russian Geographical Society, the Ministry of War and the Ministry of Foreign Affairs. Leaving Semirecheye in June 1858, Walikhanov was now transformed into Alimbai, a merchant from Tashkent. The caravan arrived at the city in October the same year and Walikhanov's diary entries provide detailed descriptions of the people he met, the languages they spoke, their customs and rites, and also detailed maps. While in the city he made a record of ancient Buddhist monuments in the region. He also discovered the fate of Adolph Schlagintweit, a German botanist and explorer who had gone missing in the city two years before.

Schlagintweit was the second of five brothers born in Munich. Together with his brother Hermann he had published a scientific study of the Alps in 1846-48. Joined by a third brother, Robert, the three men published a further study of the geography and geology of the Alps in 1854. That year, the East India Company, acting on the recommendation of Alexander von Humboldt, commissioned the brothers to make scientific investigations and particularly to study the Earth's magnetic field in India and its high mountains. They arrived in India from Southampton in October 1854 and after travelling through the Deccan, spent three years exploring the Himalayas, the Karakorum

---

14. Quoted in Scott C Matsushita Bailey, *Travel, Science and Empire: The Russian Geographical Society's Expeditions to Central Eurasia, 1845-1905*, Unpublished PhD dissertation, University of Hawai'i, May 2008, p. 105.

and the Kunlun Mountains on the border with Tibet.[15]

After many travels throughout India and the foothills of the Himalayas covering over 17,000 miles, the three brothers met up for the last time in Srinagar, capital of Kashmir, in October 1856. Robert and Hermann then decided to return to Europe by sea, arriving home in June the following year. Soon after, they published in four volumes their *Results of a Scientific Mission to India and High Asia* (Leipzig, 1860-66). Adolph, however, decided instead to attempt to return to Europe overland via Central Asia and Russia, although reports of disturbances in Turkestan prompted him to return all his belongings to Bombay (Mumbai). Nonetheless, he continued to travel into the mountains until in the summer of 1857 he was captured by the troops of Wali Khan, the ruler of Kashgar, who was in revolt against the Chinese. On 26 August 1857 Schlagintweit was summarily beheaded as a suspected Chinese spy in the courtyard of the khan's palace.

Walikhanov thus found out what had happened to Schlagintweit and according to some accounts he successfully returned to the Russian Empire with the scientist's head. The latter's notebook turned up sometime later in a Kashgar tobacconist's shop, where it was bought by a Persian trader who brought it to India. The return of his head provided a plot element in Rudyard Kipling's famous story *The Man Who Would Be King* (1888).

Walikhanov did not leave Kashgar until April 1859 and on his return was once again invited to St Petersburg, where he was at the centre of public life and received a decoration from Tsar Alexander II, a promotion to the rank of captain and a 500-rouble reward. His important articles, *On the Western Regions of the Chinese Empire* and *On Trade in Kuldja and Chuguchak*, were only circulated within military circles and were not finally published until 1962. He was also given a new job in the Asiatic Department, but in the spring of 1861 a bout of tuberculosis forced Walikhanov to leave St Petersburg and make his way back to his beloved steppe.

---

15. For a detailed examination of the careers of the Schlagintweit brothers, see Gabriel Finkelstein, "Conquerors of the Kunlun?", *History of Science*, xxxviii (2000), pp. 179-218. See https://philpapers.org/archive/FINCO.pdf

Walikhanov was dogged by poor health for the rest of his short life. In 1862 he stood for election to the post of senior sultan of the Atbasar outer district but was ruled unfit to take up the post. On 15 October 1862 he wrote to his friend, the Russian writer Fyodor Dostoyevsky:

I took a notion to become a senior sultan, in order to devote myself to benefiting my compatriots, to protecting them from officialdom and the despotism of rich Kazakhs. My main concern was to show the people of my region how an educated ruler could be of value to them... To this end, I agreed to seek election as senior sultan of the Atbasar District, but the election did not take place without a certain amount of bureaucratic chicanery. These gentlemen, both at provincial and departmental level, were, to a man, against it. You will understand why. The provincial officials would have lost several thousand, which they are presently able to extract from the senior sultan; the departmental officials were absolutely correct in supposing that if I were to become sultan they would all be sent a-begging...

Sad to relate, of all the Russian authorities only Mr Gutkovsky was on my side, who at that time occupied the office of governor and was conducting the election. Officialdom set about playing on the vanity of the rich and ambitious in the Horde and scaring them with assertions that, if Walikhanov became sultan, it would be the worse for everyone. He subscribes, they averred, to notions of equality... They also put it around that I do not believe in God and am personally at odds with Mohammad. Needless to say, that sort of thing could not but have consequences, especially when the utterances were coming from Russian "majors", as the Kazakhs call all Russian officials.

Two years after his failed election attempt, in 1864, Walikhanov joined a military expedition to South Kazakhstan under the command of General Mikhail Grigorievich Chernyayev. The general's brutal treatment of the local people at Aulie-Ata (Dzhambul) so appalled the young Kazakh and a number of sympathetic Russian officers that they decided to resign their commissions and leave the theatre of military operations immediately. He never again worked for the Russian state.

The last year of Walikhanov's life was spent in the *aoul* of Sultan Tezek, a distant relative from the Alban clan living in the Almaty region in what is now southeast Kazakhstan. Here he married Tezek's sister and continued to collect historical and ethnographic materials on the Kazakhs of the Senior *zhuz*. In April 1865 he died, probably from TB, aged only 29, leaving behind his remarkable studies on the ethnography of the Kazakhs and also more than 150 paintings. He was buried in the nearby cemetery of Kochen-Togan in present-day Almaty Province, close to Altyn Emel. On his death the Russian Geographical Society issued a statement stating that his journey to Kashgar "represented the most outstanding geographical achievement since the time of Marco Polo".[16]

Walikhanov, who always remained *inorodets* – an outsider, never quite "one-of-us" – to the Russians because of his Kazakh and religious background, turned out to be the person who provided them with the best insights into the functioning of nomadic society. He made passionate pleas to Russian governors and policy-makers to respect the legal and historical traditions of the steppe nomads, none of which were listened to. There can be little doubt that while Russian geographers, cartographers, botanists and biologists were able to map and classify the vast, newly-acquired Central Asian territories, none was able to understand its people with such clarity. After Walikhanov's death Dostoyevsky spoke warmly to a visitor about his old friend: "Do you see that big rosewood box? That is a present from my Siberian friend Shokan Walikhanov. It is very dear to me. In it I store my manuscripts, letters and those things which are dear to me in my memory."[17]

*

Meanwhile, Russian Cossacks, closely followed by large numbers of land-hungry – and highly subsidised – Russian peasants were settling in the best agricultural lands close to the mountains in the south and

16. *Ibid*, p. 186.

17. Quoted in Bailey, *op. cit.*, pp. 177-8.

southeastern regions of what was once known as Western Siberia, but soon became Turkistan. The Great Horde had submitted to Russian rule in 1846 and soon after the town of Kopal was founded as a Cossack outpost. But the problem of the Kyrgyz tribes remained. Usually called Dikokamenni by the Russians and Burut by the Chinese, these warrior tribes were difficult adversaries, able to move through the mountains and sweep down on their enemies without warning. The Russian response was to move beyond the River Ili and to take them on in their fastnesses around Lake Issyk Kul.

In 1853 a first Russian detachment under Colonel Gutkovsky was sent across the Ili. The following year the Kyrgyz fort at Tuchebek on the Kesken river was destroyed and soon the Kyrgyz tribes were submitting, while others fled to Kokand. In 1855 Fort Verniye – i.e. Fort Loyal, later to become Almaty (Town of Apples) – was founded at the head of the Almatynka Valley. Within another two years most of the Kyrgyz had been pacified.

With much of the danger of tribal conflict removed, Russian geographers were able to continue the process of exploring the mountains and valleys of the Alatau and Tian Shan Mountains. In 1856 Semenov set off to explore the more remote parts of these regions, never before seen by "scientific" outsiders. He too had been encouraged to visit these regions by Alexander von Humboldt and Carl Ritter, by whom he had been tutored during his stay in Berlin in 1853-55. Even before going to Germany he had been responsible for translating sections of Ritter's book on Asia into Russian. "Humboldt attached so much importance to the investigation, even a cursory one, of this range, that I could not look at the undertaking except in the light of a holy mission marked out for me by the Nestor of European men of science," wrote Semenov.[18]

Semenov travelled to Issyk Kul, reaching the eastern edge of the lake on 21 September 1856, with a detachment of 12 Cossacks. But fearing attack, they returned to Verniye to procure a larger force of 40 Cossacks. He returned to Issyk Kul's western end via the Buam defile at the upper course of the Chu river. Here he met large detachments of Sary-Bagysh

---

18. Semenov, *op. cit.*, p. 221.

tribesmen, recently defeated in an engagement with Russian troops. He was received hospitably but could not penetrate beyond the first exposed rocky spurs of the Celestial range, as he was worried about being attacked. He was forced to withdraw.

In spring 1857 he returned to the same region. There was fighting between the Bugus and Sary-Bagysh tribes, but a rumour spread about the approach of a strong Russian detachment with "terrible instruments of destruction" that would be used to assist the Manap Burambai of the Bugus. As a result, the Sary-Bagysh migrated some 200 *versts* to the upper course of the Narym river. This allowed the Bugus to recover their former camping grounds and to reap the crops they had planted months before. As a result the Bugus became firm allies of Semenov and gave him every assistance. This allowed him to make a detour of Issyk Kul from the south side to reach the summit of the imposing Zauku-Davan mountain pass. He also got to the source of the Narym.

Soon after he penetrated much farther into the heart of the Tian Shan, ascending the Tengri-Tag group of mountains, which included the imposing peak of Khan Tengri that was not climbed until 1931. Here he discovered the source of the Sary-Djaza, belonging to the system of the Taryn-Gol or Ergeu – the most remote river of the Asiatic continent. He was also able to correct Humboldt's theory about the volcanic origins of the Tian Shan Mountains. Nowhere did he find any evidence of volcanic activity.[19] He was also an impressive collector. His collection of insects alone included more than 700,000 examples. More than a hundred new species were named after him. With the publication of his findings on the Tian Shan in 1857 Semenov firmly cemented his reputation,[20] although he seldom returned to exploration on completion of the expedition. It was in recognition of his travels in these regions that in 1906, on the fiftieth anniversary of his great expedition, Tsar Nicholas II awarded him the honorific epithet "Tianshansky", to be added to his surname.

---

19. Thomas Atkinson had also been asked by Humboldt, whom he met in Berlin in 1846, to look into the possibility of volcanic activity in Central Asia. In his writings Atkinson specifically mentions that Humboldt's theory of the volcanic origins of an island in the middle of Lake Ala Kol was incorrect.

20. Petr Petrovich Semenov, *Travels in the Tian'-Shan' 1856-57*, The Hakluyt Society, London, 1998.

As Scott C Matsushita Bailey writes: "His journey to the Tian' Shan' Mountains at mid-century was a critical starting point in the process of scientific travel and exploration of the region. Semenov-Tian'-Shansky's journey gained immediate attention from the elite of the Russian Geographical Society and he quickly rose to prominence as one of its most celebrated leaders, enjoying a long career that closely coincided with the establishment of Russian imperial hegemony in Central Eurasia. His scholarly example would be followed by subsequent generations of Russian scholar-travellers and his direct support for training and equipping of explorers and expeditions paved the way for the success of the empire in the region."[21]

The closer involvement of the Russian Geographical Society (from 1849 the Russian Imperial Geographical Society) in the exploration of Central Asia was in part due to the need to know more about the vast lands that were coming under the control of the tsarist state. At another level they were also part of the long-running debate about whether Russia itself was a European or an Asian state. Knowing more about the people that were part of this state was seen as crucial to answering this question.

It is fascinating to note that it was a British geographer, Sir Roderick Murchison, who played an important role in the organisation's formation. During several years in the early 1840s studying the geology of the Ural Mountains – from whence he derived the concept of the Permian geologic period – Murchison lost no opportunity to encourage Russian scientists to form a geographical society, similar to those already founded in Paris, Berlin and London. The collection of both geographic and ethnographic information – along with statistics – would quickly become its major focus of interest. In 1847 Murchison, along with Humboldt and Ritter, was elected to the newly-formed society as one of its first foreign members.

And the decision to concentrate its resources on Central Asia was also a result of political and diplomatic expediency. Russia's defeat in the Crimean War in 1856 and the terms of the Treaty of Paris that year

---

21. Bailey, *op. cit.*

forced Russia to curtail its interests in that region and to expand its activities further east. The defeat of Shamil in the Caucasus also allowed Russia to consolidate its military strengths in the region. Ultimately it would lead to the subjugation of the khanates, prompted in part at least by fears of British expansion beyond India and Afghanistan.

Within a few years of Semenov's journey to the Tian Shan, the Russian Geographical Society had sponsored Nikolai Alexeevich Severtzov on a series of expeditions. Severtzov was inspired in his interest in Central Asia by his meeting with G S Karelin – whom we have already met – in 1845. Severtzov was only 18 and had been educated at the University of Moscow. In 1857 he got his first opportunity to take part in a scientific expedition on a mission organised by the Academy of Sciences to "investigate the continental climate and explain the geographical distribution of animals by physical conditions of terrestrial surface". It was not a straightforward journey by any means; he was briefly captured by Turkoman raiders and wounded in several places by sabre cuts.

Undeterred, he continued his work and in 1864 was invited to join General Mikhail Grigorevich Chernyayev's military campaign to take the city of Tashkent. Marching with just 1,000 men across the steppes, Chernyayev first captured Shymkent, part of the Khanate of Kokand, before capturing Tashkent (against explicit orders not to do so), 130 km further south, the following year. Severtzov's initial geographical findings from the expedition were published in English by the Royal Geographical Society in 1870.[22]

It was another eight years before Severtzov's important book, *The Vertical and Horizontal Distribution of Animals in Turkestan*[23] was published. The book contained the first descriptions of a number of animals, including a subspecies of argali (wild sheep) that was later named after him, *Ovis ammon severtzovi,* and Severtzov's jerboa *Allactaga severtzovi.* He also described numerous new species and

---

22. N Severtzov, "A Journey to the Western Portion of the Celestial Range (Thian-Shan), or 'Tsun-Lin' of the Ancient Chinese, from the Western Limits of the Trans-Ili region to Tashkend", *Journal of the Royal Geographical Society*, vol. 40, 1870, pp. 343-419.

23. Unpublished in English. See "Vertical and Horizontal Distribution of Turkestan Animals", in *Izvestia* of the Moscow Society of Amateurs of Natural Science (1873).

subspecies of birds, including the Spotted Great Rosefinch, *Carpodacus severtzovi*. Severtzov contributed regularly to *The Ibis*, a quarterly journal published in London by the British Ornithologists' Union.

In 1865-66 Severtzov explored the Tian Shan Mountains and the region around Lake Issyk Kul. In 1877-79 he took part in expeditions to the Pamirs, writing up his notes on birds of the region to great acclaim. He spent the last five years of his life working on scientific papers. In February 1885, when driving a carriage with a friend on a beaten track on the frozen River Ikorts, a tributary of the Don, the carriage suddenly plunged through the ice. Everyone got out, but Severtzov could not find his portfolio and went back to try to find it. Within moments he fell down in a fit and died.

From the 1860s onwards most of the Russian travellers in Central Asia were acting at the behest of the Russian Geographical Society and tasked with gathering information – including ethnographic material – that would be useful for administering these new territories. They included the Polish explorer Nikolai Mikhailovich Przhevalsky (1839-88), who mounted four major expeditions in Central Asia. Between 1870 and 1873, leaving Kiakhta south of Lake Baikal, he crossed the Gobi Desert to Beijing and then explored the upper Yangtze before crossing into Tibet. He returned with 5,000 plant specimens, 1,000 birds, 3,000 insect species, 130 mammals and 70 reptiles. Most famously, he discovered the wild progenitor of the domesticated horse, named in his honour Przehevalsky's Horse. He also furnished important information about the Islamic uprising of Yakub Beg against the Chinese.

From 1876-77 Przhevalsky travelled through the Tian Shan Mountains and on to Lop Nor Lake in an ultimately unsuccessful attempt to reach Lhasa, the capital of Tibet. From 1879-80, leading the first Tibet Expedition, he once again entered Tibet, making it to within 160 miles of Lhasa before being turned back by officials. Finally, from 1883-85, in the Second Tibet Expedition, he crossed once again from Kiakhta across the Gobi Desert to Alashan and the eastern Tian Shan Mountains. From there he returned westwards towards Lake Issyk Kul.

The regions explored by Przhevalsky were truly remote, seldom if ever visited before by outsiders. He argued that these inner Asian regions had once been much wetter and that towns and cities had been lost to the ever-encroaching sands: "What gives the traveller even more telling evidence of the depletion of life-giving water supplies and the advance of the deadly forces of the desert is the sight of once flourishing oases and sand-buried towns. We know many of those from Chinese chronicles and saw some ourselves; in fact, we heard the natives say that in olden days the area limited by Khotan, the Aksu and Lop Nor used to have 23 towns and 360 villages, now gone. At that time, one was able, legend has it, to reach Lop Nor from the town of Kucha by stepping 'on the house roofs', so densely populated was the Tarim Basin, now deserted."[24]

As for his legacy, it is best summed up by his biographer, Donald Rayfield: "No matter how we spell his name, Nikolay Przhevalsky was one of the most remarkable men born in Russia in the nineteenth century. He was an explorer and adventurer as single-minded as Livingstone. As a zoologist and botanist, he was so productive that his collections are still being analysed. As a geographer he mapped an unknown area of western China, Mongolia and Tibet even larger and more hostile than that 'black heart' of Africa. He personified the thrust of Russia's empire in Asia with the vigour of a conquistador. His four expeditions made an indelible contribution not just to our atlases and our knowledge of a vast expanse of Central Asia, but to the rivalries and tensions of the area."[25]

One might add that most of the lands through which Przhevalsky travelled never became the subject of Russian colonisation. His contribution to natural history and to geography were enormous, but despite his military swagger and extraordinary vitality, few Russians followed in his footsteps.

There were a few others who followed Przhevalsky, in particular the Cossack Grigory Nikolaevich Potanin and his wife Alexandra Viktorovna Potanina. Potanin had studied at the military academy in Omsk alongside Walikhanov, with whom he became good friends. He had also met Semenov in the same city in 1856 and it was the latter who

---

24. Quoted in Popova, *op. cit.* p. 20.

25. Donald Rayfield, *The Dream of Lhasa: The life of Nikolay Przhevalsky (1839-88), Explorer of Central Asia*, Paul Elek, London, 1976, p. xi.

later supported Potanin's expeditions to Central Asia and even assisted him in getting a university education in St Petersburg. The two men were to stay in touch with each other well into the 20th century.

Potanin became radicalised while studying in St Petersburg and his political activity eventually led him into trouble. He was kicked off his botany course and from 1865-74 he was either in prison or in exile for his views on the liberation of Siberia from Russian control. However, Semenov never lost faith in him, and his years of incarceration seem to have moderated his views. He married Alexandra in 1873 and for the rest of their lives they travelled together, even in the most remote places. Sadly, she was to die on their fourth expedition together.

With support from Semenov, the Potanins were able to organise their first expedition to northwestern Mongolia in 1866-67 and a second to Tuva in 1879-80. While Grigory collected geographical and ethnological material and folklore, Alexandra collected botanical specimens and kept a detailed diary. The couple also collected bird specimens and made the first detailed maps of the regions through which they travelled. Third and fourth expeditions followed in 1884-86 and 1892-93. These traversed the eastern areas of Tibet and the neighbouring Chinese provinces of Gansu and Sichuan. Alexandra, who had become ill even before the start of the fourth expedition, died in October 1893 and was buried at Kiakhta, on the Russian border with China. Grigory made his fifth and final expedition, to the Greater Khingan Mountains in 1899, before retiring to write up his research. Increasingly he identified with the indigenous peoples in the lands through which he had travelled, particularly in Siberia.

The Potanins were the last of the explorers sponsored by the Russian Geographical Society. Central Asia, particularly the steppelands, had been subjugated, measured and studied, and even the most remote borderlands had been crossed and re-crossed by large, well-financed scientific expeditions. In the early years of the 20th century politics and social upheaval came to dominate these regions and the focus of geographical and ethnological study changed, particularly following the creation of the Soviet state. An era had come to an end. The Great Steppe had become Tatary, had become Western Siberia, had become Turkestan, had become the Soviet Central Asian "stans". The expeditions by Przhevalsky, the Potanins and others that followed them to adjoining lands had been less about colonisation than gaining knowledge and prestige within the international scientific community. From 1917 until 1991 the only question of importance for the Soviets was how to hold it all together.

—⁓—

Shokan Walikhanov *(left)*
and Fyodor Dostoyevsky.

Overleaf: Gabriel Bonvalot.

7

THE FRENCH ARE COMING

—⁓—

FRANCE IS NOT GENERALLY KNOWN FOR ITS EXPLORATION OF CENTRAL ASIA. Whereas French travellers were among the earliest to visit Indochina, parts of India and Sri Lanka, the Near East and, of course, North Africa, there were few reasons – except during the early Middle Ages – to draw the French to the Great Steppe. It was then, when France was deeply involved in the Crusades, that Frenchmen such as the Dominican priest Andrew of Longjumeau had visited the Mongols. Longjumeau's first mission, at the behest of Pope Innocent IV, took place as early as 1247.

Two years later an almost entirely French group including Longjumeau set off on a second mission with letters and presents from King Louis to meet Güyük Khan, grandson of Genghis Khan, at his camp close to Lake Ala-Kol in present-day eastern Kazakhstan. The khan was already dead when they arrived, poisoned by rivals. His successor, Möngke Khan, the fourth Mongol khagan, had not yet been installed but, as with most of the papal emissaries and royal messengers, Longjumeau was sent back to Europe with a letter bluntly demanding that European Christians acknowledge the Mongols as rulers of the world and pay tribute.

After Longjumeau there are only a handful of French travellers in this part of the world. Jean-Baptiste Tavernier (1605-89), the French traveller and diamond dealer, made it to Persia several times and died in Moscow at the age of 85 while contemplating a final journey to Persia across the Caspian Sea, but others are rare. While the English tried to develop the Moscow Company during the 16th century to divert the Silk Road trade northwards, France concentrated its resources elsewhere.

And when interest in Central Asia began to revive in the late 18th and early 19th centuries, France was often disbarred from sending its citizens to the steppes because of rivalry between Napoleonic France and the Russian tsars.

Yet, as the 19th century progressed political conditions changed, and French travellers began to appear on the steppes. Among the earliest were the husband-and-wife team of Xavier Hommaire de Hell (1812-48) and his wife Adèle (1818-83). Xavier was educated in Dijon and in 1833 graduated as an engineer at the École des Mines in Saint-Étienne. The following year he met and married his wife Adèle Heriot and in 1835 the two of them set off for Turkey, where he was determined to work as a builder and architect. Having narrowly escaped shipwreck on the way, his first projects included a suspension bridge in Constantinople and a lighthouse on the Black Sea coast.

From here, the couple moved on to southern Russia where Xavier carried out ethnographic and geographic research. After he discovered coal deposits along the River Dnieper in Moldavia, Tsar Nicholas I awarded him St Vladimir's Cross. Xavier and his wife were to spend the following five years in southern Russia, exploring the courses of rivers and streams, mostly on horseback. He was particularly interested in the region of the Black Sea around the Sea of Azof and its possible connection to the Caspian.

"When I left Constantinople for Odessa my principal object was to investigate the geology of the Crimea and of New Russia and to arrive by positive observations at the solution of the great question of the rupture of the Bosphorus," he wrote in the preface to his book *Travels in the Steppes of the Caspian Sea*.[1] The idea that in antiquity the Black Sea had created a huge inundation when it poured through a rupture caused by a massive earthquake that created the Bosphorus fascinated many scientists, including Peter Simon Pallas, Herbert Wood and others (see Chapter 9).

The notoriously frail Xavier, who died at the age of 36, also acknowledged the debt he owed to his wife both in taking part in his

---

1. Xavier Hommaire de Hell, *Travels in the Steppes of the Caspian Sea, the Crimea, the Caucasus, etc*, Chapman and Hall, London, 1857.

journeys and also writing them down for posterity: "My wife, who has braved all hardships to accompany me in most of my journeys, has also been the partner of my literary labours in France. To her belongs all the descriptive parts of this book of travels." In fact, many sections of this book are written in her voice, which is outspoken, often expressing her repugnance at the gratuitous violence inflicted on the Russian peasants by their "noble" masters.

Xavier and Adèle left the Black Sea shores in May 1839 for the Caspian. They visited the German- and Dutch-speaking colonies of Mennonites and Moravians on the Lower Volga and also the encampments of the Kalmyks close to what is now the city of Volgograd. They then headed down the right bank of the Volga towards the island on which Astrakhan is located at the northern tip of the Caspian. Having arrived in the fabled city, the following day they set off back along the Volga on horseback to cover the 40 miles or so to the home of a Kalmyk chieftain, who was known to entertain guests at a wonderful palatial house-cum-temple – Khoshut Khurul – located on an island in the Volga. "I was quite unprepared for what I saw; and really in passing through two salons which united the most finished display of European taste with the gorgeousness of Asia, on being suddenly accosted by a young lady who welcomed me in excellent French, I felt such a thrill of delight that I could only answer by embracing her heartily," wrote Mme de Hell.[2]

The founder of the palace, part of which is still standing, and which is the only pre-revolutionary Buddhist temple that survives in Kalmykia, was Prince Serebjab Tyumen, a hero of Russia's Patriotic War of 1812 against the French. He had even taken his Kalmyk troops – who were the last to use bows and arrows in any conflict in Europe – to Paris. He was an outstanding military commander who led the Second Astrakhan Kalmyk regiment, and was also head of the Khoshut (literally "bannermen") clan of the Kalmyks. These Kalmyks were the descendants of the Kalmyk Horde that had not been able to cross the Volga and join their kin in the winter of 1771 on the great migration back to China. They had stayed behind and to prove their loyalty had

---

2. *Ibid*, p. 168.

provided regiments of mounted archers to the Russian Imperial Army.

Tyumen was aided in building Khoshut Khurul by his brother Batur-Ubashi Tyumen – a warrior, historian and writer – and a Buddhist monk called Havan Jimbe. The two brothers had visited St Petersburg in the summer of 1814, participating in celebrations to mark the victory over Napoleon. Inspired by the greatness of the city, and especially its Kazan Cathedral, they decided to perpetuate the memory of victory in their native steppes. The remarkable building was completed in 1818.

Old photographs show that the Khoshut Khurul was originally a magnificent ensemble consisting of a central three-nave tower (*sume*) and two galleries that separated from it in a semicircle and ended with two small towers (*tsatsa*), as well as several outbuildings and a cobblestone fence on brick poles. Although it was both a palace and temple, the prince himself lived in a small building hidden away in the garden. In the 1920s, the Khoshut Khurul was closed by the Bolsheviks. Later it was used as a club and in the 1950s as a granary.

After the restoration of the Kalmyk ASSR in 1957, the territory where the Khoshut Khurul was located was transferred to the Astrakhan Region. In the 1960s, most of the building was dismantled for the construction of a barn. Later, the rest of it was abandoned, and it gradually began to collapse. The three-nave main tower is the only one to have survived. Now, at last, the gradual restoration of the Khurul is under way.

Mme de Hell noted that soon after she and her husband arrived the room began to fill with Russian and Cossack officers and then the prince himself arrived. The palace was decked out in the finest European furniture and silver: "In vain I looked for anything that could remind me of the Kalmyks; nothing around me had a tinge of *couleur locale*; all seemed rather to bespeak the abode of a rich Asiatic nabob. And with a little effort of imagination, I might easily have fancied myself transported into the marvellous world of the fairies, as I beheld that magnificent palace encircled with water, with its exterior fretted all over with balconies and fantastic ornaments, and its interior all filled with velvets, tapestries and crystals, as though the touch of a wand had made all these wonders start from the bosom of the Volga!"

Mme de Hell spent some time with the prince's gorgeously-attired and beautiful sister-in-law in the large yurt in the palace grounds in which she lived during the summer, who questioned her closely on any number of issues. Afterwards they were given a dramatic display of bareback horsemanship and then taken into dinner. "The cookery, which was half Russian, half French, left us nothing to desire as regarded the choice or the savour of the dishes," she wrote. "Everything was served up in silver and the wines of France and Spain, champagne especially, were supplied in princely profusion. Many toasts were given, foremost among which were those in honour of the Emperor of Russia and the King of the French."[3]

Afterwards they visited the prince's personal rooms, where they were shown some ancient curiosities, including a pair of 15th-century Florentine pistols, coats of chain mail, damascened swords and a visitors' book which included the names of various English, German and Russian dignitaries, including von Humboldt, who had visited Khoshut Khurul in 1829. The entertainment did not stop there, as the couple, together with the army officers and the prince's household, danced all night.

The following day the couple returned to hot and dusty Astrakhan, the ancient capital of the Golden Horde, which then had a population of around 45,000. It had once been a major transit point for Indian and Chinese goods taken from there by land across to the Black Sea for shipment onwards to Constantinople and Europe – a trade that was once in the hands of the Genoese and Venetians. That had ended with the predations of Tamerlane and the expansion of the Ottoman Empire and finally with the opening up of the sea routes to India and China. By the 1830s, despite the efforts of Peter the Great to reinvigorate the old trade routes, it was a backwater.

A few weeks later they left the city, crossing the Volga, which took more than an hour. Once on the western side they were struck by the differences: "When we reached the opposite bank, we might have fancied ourselves transported suddenly to a distance of a hundred versts from Astrakhan. Kalmyks, sand, felt tents, camels, in a word, the desert and its tenants were all that now met our view."[4]

---

3. *Ibid*, p. 174.

4. *Ibid*, p. 202.

Now they were heading south, along the western shores of the Caspian towards Kizlyar in modern-day Daghestan. It was a dreary road, mostly loose sand, enlivened only by the hawk of a Tatar officer who accompanied them and which kept them in fresh game for dinner. He would let it go and follow it to a nearby pool of brackish water, all the while beating a small drum fastened to his saddle. There he would find the bird, its claws firmly fixed into the back of a duck or goose, waiting for its master to arrive. The drumbeat was to discourage other geese from attacking the hawk and trying to free its victim.

As they progressed on their journey, Xavier Hommaire de Hell would stop every ten minutes or so to take a level, so that he could work out the difference in height between the Caspian Sea and the Black Sea. They would stop for lunch, erecting their tents and cooking some of the birds brought down by the officer's hawk. Mme de Hell describes her travelling outfit: "I myself figured in my huge bonnet, dressed as usual in wide pantaloons, with a Gaulish tunic gathered round my waist by a leathern belt." She tried riding a camel, but decided against it, finding that after just two *verst*s she was "totally exhausted when I dismounted".

Mme de Hell discusses in detail the history of the Kalmyks and their relations with both St Petersburg and Beijing. She quotes in full the document written by the Qianlong emperor in which he describes the saga of the Kalmyk return to China in 1771.[5] She also sets out in detail the ethnographic distribution of tribes in the northern Caspian region, on either side of the Volga, as well as the administrative arrangements through which the Russians governed this part of the steppe. She mentions, for example, the Turkoman tribes, the Nogais, the Sirtof Horde of Tatars and the baptised Kalmyks, as well as the Junior Horde of the Kazakhs, who in the early 1800s moved into the steppe regions left empty following the migration of the bulk of the Kalmyks back to China.

Most of these people were involved in stock breeding, particularly horses, which were used extensively by the Russian cavalry. They even exported horses to Poland at one time. Mme de Hell estimated the numbers of animals held by the Kalmyks in 1838 at from 250,000

---

5. *Ibid*, pp. 229-35.

to 300,000 horses, about 60,000 oxen, 180,000 camels and nearly a million sheep. Agriculture was not only against the traditions of the steppe nomads, but was almost impossible; in these regions in particular the land was salty and lacked fresh water. The flatness of the land meant that the winter winds were formidable. As she comments: "A nomad life seems therefore to me a necessity for the Kalmyks and until the development of civilisation among them shall make them feel the need for fixed dwellings, they must be left free to wander over their steppes."

Mme de Hell also discusses in some detail the Kazakhs who lived in the Caspian steppes. When she was writing these tribes held around seven million hectares of land, paid no tax and had their own sovereign khan. Their only obligation was to provide a corps of cavalry in time of war. She says that a Russian survey of 1841 indicated around 16,550 tents, although she estimates that the real number was around half that figure. Whatever the truth, she says they were "imprisoned" between two lines of Cossacks along the Ural and Volga.

Although the Kazakhs and Kalmyks had been implacable foes from time immemorial, during the time described by the French couple there were good relations. The Kazakh khan, Giangour Bukevich, often visited Prince Tyumen and in 1836 more than 2,000 Kazakhs camped on the banks of the Volga and took part in grand entertainments offered by the prince to government officials. The Russian Emperor Nicholas I had built a wooden house for him in the Ryn-Peski Desert in present-day northwest Kazakhstan.

Having spent time in the Caucasus, the de Hells headed back towards the Crimea and then, due to Xavier's ill health, back to France in 1842, where he received many awards, including the Légion d'honneur. The couple were to travel again in 1845, first to Turkey and later, in June 1847, to Persia, where Xavier died of cholera a few months later. They were remarkable travellers and Mme de Hell in particular deserves more recognition, both for her travels and for her writings, which are full of insights.

*

After Xavier and Adèle Hommaire de Hell there was a gap of almost 40 years before once more we began to see French travellers in Central Asia. The immediate reason for the increase in visitors, not just French, was the defeat by the Russians of the Central Asian khanates, a process that began in the early 1860s. Russia's immediate requirement was knowledge about the vast new territories of the Great Steppe it had brought under its control, and its ministers were open to assistance from scientists from outside the country.

However, with a few notable exceptions – the Atkinsons in particular – Central Asia was largely closed to the British in this period. The mutually perceived threats that informed and exacerbated the Great Game were now in play. As for the French, Russia had few quarrels at this point with Paris and was not concerned about any kind of neo-colonial agenda in this region by its former rival. Russia backed the idea of French expeditions to Central Asia, offering both protection and finance.

According to historian Svetlana Gorshenina, there were two events that stimulated French interest in Central Asia.[6] First, in 1873 Paris hosted the first International Congress of Orientalists where several sessions were dedicated to the history and culture of Turkestan. Second, the Russian decision to build a trans-Asiatic railway necessitated assistance from foreign engineers and surveyors. This, says Gorshenina, was one of the principal factors in the formation of Central Asian studies in the French language. Even Ferdinand de Lesseps, the builder of the Suez Canal, became involved at one point, although his proposal for a railway line from Orenburg to Tashkent and then on south towards the borders of Britain's Indian empire never got off the ground.

French interest in Central Asia grew rapidly at this time, with Jules Verne and Alexandre Dumas writing novels with Central Asian themes, numerous articles in the popular press, exhibitions of works of art and so on. In her book Gorshenina includes at least 30 French travellers from this period who wrote books about their journeys – although

---

6. Svetlana Gorshenina, *Explorateurs en Asie Centrale : voyageurs et aventuriers de Marco Polo à Ella Maillart*, Olizane, Geneva, 2003.

many of them took the well-trodden road from the Caspian coast to Bokhara and Samarkand and then back to Europe. Towards the end of the 19th century, most French travellers followed the line of the Transcaspian railway, which was started in 1879 and eventually ran from Krasnovodsk on the east coast of the Caspian Sea, via Bokhara and Samarkand, which it reached in 1888, before going on to Tashkent and then Andijan in the Ferghana Valley, in 1898. What was known then as the Transcaspian Military Railway that ended at Tashkent was eventually connected to the main Russian railway system in 1906.

*

One of the earliest 19th-century francophone travellers in Central Asia was Henri Moser, who described a series of four journeys he made through the Great Steppe and beyond in his marvellous and sumptuous book *A Travers L'Asie Centrale*.[7] Born in Moscow in 1844 to the son of a wealthy watchmaker and merchant, Moser was brought up in Switzerland before returning to Moscow when he was 18. After falling out with his father he briefly joined the Russian Army as a cavalry officer before setting out towards Central Asia, with little money or baggage. Another journey along the Syr Darya river took place in 1869-70, followed by a third (with his wife) to Khiva and Iran in 1883 and a fourth across the remotest parts of the Turkoman lands in 1889-90.

Moser worked as a soldier in Tashkent, as a baker and as a trainer of Turkoman horses for the Russian Army during his travels. He tried unsuccessfully to build a business importing silkworms into Europe. At one point he was even a steward in a Turkish bath. He later found time to write a book about the irrigation of Central Asia.[8]

Whatever way you look at Henri Moser, he comes across as an "enthusiast". He threw himself into everything he did. Speaking of his first journey he says, "I left Moscow with only a few hundred roubles in my pocket and a great deal of determination. The new conquests in

---

7. Henri Moser, *A Travers L'Asie Centrale*, Librairie Plon, Paris, 1885.

8. Henri Moser, *l'Irrigation en Asie Centrale: étude géographique et économique*, Société des Editions Scientifiques, Paris, 1894.

Central Asia attracted me irresistibly. With the presumption of youth I did not doubt the possibility of making an independent position for myself in those lands that would allow me to satisfy my passion for the unknown that the reading of travel accounts had excited in me since my youth."[9]

He spent a few months in Orenburg learning the language and customs of the Kazakhs. However, General N A Kriyanovsky, Governor-General of Orenburg and Deputy of the Caucasus, refused to give him permission to leave the garrison for a journey towards Tashkent and the south. This did not stop Moser, who left anyway with the support of a few of his Russian Army friends, delighted to be part of a trick played on their boss. Moser avoided the main routes and stayed mostly in the yurts of nomads in case anyone was sent after him. He took the road to Orsk across country inhabited by the Orenburg Cossacks, but once beyond this region the country changed completely. There were no more villages, just endless plains and nomads.

Moser goes into some detail about the origin of the Kazakhs, particularly those of the Junior Horde, with whom he was most familiar. He described their physiognomy, their clothing and their customs with great accuracy. In part this was because one of the friends he had made in Orenburg, Suleiman-Tiaoukin, was a direct descendant of Khan Abul Khayir, the best-known leader of the Junior Horde who during the 1720s and 1730s had brought his followers under the protection of the Russians. Moser refers to him as a sultan, although the Russians had abolished the aristocratic titles of the Kazakhs in the 1820s.

Moser records that the Junior Horde had 1,200 *kibitkas* (yurts) in the area. Suleiman's father, Mohammed Ali, was himself also a Russian *provitl* or Kazakh governor. But following various intrigues he was arrested and demoted from his functions, ending his time in a dungeon in Orenburg. "Suleiman was very attached to me during my stay at Orenburg and seeing that I was studying the Kazakh language with zeal he invited me to come with him to his aoul and travel his country while hunting," writes Moser, who was very keen to learn about horses and how they were sold: "On a beautiful day we mounted Kazakh amblers

---

9. *A Travers L'Asie Centrale, op. cit.*, p. 7 (my translation).

and entered the endless steppe. We were escorted by 30 Kazakhs, amongst whom were servants of the sultan who led our replacement horses. The first part of the journey took us to Minavnoi-Dvor, where every Monday there is an open-air market, with around 200 stalls where Russian merchants sell the products of civilisation to the Kazakhs. The Kazakhs trade whilst on horseback. The buyer and seller haggle by raising their arms in turn. To each new offer the buyer claps the hands of the seller. Sometimes this lasts for a long time. When they agree they shake hands and the deal is done."[10] Kazakh amblers in particular were highly prized. Their gait is faster than a walk, but slower than a canter and allows the horse to ride long distances while providing a smoother ride for the horseman. They could fetch at least six times as much as an ordinary horse, sometimes a lot more.

The presence of a foreigner in the market caused a sensation and Moser says that it was only with great difficulty that Suleiman managed to free him from the crowd and lead him off to his *aoul*, where Moser found that the largest yurt had been transformed into a reception room. He was led in by Suleiman, who soon arranged for fresh clothing – a light gown and slippers that had been heated by the fire. The white felt of the yurt was covered in rich rugs, and on the walls were British rifles and Kazakh weapons – including *aibalta* (long-handled axes), lances and curved sabres – and richly-decorated horse harnesses.

Moser gives a brilliant description of his stay with Suleiman.

We sit down in the oriental fashion on cushions located facing the entrance. Little by little the yurt fills with people – brothers, family and friends of the sultan. He introduces me to the names of the most influential. After drinking the traditional tea, Suleiman, with a sign, invites the spectators to take their seats. What patriarchal habits! The younger brother does not dare to sit in the presence of the head of the family unless he had been invited to do so.

When we have sufficiently showered each other with compliments, as is the tradition in the East, an attendant comes

---

10. *Ibid*, pp. 25-6.

with a great basin and another one comes with an ewer and pours warm water on our hands. A third follows equipped with a hand towel. No sooner have they disappeared that a long line of servants makes their entry to the yurt, each carrying a large tray that is lowered at our feet. It is a feast capable of satiating a squadron and yet only the host and myself are eating.

A man armed with a knife cuts the meat and serves it with his fingers onto the plate. There is sheep and horse, but not an old nag that our poor eat in Europe. It is a delicious foal that has been specially fattened for a great occasion. But the most appreciated dish, the one that only appears at banquets, is the young camel. This dish is served with mountains of rice prepared with carrots and raisins. It is the national dish that the sarts[11] call palau or pilaou or pilaf.

Politeness demands that you stuff yourself with food. I am constantly exhorted to eat. If I show any hesitation, Suleiman with his own hand chooses the biggest morsels and brings them to my mouth. Replete and stuffed, I can barely breathe, and the dishes continue to appear with a despairing profusion. But I reach the end of my strength when to finish this meal in style we are presented with tea in china cups covered with mutton grease. Better die than to swallow this emetic! I seize the moment when my host is turning around to pour the treacherous drink under the felt on which I am sitting.[12]

Moser remembered that he had some bottles of *nalifka* – fruit liqueur – in his bags and quickly sent for them. As they shared the drink, Suleiman decided to introduce his favourite wife to his guest: "Upon her arrival in the tent, Fatme dazzles me with her beauty and the riches of her costume. She is in her 20s, a fresh complexion and a body that is admirably proportioned. On her head she wears a cylindrical red velvet

---

11. City dwellers of Persian origin.

12. *A Travers L'Asie Centrale*, p. 27.

hat literally covered in precious gems and lined at the bottom with fur;[13] another scarf that falls over her left ear ends with an enormous turquoise of rare dimension. As a distinctive sign of her authority the favourite was wearing an array of heron and ostrich feathers on top of her headware."

He was clearly overcome by the beauty and charm of Fatme, who sat beside him and soon engaged him in conversation: "It was with an obvious pleasure and feminine vanity that she gave me details about her costume. From the top of her headwear muslin veils lined with golden fringes were falling on her shoulder, a kind of white satin chasuble similar to that worn by a priest was decorated with large golden ribbons and a massive gold fringe fixed behind her hat cascaded to her knees. Under the chasuble one could distinguish a *sarafan* of golden brocade. This graceful costume was completed by very thin white silk trousers embroidered in gold and tightened at the ankles, and little boots, very small in red patterned leather which were covered in golden embroideries and fine stones. Fatme complacently allowed me to admire her and received the over-the-top compliments that I was sweating to make in front of my great friend."[14]

And so it continued:

I compared her teeth to pearls, her eyes to stars, her smile to the rising sun and her face to a Swiss cheese. I was running out of metaphors after this last comparison, but this lovely lady found another thing to commend to my admiration. A married woman would never dare to show her hair but wishing to complete the good opinion I had of her, Fatme graciously showed me the tip of one of her jet black tresses. I held it delicately, but not without pulling it strongly enough to ensure whether or not they were for real. Even in Europe a woman would have been very proud of this mane. A rather long silence ensued which made me feel that it was my turn to give her a good opinion, if not of my person, at least of my country and its women. I was then wearing around my neck a medallion containing the portrait of a woman. I showed

---

13. This kind of hat is known as a *saukele* and can be up to 70 cm in height.

14. *A Travers L'Asie Centrale*, p. 28.

this. As she gave it back she asked, "Is this your favourite? Is it you that made the image?" But no, I answered very surprised. "It is a painter of my country."

"This woman does not love you if she shows herself to another so scantily clad." And without knowing, this girl had guessed right. Her astonishment was great when I told her that in our gatherings all women were dressed as little as possible and especially when I described our balls to her, where a woman goes from one arm to another.

At this point Suleiman seems to have become a little agitated, appearing not to approve of the turn of the conversation. He made a sign and three *kizdars* – young women, relatives of Fatme – made their entrance, dressed in their finery, the tallest of whom, Khalisa, came to sit next to Moser. "She presented me her white hands, which I pressed very cordially. This hospitality seemed charming to me. Tea, sweets, dried fruits, pistachios, almonds were served. Khalisa broke the pistachios with her teeth to offer them to me. Comfortably squatting on my cushions, I was taking my role as sultan very seriously."

As the evening went on Suleiman designated one of his followers as a master of ceremonies who introduced various games. This king-for-the-evening was crowned with a golden crown made of paper, whilst his two "sultans" wore felt turbans. As he was crowned, he issued an order for all his subjects to kiss their sweethearts, an order that was executed promptly and with much laughter. Suleiman's second *ukase* (command) was more rigorous: he ordered the *kizdars* to kiss their *djiggits* (young warriors), again to the accompaniment of much laughter. Then a sheep's vertebra was brought in. If after being thrown into the air it fell on its side, the player lost. If it fell straight, the player had the right to demand something from his female neighbour. "I lost and the beautiful Khalisa requested me to sing a song from my homeland," writes Moser.

He adds that a fat doctor from Orenburg who was present lost his throw and was asked to imitate a dog. The king's two sultan-helpers took great pleasure chastising him with their whips each time he attempted to stop his pitiful barking. Only when he was exhausted did the game change; this time the player had to fish with his teeth for a silver coin thrown into a bowl of curdled milk.

As the evening progressed the games became more animated and noisier, probably under the influence of the *kumyss*[15] that had been passed around. Moser realised that it was time for him to retire. As he was leaving, he noticed a ring on the finger of Khalisa and asked her about it. "Take it," she said, "it is a poor girl from the steppe that offers it to you. May it, on your finger, always press a friendly hand. This is Khalisa's wish."

"In my turn I took off from my watch an old relic and gave it to her, saying you will give it to the one you love, and I hope he will be worthy of you. What has become of this proud Amazon with whom afterwards I had so many good rides in the desert? I can still see her the day I said goodbye to her, standing on my stirrups, one hand on my forehead and the other on my heart."[16]

It is hard not to believe that Moser had been completely smitten by the young woman who had sat next to him at dinner and for whom he had asked the troubadour to play a love song on his *dombra*.

Moser writes very well about his experiences in the Great Steppe. He is one of the few who saw these regions both before and after they had been annexed by the Russians. Although he was to return for another three journeys, it was this first one that was clearly the most important to him.

As an influential foreigner on excellent terms with the Russian conquerors of Central Asia, Moser was given many treasures on his travels. Some he gave away, some he exchanged for different or better-quality objects, and still others he purchased after lengthy bargaining. The many weapons, horse equipment, ceremonial coats and saddlecloths, jewellery, metalwork and miscellaneous objects he acquired – more than 500 objects in all, and certainly one of the best private collections anywhere – he sent back to Europe. From 1890 he started another career as a businessman and a diplomat for the Austro-Hungarian Empire, basing himself in the Balkans.

---

15. Fermented mare's milk that is a staple of nomadic life. Slightly alcoholic.

16. *A Travers L'Asie Centrale*, p. 35.

In Paris, he continued to purchase mostly Caucasian artefacts at sales. In 1907 he finally made some money when speculative shares he had bought in Siberian copper and gold mines produced substantial profits. This enabled him to return to Switzerland where his collection was initially installed in a mansion at Charlottenfels – where he lived until he died in 1923, at the age of 79. He bequeathed his entire collection to the Berne Historical Museum.[17]

*

Our third traveller, Mme Marie de Ujfalvy-Bourdon, is just as exotic, perhaps more so, than Henri Moser. She was born in Chartres in 1842, had a good education and at the age of 24 married the Hungarian-born ethnographic researcher and linguist Charles-Eugène Ujfalvy de Mezőkövesd, with whom she took part in several expeditions in remote parts of Asia. When in 1876 her husband was chosen for a government-funded expedition to Central Asia to investigate the regions newly conquered by the Russians she was quick to make her intentions clear: "Je suis résolue à le suivre," she explained in the first paragraph of the book she later wrote about their journey.[18]

And so she did. The couple left Paris on 17 August 1876, making their way to St Petersburg and then Moscow by train before setting off south towards Orenburg, the usual starting point for those wishing to cross the Great Steppe. While her husband busied himself trying to find locals who would consent to have their skulls measured – physical anthropology was in its heyday – Marie would be carefully observing everything around her. As they crossed the Kara-Kum desert in a *tarantass*, she noted the road was littered with bones. "The camels have paved the way with their own carcasses along the caravan route," she writes. "When they stumble, they are mercilessly abandoned where they have fallen."[19] Whenever she could she would send a despatch back to

---

17. Details about the collection can be found at https://www.museen-bern.ch/en/institutions/ museums/bernisches-historisches-museum/

18. Mme Marie de Ujfalvy-Bourdon, *De Paris à Samarkand, le Ferghanah, Le Kouldja et La Sibérie : Impressions de Voyage d'une Parisienne*, Hachette, Paris, 1880.

19. *Ibid*, p. 77.

Paris, where her missives were eagerly read in the latest edition of the monthly travel magazine, *Tour du Monde*.

Mme Ujfalvy-Bourdon was an early pioneer, both of women's travel and also women's journalism. She wrote in a direct, clear style that was immensely popular with her mainly female readers. She was shown in the most popular Paris magazines wearing a specially made exploring costume, including high boots, male trousers and a thick leather belt.

And she provides many entertaining stories of her travels in Central Asia. At one post-station close to the Aral Sea she says her husband went to an *aoul* to visit the interior of the tents and also to make skull measurements. Each Kazakh man or woman, old or young, received a small gift. "As a result, when we leave, all these nice Kazakhs escort us with their horses. We are very proud of this wonderful escort, but the station master dampens our pride by telling us of a conversation he had had with one of the riders. 'I have, said he,' speaking the words of one of the riders, 'never seen a man so stupid as this one who gave us money to feel our head'."

Mme Ujfalvy-Bourdon accurately explains the geographical distribution of the various hordes within the Kazakh tribal structure, although she argues that there is little to separate Kazakhs from Kyrgyz – a statement that would be strongly challenged today. She also describes them physically and psychologically – again probably in terms that would unacceptable nowadays: "Morally, the Kazakhs are pleasant, frank and honest. You can trust their word entirely. He is much superior to the Sart. When a Russian wants to send merchandise to Khiva or Bokhara he prefers to entrust it to a Kazakh because he is sure it will arrive, unless there is some disaster. Since the Russians have annihilated the Turkoman hordes that used to infest the steppe right up to the north of the Aral Sea, the Kazakhs peacefully go about their business and trade is secure."

The journey of the Ujfalvy-Bourdons was not particularly hard compared to that of other travellers, even though they were travelling in an unsprung *tarantass*. They realised after a while that General Konstantin Kaufmann, Governor-General of Turkestan, who had supported their journey and to whom Mme Ujfalvy-Bourdon's book is dedicated, had given special instructions that they should be treated as well as possible on the road. Indeed, it could hardly be otherwise as Charles Ujfalvy was travelling on a French diplomatic passport.

Near Jarkand, 30 km from Kazalinsk and close to the Aral Sea, the couple were met by a Kazakh who invited them to visit his yurt. It was very clean and large with beautiful rugs covering the floor. Trunks inlayed with silver were used as furniture. "We found there only one young woman with her mother," writes Mme Ujfalvy-Bourdon. "The owner of the tent was intent on getting another wife. My husband made a comment that he could be content with just one. He said he would have another wife next spring and then another the spring after. Yet the young woman of the previous spring was charming and, most of all, very clean. She showed us her son, whom she was feeding while trying to shape his ear to the fashion of the country. It is believed that the hearing becomes more acute if the ears are flattened. The Kazakh chief offered us tea, served in two bowls, with two spoons presented on a metal casket. The other people drank their tea in bowls without spoons. Only the wife did not take anything. While we were drinking the child started to cry. The mother took him by a leg and held him on top of a water bucket and with the other hand she poured the cold water on the poor child. She then put him back in his crib, as he had stopped crying."[20]

She mentions the point that since the Russians abolished the *barantas* – raiding parties aimed at settling property disputes – and introduced vaccination against smallpox, the population of the steppe had begun to rise, although poverty had also increased. It was not something she necessarily welcomed: "Stock-rearing is no longer enough to sustain them, and numerous families are forced to start working the land. So we have this curious spectacle of a people for whom the status of a farmer is a sign of poverty and decadence. The Kazakh is a born nomad, has been so for 500 years since Rubruck and Piano Carpini visited them. By becoming a farmer and becoming sedentary he morphs and becomes a sart. By becoming civilised he loses his frankness and honesty and becomes a coward, cruel and sly, the defects that characterise the sedentary population of Central Asia."

---

20. *Ibid*, p. 87

This attitude, common in the 19th century, has at its heart the idea of Rousseau's "noble savage", the human who lives honourably in a state of nature. It is a theme that is regularly repeated throughout Mme de Ujfalvy-Bourdon's writings.

The fact that nature was alive and well in Kazakhstan at this time was illustrated by the fact that she reports three tigers being shot only 30 km from Fort Perovsky – now Kyzylorda – on the Syr Darya river: "I have to add that the Kazakhs are careful before hunting this animal to dig a hole in the earth in which they put a dead sheep. They cover it with branches and dry leaves and it is only when the tiger is in the trap that they get close enough to shoot him. They rarely kill them in any other way. The Russian government gives 20 roubles for each animal, allowing the hunter to keep the skin, which can be sold for another 10 roubles. That is not very money because today 10 roubles are only worth 30-35 francs. This execution had produced its effects because despite all the drivers' stories of travellers being devoured that we had been told in Fort Perovsky we saw none of these felines."

Tigers were reported in the 19th century around the Aral Sea, the Caspian Sea, Lake Baikal and in the Djungar Alatau Mountains. The last tiger was shot in Kazakhstan in the 1950s. However, in September 2017 the Kazakh government announced that wild tigers were set to be reintroduced into their historic range in the Ili-Balkhash region after an absence of 70 years.[21] A US$10m fund will finance the programme, which will bring Amur tigers – closely related to the now-extinct Caspian tiger – from Eastern Siberia into the new reserve.

Having made their way through Tashkent, Samarkand and Bokhara, the couple finally reached Verniye (Almaty) in the late autumn. There they were hosted by General Gerasim Alexeyevich Kolpakovsky, the first Russian commander of the Steppe region and also Ataman of the Siberian Cossacks. Kolpakovsky is a fascinating character in the history of Central Asia. He was obsessed with finding the ruins of a lost ancient Armenian monastery said to have been inundated by a rise in the water

---

21. https://www.worldwildlife.org/press-releases/wild-tigers-to-return-to-kazakhstan-70-years-after-going-extinct-there

level of Lake Issyk Kul in present-day Kyrgyzstan. In 1869 he had made a first visit to the lake and brought up two bronze cauldrons and various other objects from beneath the water.

In November 1871 he sent various artefacts to General Kaufmann, asking for assistance to help build a submarine. Working with his brother Ivan, Kolpakovsky hired two British engineers, John Norman and Emile George, to create such a vessel. Sadly, no drawings or details have survived and the submarine sank on its first sea trial. Kolpakovsky then attempted to buy the latest diving suits, recently exhibited at the Paris World Exhibition, but in the end, money ran out. Kolpakovsky remained fascinated by the subject until he returned to St Petersburg in 1889. And Mme Ujfalvy-Bourdon records the fact that he gave her various antiques that had been brought up from the bottom of the lake, as well as objects sculpted in agalmatolite, a soft greenish stone, much prized in China.

From Verniye the couple proceeded northeast, determined to visit Kuldja, which at that time was occupied by Russian soldiers, following a bloody uprising of the local Muslims against their Chinese occupiers. In the early 1870s tens of thousands of Chinese had been slaughtered, their villages torched and their crops destroyed. Russian Cossacks had seized Kuldja and other towns to bring stability – and possibly to annexe the territory if China was unable to reassert its control. Ultimately, they had to surrender control and return it to China, but for almost a decade Russia allowed foreigners to visit Kuldja and the surrounding areas, and several recorded their impressions of this formerly inaccessible and unknown region.

They made it to the city, noting on the way the ruins of Tchimpantsi, which had once housed 50,000 Chinese. On 29 September they left Kuldja and by 4 October had reached the town of Kopal, where they noticed the Russian churches. "Our hostel is decorated with a porch, which is a relative luxury and also very clean. We also find something to eat, which is a great difference with Orenburg and Tashkent," writes Mme Ujfalvy-Bourdon. While a wheel was being mended she took the opportunity to go to the chemist in the town. In almost every town in Turkestan there was a chemist that belonged to the Crown and handed out medicines for free on a doctor's prescription.

By 6 October they had arrived at Sergiopol – today Ayaguz – and from there made their way northwards across the bleak sands to Semey, which they reached on 12 October. From here it was comparatively simple to make their way back to Orenburg and then Moscow.

It was not the last journey by Mme Ujfalvy-Bourdon. In January 1877 she and her husband set off again, this time following the course of the Syr Darya river, before heading for the valley of the Zerafshan and Ferghana. They then travelled through the Wakhan Corridor in northeast Afghanistan to Kohistan to study the Galchas, believed to be an Aryan tribe. Two years later, in 1879, she returned again with her husband, travelling through the Great Steppe to Bokhara. In 1881 the couple made a voyage into the Western Himalayas where Mme Ujfalvy-Bourdon became one of the first Western women ever to visit Ladakh and Skardu. That journey too became the subject of a book.[22] Despite its sometimes-condescending tone, it has rightly been seen as a pioneering piece of travel writing by a woman.

Nor should we forget the work of her husband, Charles-Eugène Ujfalvy de Mezőkövesd. His linguistic research into Finno-Ugric and the Altai family of languages was important, but his mission to Central Asia and his anthropological and linguistic studies of its people was ground-breaking, even if physical anthropology is now seen as outdated. The mission lasted almost two years and covered a huge amount of ground. It is said to have been the inspiration for Jules Verne's novel *Claudius Bombarnac*. Charles-Eugène collected masses of natural history specimens, as well as conducting archaeological digs in Samarkand, Pendjikent and the city of Turkestan. He was able to compose an ethnographic atlas of Central Asia which appeared in his four-volume publication *L'Expédition scientifique française en Russie, en Sibérie et dans le Turkestan*.[23] By 1878 he has been given the

---

22. Marie de Ujfalvy-Bourdon, *Voyage d'une Parisienne dans L'Himalaya Occidental*, Hachette, Paris, 1887.

23. *Expédition scientifique française en Russie, en Sibérie et dans le Turkestan: résultat anthropologiques d'un voyage en Asie Centrale, communiqués au congrès anthropologique de Moscow (août 1879)*, E Leroux, Paris, 1880 (4 vols.). The four volumes are: Vol 1: *Le Kohistan, le Ferghaneh et Kouldja, avec un appendice sur la Kachgarie*, Paris, E Leroux, 1878 ; Vol II: *Le Syr-Daria, le Zérafchane, la province des Sept-Rivières et Sibérie occidentale, avec plusieurs*

permanent post of Professor of the History and Geography of Central Asia in Paris.

*

The final French traveller we are to meet is Gabriel Bonvalot, described by Svetlana Gorshenina as "one of the most celebrated travellers of the 19th century". Like Ujfalvy, Bonvalot made his first voyage in Central Asia at the demand of the Minister of Public Instruction in 1880 to study the new Asiatic territories conquered by Russia. Central Asia became a kind of departure or arrival point for all his expeditions.

For this expedition, which was recorded in his book *En Asie Centrale*,[24] Bonvalot, accompanied by his close friend, the Luxembourg-born naturalist Guillaume Capus,[25] left Moscow for Ekaterinburg and from there took a *tarantass* all the way to Tashkent. As far as Omsk he says that they were in richly cultivated lands. On entering the Baraba Steppes villages became scarce and he only saw yurts. At Pavlodar on the Irtysh he saw a steamer carrying salt pass the town. From Semey – "the last town (or rather village) of any importance that we came across in Siberia" – he could see the peaks of the Altai Mountains out to the east.

As with other writers, he found the journey from Semey to Sergiopol (Ayaguz) to be across a bleak steppe, with barely a village, the only buildings being the post-houses. "We went for 80 km with barely seeing a bird," he wrote. Carcasses of horses and camels were strewn across the route and every now and again they would come across a few Kazakh tombs.

At the second station after Semey a convoy of condemned steppe dwellers had made a halt. Chained by their feet, they were being taken to the mines at Barnaul in the Altai Mountains. They were preparing

appendices, Paris, E Leroux, 1879 ; Vol III: *Les Bachkirs, Les Vepses et les Antiquités Finno-Ougriennes et Altaiques* ; Vol IV: *Atlas anthropologique des peuples du Ferghana,* Paris, E Leroux, 1879.

24. Gabriel Bonvalot, *En Asie Centrale: de Moscou en Bactriane,* Librairie Plon, Paris, 1884.

25. Guillaume Capus (1857-1931). He later wrote several books about his travels with Bonvalot, including *A Travers le Royaume de Tamerlan (Asie Centrale): Voyage dans la Sibérie Occidentale, le Turkestan, la Boukharie, aux Bords de l'Amou-Daria, à Khiva Et dans l'Oust-Ourt,* A Hennuyer, Paris, 1892.

their pittance of food in their cooking pots, a mixture of rice and milk. They seemed resigned to their lot.

At Atchikoul, Bonvalot made a visit to some nomads. There were three people present; two of them cut dried horse meat into small pieces and threw them into a pot full of water. The third fed the fire with fuel and dried herbs. "These Kazakhs are very sweet and affable, like all those of their race that we came across later. Always we found them hospitable and accommodating and they were more honest and more masculine than their neighbours, the sedentaries of Iranian origin."[26]

Bonvalot had set off late in the season and it was already 8 October when they reached Sergiopol (today Ayaguz), at the foot of Mount Chingis. He called it the main town of Turkestan: "Although marked as a city on the map, in reality it was a small mining village, in a sad and desolate valley. A white church, a few houses with dusty roofs, huts made of crushed lime soil, enough to house 200 inhabitants, and a barracks for the soldiers – that is Sergiopol."

From here on the party would have to move more slowly. The roads were appalling and the horses were of poor quality and rare. Bonvalot noticed that many nomads were riding oxen, which they guided by pulling on a cord attached to a wooden peg that passes through the nostrils. These oxen were particularly used in the mountains, where they are known to be sure-footed. They marched on towards the south and could soon see the snowy summits of the Alatau Mountains which, he said, "form a jumble of mountains that line up, become stuck and merge into grandiose ripples that get lost in the sky." Bonvalot says he could not take his eyes away from these beautiful peaks. Now dried-up rivers were rarer; the post-stations were generally built next to a mountain stream, close to poplars or willows. There were cultivated fields, and "many little green oases where our eyes can rest from the bleaching of the sun-drenched steppe." They passed the Lepsa and the Ak-Su rivers, and noticed many *aouls*, tombs and large numbers of horses grazing the steppe.

At the Abakumovsky station Bonvalot experienced his first water-melon of the trip. He savoured it as slowly as a sorbet. Central Asian

---

26. Bonvalot, *En Asie Centrale*, p. 19.

watermelons are rightly regarded as among the best in the world. At night he often slept snuggled up in the *tarantass*, shaken by the wind. The next morning he started up the Gasfort Pass towards Kopal. This rough track, which still exists, is sunk between the hills, turning from left to right as it climbs a steep gradient. To make it easier for the horses they got out of the carriage and walked. At the top there is a natural platform of granite from where one can see the track snaking across the steppe at the foot of the mountains, with the green plateau of Ghildergaraghi to the right where the nomads scattered their tents, looking, as Bonvalot says, "like very small molehills at the foot of the mountains".

From the top of the pass, the descent towards Kopal is very quick. Kopal, which then had a population of 4,000 inhabitants, was an important little trade town. With its neatly aligned Russian-style houses made of wood and surrounded by vegetable gardens, it seemed infinitely preferable to drab Sergiopol. Kopal was the first Cossack outpost to become a trade centre thanks to its position on the road from Tashkent and Verniye to Siberia. As they left the town it began to rain, followed soon by hail and then snow. The temperature dropped brutally, in the space of 24 hours falling from 25 plus to -3°C, with a glacial wind blowing from the southwest.

At Altyn Emel there was a Russian picquet on this road that leads to China where Bonvalot was very happy to be able to warm himself. Instead of spending the night in the carriage, he took refuge with Russian officers who kindly offered him a place next to a burning stove. He noticed the large number of troops billeted around, in anticipation, he says, of war with China. Russian troops were still occupying the Ili Valley and Kuldja at this point and even though an agreement was in place for their withdrawal, this had still not happened.

On the road, Bonvalot now began to see bullock carts with huge wheels (*arba*), driven by farmers and traders on their way to market. They arrived at Tschingil, on the banks of the River Ili, precisely at the moment of the migration of the mountain partridges. "The flocks hurry above our heads," he wrote. "I do not dare to give an approximate number that pass in three hours. It would certainly seem exaggerated to our French hunters who consider themselves happy when they are able to spot a hundred in a day." Another sign that winter was approaching.

From here they crossed the Ili on a ferry and made their way through the steppe and cultivated fields and then along a poplar-lined avenue towards Verniye (Almaty), capital of the Seven Rivers province which nestles at the foot of the Trans-Ili Alatau, crowned by pine forests. Having been founded as a Cossack outpost in 1853, by the time Bonvalot arrived there were more than 20,000 inhabitants. He was clearly impressed by the city, noting that it was crossed by beautiful and wide boulevards, planted with trees and watered by streams of running water.

Bonvalot's route was now westwards, along the base of the Alexandrovsky Mountains, where the first snows already covered the peaks. Soon they reached the River Chu, where there were still tigers and wild boars. Wolves also abounded and Bonvalot says he saw one cross the road about 100 m in front of him, scratching the soil here and there in search of rodents. In the mountains above were lynx, snow leopards and bears. Beyond the Chu, at the point where the road forks to the east towards Lake Issyk Kul and to the west towards Aulie Ata, they saw the old Kokandian fortress of Pishpek – now Bishkek, the capital of Kyrgyzstan – which is described as little more than a pretty village of pleasant aspect, with houses surrounded by poplars and willows.

Increasingly Bonvalot noticed the number of well-established and prosperous villages, many of them inhabited by migrants from southern Russia. He contrasts these well-ordered villages with those of the Cossacks, remarking that the latter did not make good colonists, as they preferred being in the saddle to cultivating the land. "They have not sufficiently forgotten the habits of the sabre to enjoy using a spade," he says. In the large village of Merke, which had once been a Kokandi fort, there was a large cross erected in the ruins of the fortress to commemorate the Russian soldiers who died when they captured it. As Bonvalot was leaving in the morning a wolf caused a panic after it entered a yard to catch some hens. It was pursued down the street by locals armed with pitchforks or sticks trying to catch or kill it. It got away.

Soon he was well on the way to Samarkand and Bokhara, Khiva and then across the Caspian Sea to Baku in present-day Azerbaijan and thence back to Europe. In 1882, still accompanied by Guillaume Capus, he retraced much of this journey, taking in the upper valleys of

Zerafshan and the Amu-darya, including the mountainous districts of Kohistan, the famous Transcaspian railway and the Caucasus. The goal of his third expedition, on which he was again accompanied by Capus together with the artist Albert Pepin, was to complete the information gathered between 1880 and 1882 about the areas to the north of the Oxus, by the study of the area to the south. This mission left Tiflis in March 1886, heading towards the Caspian and passing through Resht and Qazvin to reach Teheran, then after 25 days on the road in a *tarantass*, the city of Mashhad, holy to the Shi'as.

From here the travellers hoped to cross into Afghanistan to study the sources of the River Koshka and to visit Herat, but the Afghan authorities would not let them in. The mission was instead forced to leave northwards for Sarakhs and Merv across the sands of the Kara-Kum desert. From there, they tried in vain to get into Afghanistan via Andchui and Maimana. Having failed, they set off to cross the desert, crossed the Amu Darya and then passed via Karakol and Bokhara, to Samarkand, where they stayed for the month of August.

After a dangerous attempt to reach Balkh and Faizabad in northern Afghanistan again failed, Bonvalot and his companions stayed in Samarkand during the winter of 1886-87 and there developed a project to cross the Pamir Mountains from north to south by following the direct route connecting the Russian territories to British India. In March 1887 the expedition left Osh – the traditional point of departure for all expeditions to the Pamir – in the company of a Russian traveller (and spy), Bronislav L Grombtchevsky, and crossed the Alai and the Pamir Mountains to reach Chitral. From here they crossed the high mountains into the unknown region of Kafiristan where they were captured by Chitrali tribesmen, but after 40 days and thanks to the intervention of the Indian viceroy, Lord Dufferin, the mission was able to return to its route towards India, Kashmir and Karachi. The return to France in September 1887 was by ship. This expedition brought Bonvalot a gold medal from the Société de Géographie de Paris, as well as the title of Chevalier of the Légion d'honneur. It also resulted in another book.[27]

---

27. Gabriel Bonvalot, *Through the Heart of Asia, Over the Pamïr to India*, London, Chapman and

In July 1889 Bonvalot made his final adventure into Asia with an attempt to cross Tibet from east to west, a project underwritten by the Duke of Chartres whose son, the young Prince Henri d'Orléans, was a participant. After 3,000 km, of which 2,500 were in unexplored territory, the travellers reached the mountains of the Tien Shan and the Tarim Valley and Lake Lop-Nor, not far from the environs of Lhasa. Having crossed eastern Tibet, they were unable to proceed further and returned to Hanoi, which they reached by the end of September. The success of the voyage brought on their return a triumphal welcome and another gold explorer's medal. This expedition to the Pamirs is probably the only one where Bonvalot travelled on routes never travelled by his Russian or English predecessors.

There were other French travellers through Central Asia, but by the turn of the 19th century they were becoming fewer and fewer. The window that had been opened to the French by the Russians was firmly closed by the advent of the First World War and the victory of the Bolshevik Revolution. The French had been responsible for little new exploration and those who travelled were mostly concerned with engineering projects or simply providing useful information to the French Foreign Ministry.

But special mention should be made of the two women who accompanied their husbands during their scientific explorations. Both Adèle Hommaire de Hell and Marie de Ujfalvy-Bourdon belonged to a new category of writer that emerged in the early 19th century: the wife of the explorer. Both used their status as wives to overcome their social handicap as women. As wives it was their duty to follow and support their husbands in adventures that as women they would be deemed too weak to embark on themselves. Adèle justifies her presence by acting as her husband's assistant. She had the official role of writing about the details of the trip while he was in charge of reporting on the historical and scientific aspects. In the end, it is largely thanks to her that we know about her husband's scientific endeavours.

Hall, 1889 (2 vols.). It was illustrated by Albert Pepin. The English edition is dedicated to Lord Dufferin.

Marie's justification is that it is her duty to be with her husband. She does not have any official role and claims to write only to encourage other women to travel. Yet her writing was influenced by her husband's research and complements it with picturesque descriptions of landscapes and by comments on social matters, such as the role of 'women – an aspect that her husband is not able to access. The same is true in part of Lucy Atkinson, although in her case it is difficult to separate her achievements as an explorer from those of her husband.

What is true is that all three of these women have largely been excluded from the pantheon of travellers and explorers. Even today in France the names of Adèle and Marie are barely known. Now is the time to put that right.

—m—

Right: Mme Marie de Ujfalvy-Bourdon
in her very fashionable travel clothes.
Overleaf: A page from William
Bateson's notebook.

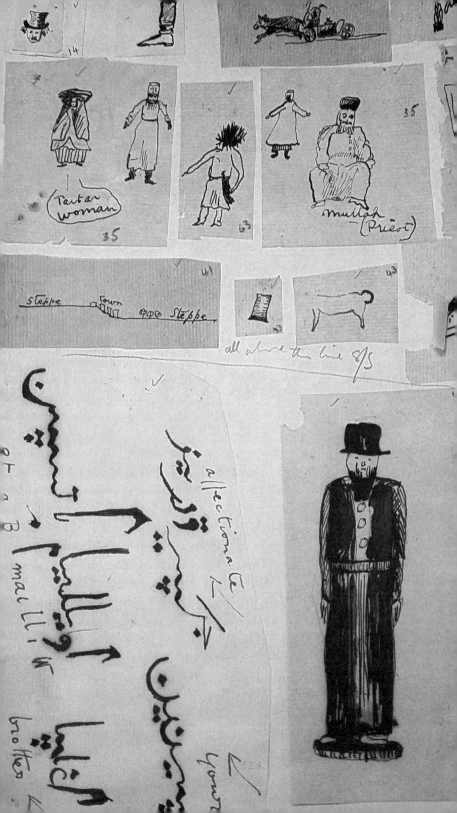

Taitar
woman

35

mullah
(Priest)

Steppe   Town   Steppe

all about the line 8/5

affectionate

yours

8

SCIENCE IN THE STEPPE

Johann Peter Falk, Herbert Wood
and William Bateson

—ᴡᴡ—

IT WAS PETER SIMON PALLAS AND HIS ASSISTANTS who in the 1760s began the process of understanding the scientific importance of Central Asia and classifying its plants and animal species. Pallas was a German, born in Berlin. After studying in Holland and London, in 1767 he was invited by the Empress Catherine II of Russia to become a professor at the Academy of Sciences in St Petersburg. From here he set out the following year on an extensive expedition to the central Russian provinces, the Urals, the Altai and Western Siberia and the Transbaikal, to collect natural history specimens. He personally explored the Caspian Sea, the Ural and Altai Mountains and regularly sent his reports to St Petersburg where they were published as *Reise durch verschiedene Provinzen des Russischen Reichs* between 1771 and 1776 – a monumental work that, sadly, has never been published in English.

Pallas was accompanied by a band of young scientists, mostly of German origin, who all contributed to his work. They included such important figures as Samuel Gottlieb Gmelin, Johann Gottlieb Georgi and Georg Wilhelm Steller. But the one person who spent more time in Central Asia than any of the other assistants was a Swede called Johann Peter Falk. Falk studied at the University of Uppsala under Carl Linnaeus before travelling to Russia in 1763, where he became Curator for the Cabinet of Natural History in St Petersburg. Between 1768 and 1774 he participated in Pallas' expedition. Travelling with his assistant

Christoph Bardanes he spent time in the northern steppes trying to find out if there had ever been any connection between the Caspian Sea and the Aral Sea. He also spent much time analysing water samples from lakes across the Kazakh Steppe and developed a classification system for differentiating between different kinds of water.

Falk was later joined by Johann Gottlieb Georgi, a young scientist who was sent to relieve Falk from the rigours of organising the expedition. They met first in Uralsk in July 1770 before arriving in Orenburg, where they stayed until the end of that year. From there the two men moved on to Omsk, the Barabinsk Steppe and then into the Altai. It soon became clear that they could not get on with each other, and Falk, who was beginning to suffer from depression, finally got rid of his rival by sending him to join Pallas in Tomsk.

Meanwhile Falk continued his work collecting specimens on the steppe and compiling his voluminous notebooks. He spent much time in the company of Kazakhs from the Junior Horde, including Nurali Sultan, the son of Abul Khayir. He outlines the clan structure of the hordes and gives many details about their organisation: "The khans have no income other than that which derives from their own herds. Nurali khan told me he had as many as 100 camels, 3,000 horses, 1,000 head of cattle, 5,000 sheep, 1,000 goats and over 100 steppe donkeys. Ablai khan is even wealthier, though the khan exceeds him in Russian gifts, which include 600 roubles in cash annually."[1]

Falk also provides detailed descriptions of Kazakh food, including *beshparmak* (boiled horsemeat), *korta* (sausages), *krut* (cheese), *kudyo* (soup) and *kosum* (fatty smoked horse ribs). "In their mild healthy climate and with their simple, sober and carefree mode of existence," says Falk, "they live to a happy and healthy old age. If they fall ill, they seek shamanistic help or use household remedies and shamans together. They are so fond of their beloved steppes that they would probably be content to roam around them until Judgement Day, and they regard death as utterly abhorrent."[2]

---

1. See Lars Hansen (ed.), *The Linnaeus Apostles*, vol. 2, book 2: Johan Peter Falck, IK Foundation, London, 2007, p. 672.

2. *Ibid*, p. 677.

Falk is said to have suffered from depression for much of his short life and during his time on the steppe he appears to have become addicted to opium. In March 1774 he took his own life while staying in the town of Kazan. His notes were edited by Georgi in German in 1785-87. Later, when Georgi published his own work in 1798 there was controversy, particularly over his water classification system, which seems to have been largely based on the work of Falk.

Pallas and his collaborators were the first to put Central Asia onto the scientific agenda, but it was Alexander von Humboldt who really put the region on the map with the publication of his three-volume *Asie Centrale* in 1843 which, as with Pallas' great work, has never been translated into English.[3]

Humboldt had wanted to travel to Central Asia ever since he returned from his ground-breaking journey to South America in 1804. The two journeys were aimed at complementing each other – one in the eastern hemisphere, the other in the west. But various things prevented him from making a trip until 1829, when, on the invitation of Georg Cancrin, minister of finance to Tsar Nicholas I, he was able to bring his long-held desire to fruition. Humboldt set off from Berlin in May 1829, taking with him the mineralogist Gustav Rose and botanist Christian Gottfried Ehrenberg. Their journey would last until the end of the year.

Humboldt later complained about the restrictions imposed on him during his trip. He was not permitted to decide his own route and was accompanied at all times by a troop of Cossacks. The Russians were interested in the presence of platinum in Asian Russia beyond the Urals and the possible presence of diamonds, but Humboldt's aims were much more scientific. Nor was he to comment in any way on the social or political conditions he experienced on his journey, a constraint that he bitterly resented. He refused to return, despite many invitations. He was able to travel as far as Barnaul in southern Siberia and pass through the Altai Mountains on to the northern outskirts of the Great Steppe at Ust-Kamenogorsk (today Oskemen, in northeast Kazakhstan) and Lake

---

3. Alexander von Humboldt, *Asie centrale: recherches sur les chaînes de montagnes et la climatologie comparée*, Gide, Paris, 1843, (3 vols.).

Nur Zaisan, before heading back to European Russia via Semipalatinsk, Orsk, Orenburg, Uralsk, Saratov, Astrakhan and Volgograd.

Humboldt was the first scientist of the modern era to show an interest in the region that we today refer to as Central Asia. He remained preoccupied by its geographical importance for the rest of his life and inspired many others, including Sir Roderick Murchison, Thomas Witlam Atkinson and the Russian explorer and geographer Petr Petrovich Semenov to travel to these remote regions and send him information.

*

It is thus interesting to note that Major Herbert Wood begins his book on the Aral Sea with a quote from Humboldt. Nor was Wood any the less fascinated by the region. As he wrote: "West Turkestan presents perhaps the greatest number of interesting points that could be found collected in any one single locality for the consideration of mankind... Though the earliest historical records inform us how solitude and sterility were the marked characteristics of North-western Asia, there are certain indications of a previous local civilisation and culture, which were overwhelmed by the devastating torrent of perpetually encroaching barbarism; and such dim testimonies to a pre-historic state gain form and substance daily from observations of the signs that are graven on the face of Nature herself."[4]

Wood was the son of a lieutenant-colonel in the Madras Native Infantry, also an engineer. After education at Cheltenham and the East India Military College at Addiscombe he first went to India in 1855, aged 18. He fought in several of the battles of the Indian Rebellion in 1857 and then was appointed to the Public Works Department. In 1868 he spent six months as a field engineer in Abyssinia (Ethiopia), but by 1873 he was given a three-year leave of absence from India due to ill health. Yet by the following year, despite his lack of previous experience of the region, he had been invited by the Russians to join an expedition to the Aral Sea.

---

4. Herbert Wood, *The Shores of Lake Aral*, Smith Elder and Co, London, 1876.

What brought this British Army engineering officer to Central Asia to study the Aral Sea? His invitation came from the liberal Grand Duke Constantine Nikolayevitch, brother of Tsar Alexander II and president of the Imperial Russian Geographical Society, who asked him to accompany an expedition being sent by that august body to study the Amu Darya river and the Aral Sea, one of several similar expeditions sent by the Russians as they tried to make scientific sense of their newly-conquered territories. It took place in 1874, the year after the Russian conquest of Khiva, the khanate based around the southeastern corner of the Aral Sea, which made it possible for the first time to send scientists to this region without fear of kidnap or murder.

A clue to why Wood was specifically invited to join the Russian expedition may lie in the dedication printed in the front of his book which reads: "To Charlotte and Athenais de Bodisco this book is inscribed by their obliged friend and servant, The Author." Thereby hangs a scandalous tale, relating to Baron Alexander de Bodisco, a former Russian Ambassador to the United States. In Washington in 1840 the 54-year-old baron married the beautiful 16-year-old Harriet Beall Williams, much to the consternation of her family, a marriage that was reported with relish in London and elsewhere and was probably one of the grandest ever to take place in Washington. Charlotte de Bodisco was the wife of Constantine, one of Harriet's seven children.

After the baron died in 1854 Harriet de Bodisco travelled to India where she met Captain (later Major-General) Douglas Gordon Scott (1827-1911). Their marriage in 1860 at St John's Episcopal Church opposite the White House in Washington was a grand affair and she was given away by US President James Buchanan. After their marriage Scott was posted to India, where the couple spent several years. Scott and Wood were close army friends in the Madras Native Infantry, so it is likely that the invitation had something to do with the well-connected ambassador's widow, who died in London in 1890.

According to *The Aral Sea Encyclopedia*, the Aral Sea Expedition comprised three units: the first was organised by the Natural Scientist Society and included geologist N P Barbot-de-Marni and zoologists V D Alenitsyn and Bogdanov. They aimed to study the geology of the Aral coasts and the Aral and Caspian fauna. The second was a surveying unit led by General A A Tillo, and the third was a natural science and historical unit led by General N G Stoletov. The latter unit also included the famous scientist N A Severtzov, meteorologist F Dorandt, hydrographer Zubov and Major Wood.[5]

Wood was to spend several months in the regions around the Aral Sea. He believed that the Russian annexation of the Amu Darya territory would open up a new era in the history of Turkestan. Once it had been thought that this great waterway, which rises in the Pamir Mountains on the borders of India, would offer a new trade route between India and Europe, but even though this was not to be the case, Wood believed that "the moral and material regeneration of Central Asia" was dependent on the river.

As an engineering officer, Wood suggested that the river's waters could be diverted south by canals for irrigation. "In this way a belt of desert country may be reclaimed and settled, industrious populations may once more be established upon broad lands, from whence the ancestors of European peoples were expelled by barbarian hordes... It would be for the benefit of Russia more particularly, were the deserts south of Khiva changed into productive cotton-fields, and into habitable territory across which the ancient silk trade, that was destroyed by Mohammedan fanaticism, might once more be established between Europe and Central Asia."[6] It was very much part of Wood's belief that the region had once been vastly more productive but that the destruction wrought by the Mongols of Genghis Khan, by Tamerlane and others had reduced this once-flourishing region to a shadow of its former self.

Bucking the trend of Great Game rhetoric, Wood argued that although British security for its Indian empire was important, Russian expansion into Central Asia could, in fact, be useful. Development did not have to take place close to the borders and thus "the question of Russian boundaries on the Perso-Afghan frontier might be ultimately solved in a satisfactory way to both Powers."

Wood spent much of his time during the expedition examining the

---

5. Igor S Zonn *et al, The Aral Sea Encyclopedia*, Springer-Verlag, Berlin, 2009, p. 251.

6. Wood, *op. cit.*, p. xii.

existing and historical channels of the Syr Darya and Amu Darya rivers. He was based at Kazala (Kazaly, and later Kazalinsk) on the Syr Darya for much of this time, which was the headquarters of the Aral Flotilla, the first vessels of which had been brought across the steppe from Sweden and England in pieces and assembled on the banks of the river. It comprised half-a-dozen paddle steamers, some steam launches and a dozen flat-bottomed barges. The waterway itself was only open from May to October and there were constant navigation difficulties due to sandbanks and strong currents. During the summer the river was only about two metres deep. Wood estimated the surface area of Aral then at 24,500 sq miles (63,500 sq km) – the size of Scotland – making it the fourth largest lake in the world.[7]

Even then it was evident that the Aral was shrinking. Wood was remarkably prescient in his comments on the waterflow into the lake, noting that "a very few figures would show that about double the supply of water which it now receives would soon again raise its level to overflowing, while on the other hand, if the present supply were cut off, about ninety years only would suffice to dry up the lake entirely. Replenished as this basin is with a very limited amount of rainfall, the existence of the body of water it contains practically depends on the single condition, that the quantity emptied into it by its tributary rivers shall equal that which is evaporated from its surface."[8] Sadly, Soviet planners paid no heed to such warnings.

Wood devotes considerable space in his book to considering the possibility that the Black Sea, the Caspian and Aral Seas had once been a single body of water. He notes that this theory had first been developed in modern times by the French botanist Joseph Pitton de Tournefort in the late 17th century and supported by his countryman, naturalist Georges-Louis Leclerc, Comte de Buffon. Peter Simon Pallas, the great scientist who travelled throughout the south of Russia and Siberia in the second half of the 18th century, also supported this theory, writing thus:

---

7. By 2007 it had fallen to around 10 per cent of this figure and increasing salinity had killed off most of its flora and fauna.

8. Wood, *op. cit.*, p. 114.

"The idea of the indefatigable Tournefort, and of the Count de Buffon, concerning the ancient state of the Black Sea and of its communication with the Caspian is more and more confirmed by the observations of travellers. The phocae, some fish and some shells, which the Caspian has in common with the Black Sea render this ancient communication almost indubitable; and these very circumstances also prove that the Lake Aral was once joined to the Caspian. I have traced (in the third volume of my *Travels*) the ancient extent of this sea over the whole desert of Astrakhan and beyond the Jaik [the Ural], by the symptoms of coast with which the elevated plains of Russia border this desert, by the state and the fossil productions of this ancient coast and by the saline mud, mingled with sea-shells, calcined, which covers the whole surface of the desert itself."[9]

This great freshwater lake, according to the theory, had once covered the plains of the lower Danube, southern Russia and extended eastwards and northeastwards to include the basins of the Black, Caspian and Aral Seas. In some versions of this theory, the Volga itself linked this lake to the ocean in the far north of Russia.[10] Wood believed it was possible that the separation of the three basins resulted from the rupture of the Straits of the Bosphorus due to a massive series of earthquakes, estimated to have taken place in 1529 BCE and known as the Deluge of Deucalion, an event that was mentioned by numerous ancient writers and is an early Greek version of the biblical story of Noah and the Flood.

Wood states that if the outlet of the Bosphorus was closed to the height of 220 ft above sea level the water that now flows into the Mediterranean would rise and flood the southern Russian steppes and lower Danube plains, although the coast of Asia Minor would be little affected, as it is so high and steep. After rising 23 ft the waters would escape into the basin of the Caspian and would then flood the country towards the Aral. For his book Wood also draws on the research of the French engineer, Xavier Hommaire de Hell, who from 1838 onwards spent five years in southern

---

9. Quoted in "On the Primeval Form of Europe", *The Monthly Magazine or British Register,* vol. II., March 1796, p. 97.

10. The geographer Sir Roderick Murchison also wrote about this subject following his three visits to Russia in the early 1840s. See *The Geology of Russia in Europe and The Ural Mountains,* John Murray, London 1855 (2 vols.).

Russia investigating this subject (see Chapter 7).[11]

As Wood notes: "In this imaginary reconstruction of the Asiatic Mediterranean, the moment the rising waters reached a point at about 210 feet above the sea, and which is situated at the head of the now dry gulf Abougir, they would have entered into and filled up the basin of Lake Aral. A glance at the map will show this lowest point in the ground enclosing the basin to have been actually worn down from some greater height by an escape of the waters in a southerly direction, which took place in historical times."[12]

To back up his research, Wood also refers to the writings of the Greeks. The fourth book of Herodotus, for example, states clearly that the Caspian and Aral had once been connected and that the Aral overflowed towards the north. Wood's view is that the linkage of the Aral and Caspian was intermittent; sometimes there was a continuous expanse of water and at other times merely a succession of swampy channels connecting the two basins.

The Roman authors Strabo, Pomponius Mela and Pliny also wrote on this subject, all of them accepting the idea of a connection between the two bodies of water, and Chinese writers recorded in the first century of the Christian era that the Aral and Caspian appeared to be a single body of water.[13] Persian writers such as Ibn Khordadbeh (c.820-912 CE) and Ahmad al Yaqubi (d.897 CE) also considered the Aral and Caspian to have been a single sheet of water. Even the adventurer and merchant Anthony Jenkinson, the first Briton to reach Bokhara, writing in the 16th century, noted that the two seas were connected in antiquity.

Wood also reports that he heard reports locally that until about 50 years before his visit it was still possible to find seals in the Aral Sea – although no physical evidence for this has been found – while Herodotus described people from the Aral region being clothed in sealskins.[14] Seals

---

11. See Xavier Hommaire de Hell, *Travels in the Steppes of the Caspian Sea, the Crimea, the Caucasus, etc*, Chapman and Hall, London, 1868.

12. Wood, *op. cit.*, p. 120.

13 *Ibid*, p. 137.

14. Herodotus, *The Histories*, Tom Holland (trans.), Penguin, London, 2013, Book 1, (202).

continue to survive in the Caspian, which clearly denotes a previous connection to the northern ocean.

Wood is convinced that large parts of Central Asia were previously much more fertile than in modern times. "In remote ages equatorial winds may have carried moisture to Western Asia, from the broad expanse of Central African seas, instead of the dry air which now blows from burning Sahara sands. The banks of the Oxus may have, at that time, been covered with flower-enamelled pasturages, where the posterity of Japhet led the lives of shepherds and tended their flocks and herds. Increasing in numbers, the ancient Aryans would have brought cattle under the yoke, and have learned to labour the earth, with the aid of the vivifying waters which were bountifully supplied by rivers flowing down from the primeval Paradise."[15] He wonders if the "nine and thirty northern arms of the Araxes" mentioned by Herodotus might not have been former artificial canals from the Amu Darya which had been swept away by the Massagetic hordes several hundred years before the latter was writing. Wood also thought that the Amu Darya once flowed into the Caspian directly, but that its lower stream was redirected towards the Aral in comparatively recent times.

As well as his geographical and hydrographical observations, Wood travelled extensively in the region of the Aral on horseback. He describes one ride he did from the town of Nukus, south of the lake, to Fort Perovsky on the Syr Darya, a formidable journey by any standards and one which would have been impossible for a foreigner until the Russians captured Khiva. He is particularly in awe of the Kazakh horses: "These seldom stand more than 13 ½ hands in height, but their lack of size is amply compensated by wonderful powers of endurance, as may be judged from the fact that an animal which in England would be nothing more than a coarse pony, carried me and my saddle-bags – a weight, perhaps, of 16 stone – more than 30 miles a day for 10 days in succession. Nor was he a bit the worse for the performance, though he had but very short rations of grain, no grass and a little water during the whole of the trip."[16]

---

15. Wood, *op. cit.*, p. 273.

16. *Ibid*, p. 319.

Wood was clearly enamoured of the yurt as a form of dwelling, stating that nothing compares to it for snugness and for comfort. "Sheltered behind its felt-covered walls from the howling wind outside and basking in the flames of the fire, whose wreaths of smoke rise gracefully to the opening in the roof, the dreariness of the desert is forgotten and fatigue soon passes, as, wrapped up in lambskins, one blesses, with honest Sancho, the man who first invented sleep."

Often during his travels, Wood came across large caravans of Kazakhs migrating from their winter to their summer pasturages, their camels laden with all their worldly possessions and surrounded by their flocks and herds. "Such wanderings of the nomads are methodical and their movements take place in a known and predetermined circle of change; so that any man of a certain family, of a specified *aoul*, belonging to a particular tribes of Kazakhs, can generally be found by the Russian authorities when he is wanted." He says that in the spring the main movement was from the eastern shores of the Caspian and the Aral northwards towards the River Tobol. In winter they returned to the low-lying country alongside the lakes covered with high rushes that provided fuel as well as shelter against the rigours of the climate.

He notes in particular the contrast between the dreary desert of the Kara-Kum and the much more fertile land along the banks of the Syr Darya. "The country does not indeed present a very fertile aspect, but with the aid of irrigation, cereal crops give moderately good returns, fruit trees and the vine are productive and madder and other dye roots thrive. The mulberry flourishes and sericulture, which is a lucrative industry on the upper courses of the river, promises to be a success in the government of the Syr Darya, judging from the experiments which have already been made."[17]

At the time he was writing in 1874, Wood estimated the total population of Central Asia to be around two million in Russian Turkestan, a million more in Bokhara, 900,000 in Kokand and 300,000 in Khiva. On the Syr Darya local estimates suggested around 12,500 nomads were living. However, he writes that of the million

---

17. *Ibid*, p. 63.

or so Kazakhs who nomadized the Great Steppe, probably no more than a third were to be found on the lower courses of the Syr Darya, although these were significantly richer than the surrounding tribes of Karakalpaks, Turkomans and Uzbeks. He thought they owned around 100,000 camels, 200,000 horses and 2,000,000 sheep and goats.

With large herds, the better-off families were very wealthy and their yurts, furs and clothing were generally of a better quality than usual. Silks from Samarkand and Bokhara, together with bright chintzes and woollen cloth from Europe, were worn by both men and women, while gold coins were in great demand as ornaments. They were well-fed and good-looking. Some had even taken up living in houses in Kazalinsk and Fort Perovsky. "The carpeted rooms and the quality of brass-bound boxes to be seen in their residences attest the comfortable circumstances of such families, whose relations frequently come in from an *aoul* in the country and are entertained with tea for the females and bottled English stout and vodka, to which they are too much attached, for the males."[18]

Major Wood returned to England in mid-1874 and began to write up his experiences, publishing a detailed paper for the Royal Geographical Society and working on his book. He returned to India in June 1876 and resumed official duties. In February 1879 he was appointed Superintending Engineer of the Madras circle, but by then his health was in serious decline. By October that year he suffered a stroke and died, aged only 42.

Today, Wood's book is almost forgotten, even though it remains a substantial achievement. At a time when relations between Britain and Russia were tense, particularly in Central Asia, he was able to take part in a major scientific expedition and come to some credible conclusions about the hydrology of Central Asia, all the while refusing to become involved in the machinations of the Great Game. But was he right about the Deluge of Deucalion?

Certainly in terms of dates he was probably wrong. The date of 1573 BCE was far too early and would probably have shown up in the annals of the Ancient Egyptians or other civilisations, not as a myth,

18. *Ibid*, p. 72.

but as a contemporary event. But the idea of some kind of rupture of the Bosphorus has received substantial scientific backing in recent years. In 1997 William Ryan, Walter Pitman and others published a new hypothesis for a Black Sea deluge.[19] This argued that glacial meltwater had turned the Black and Caspian Seas into vast freshwater lakes that drained into the Aegean. Retreating glaciers meant that the amount of water draining into the Black Sea declined at a time that overall sea levels rose. About 8,000 years ago, the rising Mediterranean finally spilled over a rocky sill at the Bosphorus leading to more than 60,000 sq miles of land being flooded, much of it in Asia.

In 2007 Andrei L Chepalyga argued that around 14,000-17,000 years ago the Black Sea rose as a result of glacial meltwater overflowing from the Caspian Sea and that this too led to inundations.[20] Further theories have been put forward and today the subject remains unresolved, with many academic papers continuing the controversy.

SEARCHING FOR SNAIL SHELLS ON THE SHORES OF CENTRAL ASIAN LAKES

Major Wood was not the only person in the late 19th century interested in the origin of the bodies of water in Central Asia. The name of William Bateson (1861-1926), the first Professor of Biology at Cambridge and later director of the John Innes Horticultural Institution in Surrey, is not well-known today. His unorthodox approach to his subject – and his argumentative personality – may have had something to do with that. But in fact, Bateson was a pioneering figure in what became the science of genetics – a word, incidentally, that he coined. He rediscovered and translated the work of Gregor Mendel on plant hybridisation into English and disputed aspects of the Darwinian theory of evolution.

Today, after almost a century of obscurity, his writings are drawing

---

19. Ryan, W B F; Pitman, W C; Major, C O; Shimkus, K; Moskalenko, V; Jones, G A; Dimitrov, P; Gorür, N; Sakinç, M, *"An abrupt drowning of the Black Sea shelf"* (PDF). Marine Geology. 138 (1-2), 1997, 119-126. *CiteSeerX 10.1.1.598.2866. doi:10.1016/s0025-3227(97)00007-8.* Archived from the original (PDF) on 2016-03-04. Retrieved 2014-12-23.

20. Chepalyga, A L, "The late glacial great flood in the Ponto-Caspian basin". In Yanko-Hombach, V; Gilbert, A S; Panin, N; Dolukhanov, P M (eds.), *The Black Sea Flood Question: Changes in Coastline, Climate, and Human Settlement.* Springer, Dordrecht, 2007, pp. 118-48.

a new audience who perhaps recognise that Bateson had a point or two. Alan G Cock and Donald R Forsdyke note in their 2008 biography of Bateson that not only did he bring Mendel's work to the attention of the English-speaking world, but he also dominated the biological sciences in the decades after Darwin's death in 1882.[21] In more recent times, the newly-formed discipline of Evolutionary Bioinformatics, which synthesises the theories of Darwin and Mendel, owes its existence to his work. His contribution to the early development of genetics is still playing out today.

Born in the port of Whitby in North Yorkshire, Bateson was the son of William Henry Bateson, Master of St John's College, Cambridge, so it was perhaps not surprising that after school at Rugby he too went to St John's where in 1883 he graduated with a first in natural sciences.

Soon after, Bateson decided to take up embryology and travelled to the United States to investigate the development of a tiny, worm-like snail called *Balanoglossus*. That in turn led to an interest in the origin of vertebrates. He spent 1883-84 at the laboratory of William Keith Brooks at the Chesapeake Zoological Laboratory in Hampton, Virginia. On his return to St John's as a Fellow he took up the study of morphology and evolution and decided to concentrate on variation and heredity. That, in the short term, took him to Central Asia.

It may seem odd to think about a Cambridge academic wandering around the Great Steppe without let or hindrance in the 19th century. But by this time Russia was in control of the whole region. The Khanate of Kokand had finally been incorporated into the Russian Empire in 1876 and Geok Tepe, the last great bastion of the Tekke Turkomans, had fallen in 1881, thus completing the conquest of Central Asia.

Why Central Asia? Because of his interest in evolution. In 1886-87 Bateson set off from London to spend months alone in the Great Steppe of what is now northern Kazakhstan collecting tiny snail fossils. He set himself the task of examining the fauna of the lakes and dried-out lake basins in this remote part of the world with two objectives:

21. Alan G Cock and Donald R Forsdyke, *Treasure Your Exceptions: The Science and Life of William Bateson*, Springer, New York, 2008.

first, to find creatures that still survived from the days of a vast Asiatic Mediterranean sea that once covered this region; and second, to study the salt lakes in the steppe to learn how far the infinite variation of conditions affected and changed the forms of their fauna.

According to his biography, "He wanted to obtain evidence from lake and marine organisms (i) of the existence of an 'Asiatic Mediterranean Sea', perhaps extending so far as to take in Lake Balkhash and the Aral, Caspian and Black Seas, and (ii) of environment effects, especially the degree of salinity, on animal forms."[22] So Bateson and Wood were united in their desire to find out if a large body of water had once existed in Central Asia, with the former looking at the fossil record for proof and the latter at the geological record.

In a letter he wrote to the Governor-General of Turkestan Bateson explained his travel plans in more detail: "It is no doubt well known to you that it is generally held by geologists that the whole plain in which these seas exist... in past times formed one sea, which probably communicated with the Arctic Ocean. Upon the drying up of the sea for some unexplained reason, it is to be expected that the marine animals inhabiting it would be isolated in the various basins which would then be separated. The question, then, that I am engaged in investigating is firstly, whether such traces of marine life do exist in these waters and secondly what variations they have undergone."[23]

Bateson hoped that if in the distant past one part of the sea had separated from another, this would show up in the record. If they had arisen separately, ancestral forms of the snails he studied would be different and show fewer similarities with others from different waters. He also thought that different bodies of water, with different chemical compositions, could be used to show Darwinian natural selection. Lack of change would suggest a reduced role for natural selection.

Bateson received funding from both the Royal Society and Cambridge University to support his journey to the Great Steppe, packing scientific equipment such as microscopes and hydrometers, even a Berthon

22. *Ibid*, p. 22.

23. *Ibid*.

collapsible boat, as well as a wardrobe for all occasions, including a court suit, cocked hat and sword. He also took with him a camera, allowing him to take some of the earliest photographs of steppe life. Many of his photographs are now held in the collection of the University of Cambridge library. These, together with the letters he sent home and the copious diary notes he compiled during his 18-month stint on the steppe, provide some fascinating insights into both the man and his expedition.

He set off for Russia in the spring of 1886 and soon reached St Petersburg, where he was invited to dine at the British Embassy. As he records in his notes: "Dined at Embassy. Sir R Morier [the ambassador, Sir Robert Morier 1826-93] rather a loud person, but decidedly clever and well informed on his own subject, but knows no Russian (not even written characters). Somewhat civic in style. Lady Morier a sultry, ignorant, contemptuous person, evidently regarded the entertainment of scientific strangers as an evil hardly to be borne, which view she was at no pains to conceal. Neither of these persons were aware that the Hermitage contained any Spanish pictures, which was remarkable. NB Sir R. until recently was Spanish ambassador."

Clearly Bateson did not suffer fools gladly. Nor was he a shrinking violet himself. One diary entry mentions his armed pursuit for many miles of a group of camel thieves. He also describes another tricky moment close to the Aral Sea. Having found a waterhole for his horses, he was shocked when a caravan of 40 camels arrived, threatening to drink all the water and turn it into a muddy trough: "The camels were herding around. Much objection and now, when I drew my revolver and roared out that I shd. shoot the first camel that drank there, that there was water higher up, good enough for the camels, it was true. No camels did drink and were hastily removed."

A few days later, at the end of August, he describes the custom of bride-chasing that still exists in parts of Kazakhstan and Kyrgyzstan: "Then a girl came out on a horse. She was dressed in crimson plush which is much affected by these ladies. She rode a mile or two and two or three of us tried to catch her, which is done by stroking the back and that of the horse with a whip. I failed to catch her. She had an excellent horse which had the action of a thoroughbred (a Turcoman?)."

Bateson also offers one of the earliest accounts of *Kokpar*, an ancient sport involving large groups of men on horseback fighting over the carcass of a dead headless goat. The game is still played today in many countries across Central Asia: "The goat is beheaded and laid on ground and all try to pick it up from the saddle. When a man gets it up he is allowed to start full speed and all try to grab the goat. This goes on for an irregular time and at last someone who has ridden a long way with it makes for someone's tent and throws the goat at the door. The woman of the tent is then expected to find him a present." Bateson adds that he was then asked to pay for a goat for a session of the game: "I then bought a goat and threw it to be raced for. The wretches brought it back to me – now I had again to fork out!"

The notebooks contain countless such stories and the Bateson files also include dozens of his remarkable photographs, some of them developed at what must have been one of the earliest photography studios in Siberia, based in Orenburg. His fine photographic portraits of the Kazakh nomads in particular are both accomplished and remarkable for their rarity.

During his long and lonely sojourn on the steppes Bateson also kept in regular contact with his family, sending letters back to England which are full of detail of the people he met – the Kazakh nomads, the Tatars, Kalmyks and, of course, the Russians. Many of them had been found in a trunk after his mother died in 1818. Some of those, along with extracts from his notes, were published by his wife Beatrice in 1928.[24] Bateson's letters are often very amusing, particularly his lively correspondence with his mother. By the mid-1880s communication was not too difficult. Providing he could get someone to take his mail to a town he could easily send telegram cables back to London with his instructions for books and magazines he wanted, even a recipe for plum pudding.

Bateson's research technique was either to walk in the shallows of the various lakes he came across – of which there are literally tens of

---

24. William Bateson, *Letters from the Steppe: Written in the Years 1886-87*, Methuen & Co, London, 1928.

thousands across the north of the Great Steppe, ranging from a few metres across to hundreds of miles – and dredge the mud with a bucket which was then taken back to his camp for closer inspection, or to use his boat in deeper water. He describes a typical outing: "Yesterday I drove to a large lake near here – Djalamgatch (brackish); did not get much, but have hopes later on. The boat very fairly satisfactory. Wind heavy and we shipped only one sea, though there was a good deal of swell; she dredges fairly well also."[25]

He quickly settled into a routine: up at sunrise, tea, preparing his four camels (45 mins) and then off he would go: "Kumuk Bai, the camel driver, rides the first camel; Abdul, my man, the *Djiggit*, and self on horses. We move very slowly, and I ride about to neighbouring waters, etc, to inspect. About twelve or one o'clock we halt – generally another samovar then, or *Kumyss*, if there is any in the skins, and more bread pellets. Then on again till about 5pm, when evening halt is made; boiled mutton and soup then occur, and to bed. I sleep outside tent, which is much pleasanter than inside. Thus we do about 15 miles a day only."[26]

As he indicates, there was little variation in his diet of mutton soup and *kumyss*, the staples of nomadic cuisine. It is hardly surprising that he sought almost anything to spice up this dull diet and that he would write fondly of the little treats he could sometimes allow himself: "The desire for something which has a taste becomes a perfect passion after a time. I found some wild onions and ate them with delight one day – today I have had some southernwood put into the soup as an experiment; I don't know how it will turn out. Of course, the worst time has not come yet, as a good many of the stores hold out. I have still a tin of bloater paste, which costs 6d in England and 2s. in St Petersburg; here I would give 5s. for another. Also a few lemons remain. They are brown outside and inside too, but are kept for great days. Likewise, a few drops of a beef-steak sauce remain. But I hope to get down to Kazakh level by and by."[27]

Despite the privations, Bateson soon adapted to his life on the steppe

---

25. *Ibid*, p. 40.

26. *Ibid*, p. 58.

27. *Ibid*, p. 62.

and appears not to have been discouraged by the lack of society and the primitive conditions under which he was required to exist:

> I am the colour which is half-way between the "boiled lobster" and the "berry" stage. The helmet is a wonderful invention and makes work possible in a sun that would knock one down at once without it. I have a very small and very unpleasant, straggling yellow beard of the type which one associates with the dispensing of groceries by retail and adult baptism. I wear the clothes in which I had the honour of exhibiting myself at Harvey Road. The only portions of my court suit that are with me are the cocked hat and sword – in which I dined with the Sultan Shippun (as will hereafter be described). I ride generally first or last in my caravan, which moves in single file as a rule, each animal thinking it thus gets a little shade. My hair is as short as it will go without shaving. On non-travelling days I wear only a shirt – unbuttoned in front and sleeves rolled up, knickerbockers, stockings and boots – belt and revolver and knife always. The belt is most useful and much admired by the natives.
>
> Horses: one yellow, which Abdul rides. I think of him as "Johnson"; he is very patient. Johnson has a fearful sore back and is now unrideable. Abdul will go on a camel tomorrow. I have seen on Johnson the whole history of "sore-back", from the "warble" stage onwards... My horse is very common-place in his ideas. To me he is "Jones", the name Johnson being already bespoke. He suffers from the *bot*. Into the details of this exhilarating complaint I will not enter. I shall come home a complete vet.[28]

Bateson says that he took Francis Galton's advice to wash as little as possible when travelling in remote parts, but that whenever he did so it was a source of great fascination to his camp. It was the sponge he had brought with him that was the chief object of interest. The horsemen

---

28. *Ibid*, p. 63.

and camel drivers looked on in amazement as the water was poured onto the sponge and disappeared, and would then shout in unison, "Oitoboi! Oitoboi!" when it was squeezed, and the water reappeared. Each time he repeated the action he would get the same response.

The wedding breakfast to which Bateson was invited by Sultan Shippun proved to be one of the highlights of his journey through the Great Steppe. Guests arrived riding on horses, cows and camels and once at the *aoul*, drew up in a single rank of about 40 people to salute the sultan, who rode out to greet them. No-one arrived on foot. All the guests were shown into a large yurt with Bateson himself sitting on the right side of the sultan. A woman in traditional dress came in and began to throw plugs of hard cheese and fried dough pellets at the guests, who scrambled to grab them. Then eight huge bowls of meat were put before them. Unusually, it was boiled beef, the only time Bateson saw it during his trip. Once this was finished a further bowl was brought it, from which the sultan fed each of those present, some by placing pieces of meat directly into their mouths, others – Bateson included – by handing them the food.

After eating Bateson went to inspect the young couple who had just been married and who were sitting in a separate yurt. "No-one else bothered about them, or, I believe, even spoke of them, the object of our meeting being entirely lost sight of. I presented the bride, 15, with a handsome gold bracelet, price 2s. 6d., 'A present from Birmingham,' and the bridegroom, 17, with a handsome gentleman's signet ring, price 1s., also being a souvenir of that metropolis of handicraft."[29]

After the breakfast the guests rode out to a nearby sandy knoll to take part in horse races. The first was a simple race between four people, but this was followed by racing for strips of calico, which had to be snatched from competing riders. After these festivities Bateson rode back to the sultan's *aoul*, where he met the rest of his family. A pencil sketch he made of one of the women there caused a sensation and was eventually "annexed" by the sultan. The following night he gave a great feast in Bateson's honour at the end of which he asked the scientist to choose a gift from amongst his possessions – a horse, a cow or a yurt,

29. *Ibid*, p. 68.

perhaps? "I asked for a hat; he then reached down two of his son's hats and ordered another relative to pass me the hat he was wearing, for me to choose from. I selected one which I will wear in Harvey Road [his mother's house in Cambridge] hereafter. I had been till that moment attired in old knickerbockers, black round tailcoat and cocked hat and sword. I then put on Kazakh hat instead of Court hat and a fine figure of fun I looked, I presume."[30]

A musician then appeared and played his *dombra* and sang for the next hour, after which Bateson was asked to sing. "In a pleasing voice I then rendered that popular and touching strain, '*From Greenland's Icy Mountains.*' As the three verses which I knew were obviously insufficient in quantity after the stupendous performance of the first songster, I made it up to a total of five stanzas from various sources, sacred and profane. They asked me to translate it. I said that it was the ditty which our Mullahs (priests) sing when one of their number is about to undertake a journey into foreign parts, and was therefore appropriate to the occasion. They gave me a well-earned encore." He concluded with "Ich Hatt" and "John Brown's Body Lies Mouldering in the Grave".

Towards the autumn of 1886 Bateson decided to base himself at Kazalinsk on the Syr Darya, the same place Major Wood had been stationed more than a decade before. His intention was to go around the north shore of Lake Aral, down the west shore, across the Ust Urt desert via the chain of lakes and then winter in Astrakhan via Guryev to the north of the Caspian. In fact, he spent the winter in the Hotel Morozov in Kazalinsk, where he arrived on 20 November. There then followed a correspondence with his mother concerning her plum pudding recipe. It eventually arrived in the post on the last day of the year: "It had probably formed subject of special commission of inquiry and thus been delayed," he told her.

Bateson's collapsible Berthon boat stimulated great interest out on the steppe. "The Kazakhs have already invented a complete series of myths, which originated in my collapsible boat. It is freely reported that I have a boat which can make itself invisible; others say that it goes

---

30. *Ibid*, p. 71.

under the water, etc. I think it will probably play a part in the religious history of the race," he wrote to his mother.[31]

He also wrote about his photography in a letter to his sister Margaret, dated 6 February 1887: "I did some moderate decent photos yesterday, and will send them when ready. Of course, one's only chance is to pitch one's camera in the bazaar and photo the crowd which instantly collects. The difficulty is to get any one to go into the field; they all run to the side, as though it were a cannon about to be fired. The Sarts (Bokhariots) are the worst, as they are awfully superstitious. I caught a few in one picture. In another I have a policeman and some thorough rascals. I look forward to getting some quaint things next time – I see now how to manage it in the Steppe."

A few months later, in July and writing from Pavlodar in northeast Kazakhstan, Bateson was able to put his skills to the test when photographing Kazakh women arriving with the bride for a marriage ceremony. He was particularly enamoured of their singing and their voices. "I am particularly fond of good voices and had half thought of inviting one young lady, the daughter of a judge, to share my future fortunes," he wrote. But the thought that she would not be able easily to share his quirky sense of humour put him off the idea, no doubt to the intense relief of his family in England.

Bateson set off for Lake Balkhash in the east of the Great Steppe on 20 March 1887. His aim was to move on from there to Karkaralinsk and then on to Omsk, from where he would be able to return to St Petersburg. On 11 June he wrote to his family from the Tara Ghul silver mine on the north shore of Lake Balkhash, reporting that he had also made a seven-day journey to Lake Ala Kol. A couple of weeks later, writing from Karkaralinsk, he brought them the news that he had experienced his first earthquake: "On the 16th May (N.S.) at sunrise I was awakened by a very decided earthquake, which was the first I ever felt. It lasted about fifteen minutes and was a most curious sensation. I was lying flat on the ground, as usual, and felt it very well. It was not spasmodic, as I supposed they are, but pulsated quite regularly, beating

31. *Ibid*, p. 151.

about half-seconds. It was, I suppose, very slight where we were, only succeeding in knocking a coffee-pot off the table. On reaching here, we learned that it completely destroyed the town of Vyernie [Almaty], on the Chinese frontier, killing 112 and wounding 140 people, and caused further damage at other places."[32]

In fact, this could not have been the earthquake that destroyed Almaty, as that terrible event, with a magnitude of 7.3 on the Richter scale, took place on 9 June 1887. What he may have experienced is likely to have been a precursor to the main quake. Earthquakes are not uncommon in the regions close to the Tien Shan Mountains and Almaty – once the capital of Kazakhstan – has been destroyed on several occasions since it was founded in 1854.

By this time, Bateson was becoming somewhat despondent about his research. He had collected samples from more than 450 separate locations, each carefully analysed and noted in his research diaries. But his data was not clear enough to allow him to draw any conclusions about the two great questions that had motivated his research in the first place. He did not find creatures that survived from the days of an Asiatic Mediterranean and he was not able to establish how, if at all, the infinite variation of conditions of all the lakes he sampled had affected and changed the forms of their fauna.

"The Balkhash episode is over," he wrote from the Tara Ghul silver mine. "We leave it behind us tomorrow and with it, I leave all hope of getting any marine things at all. It was a poor chance, although I clung to it until it was clearly hopeless… But I did not much expect to get sea things here, seeing that the Aral had failed to show any, so that though very vexed, I don't feel exactly disappointed. So the dream of finding a 'Tertiary fauna' holding on here must be awakened from."

He still hoped that he might be able to show that variation could occur in the small lakes from which he had taken hundreds of samples, suggesting even that he might be able to reproduce these conditions in an aquarium back in England, "and if this comes off I believe it will be the first instance of a 'natural' variety produced artificially and ought to

---

32. *Ibid*, p. 179.

mean a perfect revolution in Biology." It was not to be.

Bateson seldom referred again to his research on the Great Steppe. He went on to great things, although he was always cast as an opponent of Darwinian ideas of natural selection and was thus out of favour in the scientific community for many years. Recent research has corrected some of the misunderstandings about his work and allowed a synthesis with Darwin's theories to take place.

But what Bateson failed to do in terms of his scientific studies he amply made up for in his ethnographic observations. His comments are full of insights and humour, and his warmth of feeling for the people who protected him and looked after him during those long months on the steppe are very clear. There are few accounts of nomadic life at that time that come anywhere near the stories recounted by Bateson in his wonderful letters to his family.

As his wife Beatrice wrote in the introduction to *Letters from the Steppe*: "As a matter of course, he lived the life of the people amongst whom he found himself; the Kazakhs seem to have accepted him quite as simply, letting him share, almost as one of themselves, in their life. His scrutiny of shells and waters was, of course, inexplicable to them, but he told me that they comfortably assumed that he was looking for treasure and manifested no surprise, nor more than a gossiping interest."

And as he wrote himself in a paper he submitted to the Journal of the Royal Society: "... though this page may never reach them, I cannot let this opportunity pass without expressing my gratitude for the courtesy and hospitality which I everywhere met with at the hands of the Kazakh people."

—⚭—

EASTERN KAZAKHSTAN

Portrait of Rev. Henry Lansdell
in Bokharan armour.

9

THE VENERABLE DR LANSDELL, THE INDEFATIGABLE MISSIONARY

—ɯɯ—

It is hard to categorise the Victorian Reverend Dr Henry Lansdell. He was certainly one of the most prolific travellers of his generation, making at least five visits to the Russian Empire, including Siberia, before setting out for Russian Central Asia and, later, Chinese Central Asia and India. His adventures were recorded in three remarkably well-informed double-volumes of travels.

And yet it was not travel itself that inspired Dr Lansdell, but his unremitting desire to distribute religious publications throughout the lands in which he travelled. In fact, he set out with the remarkable aim of leaving copies of the New Testament and the Four Gospels in every room of every prison and every hospital he came across in Siberia and Central Asia, despite Russian antipathy towards any form of foreign missionary activity, either in the Orthodox heartlands or in the newly-conquered territories of Central Asia.

Missionary work had long been controversial in Russia. Between the conquest of Kazan in 1552 and the reign of Catherine the Great II the Russians had simply been concerned to baptise as many Muslims and animists as possible, with scant regard for their existing religious beliefs. Coercion was used, including the use of tax concessions, to encourage conversion as well as harassment of those who did not convert to Orthodoxy. This policy was generally unsuccessful and led to what one writer has called "the creation of a large number of pseudo-Christians.

These people were officially registered as Christians, but continued to practice their old religions."[1]

Even more severe measures, such as forbidding converts to mix with unbaptised people, failed to work. In the 17th century, for example, Tatar landowners were threatened with expropriation if they did not convert. All to no avail. Peter the Great re-emphasised the importance of missionary works as part of his attempt to streamline and simplify the structure of Russian society. He did not want to see the existence of dozens of separate religious sects and introduced laws that discriminated against Muslims and rewarded those who converted to Christianity, particularly those from such groups as the Finnish Cheremis (Mari), who were strongest in their opposition to forced conversion. Children were taken from their communities and sent to Kazan for indoctrination into Christianity, although few if any of them ever became priests. Missionary priests, usually accompanied by a group of soldiers, would visit a settlement, baptise everyone they could find and leave presents of food and drink in an effort to create a good impression of Christianity.

But it soon became apparent that such strategies did not work. Reports revealed that priests were fabricating the numbers of converts and that even those who professed to be Christians knew nothing about the religion. Harsh laws included one from 1756 that decreed if more than 10 per cent of the inhabitants of a particular town were baptised, all those who were unbaptised were required to leave. Likewise, if fewer than 10 per cent were baptised, they were required to move to a Russian town.

Catherine II brought an end to many of these harsh religious compliance laws. She began to support the Muslim Tatars, recognising that they could bring stability to the southern Russian provinces, as well as being able to trade with the Central Asian khanates. Better that her subjects were Muslims than animists, ran the logic. Christian missionary activity came to an almost complete standstill. They were recalled from Baskhkir territory in 1789, for example.[2]

---

1   See Frank T McCarthy, "The Kazan Missionary Congress", *Cahiers du monde russe et soviétique*, vol. 14, n°3, July-September 1973, pp. 308-32: https://doi.org/10.3406/cmr.1973.1179

2. *Ibid*, p. 313.

By the time Tsar Nicholas I came to power in 1825 the pendulum was once again beginning to swing back towards missionary work and conversion. Russian nationalism was resurgent under the state's official ideology of "Orthodoxy, Autocracy and Nationality". When a delegation of Tatars petitioned the tsar to return to Islam in 1827 after they claimed they had been baptised by force, the Senate recommended they should be ignored. Priests were sent out to Tatar towns where the entire population would be assembled. "Then the priest would harangue the people and would not permit them to go home until they had promised to return to Christianity. This process might take 48 hours, but almost all of the apostates eventually conceded."[3] Despite such harsh measures Tatars continued to revert to Islam. In 1866, for example, 11,000 Tatars in Kazan reverted, even though 50 of their leaders were arrested and sentenced to internal exile.

Despite the renewed emphasis on missionary work by the Russian state, there was a complete ban on foreign missionaries working anywhere within the realms of the empire. It is all the more surprising, then, that the Lutheran Protestant Lansdell was able to spend so much time within the Russian Empire distributing religious material. During his visits to Siberia he had distributed tens of thousands of bibles and religious tracts.[4] In 1879, for example, he tells us that he distributed more than 50,000 tracts and other religious publications and in addition gave the authorities more than sufficient copies of the New Testament and the Four Gospels to achieve his aim in the prisons and hospitals of Siberia.[5] He intended to do the same during his travels in Central Asia in 1882.

The Russians were content to let him travel and to distribute his bibles and pamphlets with one very clear proviso – which he readily agreed to – that he did not engage in preaching or attempt to convert people he met to his religious beliefs. This may have been difficult for Lansdell, who had studied at the London College of Divinity before his ordination as a deacon

---

3. *Ibid*, p. 315.

4. These journeys formed the substance of his first travel book, *Through Siberia*, Sampson Low, Marston, Searle and Rivington, 1882, (2 vols.).

5. Henry Lansdell, *Russian Central Asia including Kuldja, Bokhara, Khiva and Merv*, Sampson Low, Marston, Searle and Rivington, London 1885, vol. 1, p. 6.

in 1868. However, it was a price he was willing to pay for access to these remote lands. Lansdell himself was remarkably open to different cultures and his travel writing is free of the racial and religious prejudices that were typical of the period. Instead, he harboured an almost insatiable appetite for knowledge, collecting documents and anecdotes wherever he went.

His goal in 1882 was to leave Orenburg in southern Siberia using the post road to travel in a circuit around Russian Central Asia, starting from the northeast – a journey of more than 12,000 miles. Having already spent five summers in remote parts of Russian and Siberia, the journey itself held few terrors. Instead he eagerly contemplated the number of people he would pass by on his travels. He worked out in advance that even without entering Kuldja in Chinese Turkestan – at that time under Russian occupation – or Bokhara or Khiva, he would cross eight provinces with a total population of nearly five million people and that he would pass through 20 towns with populations of between 1,000 and 80,000. "Of all these towns I knew of only one (or perhaps two) to which the British and Foreign Bible Society had been able to send a consignment of Scriptures, and, judging from my experience in other parts of the Empire, I fully anticipated that the prisons, hospitals, barracks and schools would be insufficiently supplied, or not supplied at all, with the Scriptures or other religious reading."[6]

Lansdell calculated that the journey could be completed in four or five months and would cost him around £400, which he raised from various religious societies in England. At no time does he appear to have had official backing from the Church of England. But he also had other, non-religious, objectives. One friend asked him to make a collection of flower seeds, botanical specimens, beetles and butterflies. Augustus Franks asked him to collect ethnographical specimens and antiquities for the British Museum and his neighbour, James Glaisher FRS, lent him various meteorological instruments for taking measurements. Undoubtedly, he was going to be very busy on his journey, which was likely to be the most dangerous he had ever undertaken. Not surprisingly, he decided he would make his will before he set off.

---

6. *Ibid*, p. 3.

His route to Central Asia took him from London to St Petersburg, on to Moscow and Nijni Novgorod, then by steamer to Perm, by rail and post to Tyumen and then down the River Irtysh by steamer to Semipolatinsk. He left London on 26 June 1882, reaching St Petersburg three days later, where he was met at the terminus by a messenger from the Grand Duke Michael, uncle of the emperor, who invited him to lunch at the Mikhailovsky Palace the following day.

Lansdell explained his project to the Grand Duke, who told him that he might have a few difficulties on his route, but also gave him a letter of introduction to the interior minister, Count Tolstoy. The count was also supportive and a few days later he received an official letter to the governor of each of the provinces through which he was due to pass. He also received an open letter from the recently-appointed Governor-General of Turkistan, General Mikhail Chernyayev and a letter from the Post Office authorities to assist him in obtaining horses at the post stations.

Further introductions followed, to Dr Gustav Sievers, curator of the Romanov natural history collection and discoverer of the famous Sievers Apple, Dr Strauch of the Zoological Museum, Per Petrovich Semenov of the Imperial Russian Geographical Society and many other important scientists. In Moscow he met more intellectuals. He also inspected the newly-finished Cathedral of the Saviour, built in the Graeco-Byzantine style and decorated with 900 lb of gold on its five cupolas. The largest of its 13 bells weighed over half as much again as "Great Paul" in London and one of the doors weighed 13 tons.

At Perm, where Lansdell arrived on 29 July, he bought a horse-drawn *tarantass* in which he would travel for much of the next 3,000 miles, and also met up with his translator, an Austrian doctor called Alfred Sevier. His *tarantass* was 6ft 8in long by 3ft 8in wide and 4ft 4in from the floor to the top of the hood. Like all of these vehicles, it had no springs. Thankfully, most of the thousands of religious texts he intended to distribute were sent separately and carried in a *telega* springless cart.

He travelled on to Ekaterinburg by rail before posting – journeying by horse-drawn carriage – to Tyumen, which he left on 19 August by steamer for the five-day journey to Omsk, stopping only to load up wood for fuel. From Omsk he decided to travel by post for the final 500 miles to Semipolatinsk – today Semey in the northeast of Kazakhstan. The journey would take him through 31 post-houses where he would change horses and get what refreshment he could.

Soon he was in the steppe for the first time, which, he said, reminded him of the ocean. "The soil is yielding, stoneless and sandy, thus making the smoothest of roads, on which our horses dashed along. The country is nearly treeless and the ground almost without vegetation, so that one had only to picture the surface covered with snow to see the necessity for the roadside wickerwork erections to mark the route in winter."[7] He also noted the innumerable ponds and lakes, filled with both sweet and brackish water.

Lansdell arrived in Pavlodar, half-way to Semipolatinsk, on 21 August, covering the 260 miles from Omsk in 44 hours. Here he hoped to meet the newly-appointed Governor-General of the Steppe, who was on his way up to Omsk from Vierney (Almaty) and was somewhere in the vicinity. He tells us that in the post-houses he would usually try to pin an engraving of *The Return of the Prodigal Son* beneath the *ikon* that was invariably in the corner of the main room. This in turn would stimulate conversation and sometimes the sale of his books. It was here in Pavlodar that he was reunited with his large consignment of religious books, which included copies of the New Testament translated into Kazakh. "I had not the least trouble in selling my Kazakh Testaments at catalogue price," he records.

The area around Pavlodar was mostly concerned with mining for coal and metals, including silver, copper and iron ores. He noted in particular the striking green Dioptase copper crystals, which come from mines in nearby Karaganda.

Lansdell also obtained some interesting figures on the composition of the Russian military forces in Central Asia. Of 33,502 soldiers examined in Western Siberia – which included the steppe – in 1879, 98 per cent were Russians, nearly one per cent were Tatars and the remaining one per cent made up of Jews, Mordvins, Poles, Finns, Mongols, Gypsies, etc. Of these men, 1,572 were 5ft 2in high, with 4,693 measuring 5ft

---

7. *Ibid*, p. 68.

6in. Just over 1,000 were 5ft 10in. The average stature was 5ft 5½in, with an average chest measurement of 34½in.

Another 50 miles down the road and in the town of Cherna he finally came across the Governor-General of the Steppe, Lieutenant-General Gerasim Kolpakovsky, as his entourage arrived – 11 *tarantasses* in total. He provided Lansdell with a letter of recommendation to post-house staff that guaranteed him interpreters and guides and access to horses. "Gentlemen of England, who live at home at ease, or who, when they voyage to the south of France, telegraph to Paris for compartments reserved and write to *The Times* if they are not satisfied – velvet-cushion travellers such as these can only feebly appreciate the value of such a telegram in the steppes of Central Asia," wrote the good doctor.[8] Some years before, Thomas Atkinson had written in similar glowing terms about the passport he received from Tsar Nicholas I, without which, he said, he could never have completed his journey.[9]

Soon Lansdell was on the road again, posting through the night, mostly following the course of the Irtysh where, he says, the Cossacks fished for pike, nielma salmon, yass, perch and bream. Sturgeon and sterlet could also be found. He also noted many species of birds as he moved south, including hawks (Brahminy Kites, Red-footed Falcons, ospreys and eagles), bustards, crows, gulls, oyster-catchers, sand martins and larks. Where there were few trees the Cossacks often put nest boxes on top of poles for the sparrows and starlings. His interest in birds was shown by the fact that in Omsk he bought a collection of birds' eggs, butterflies and beetles, which was eventually donated to the Natural History Museum in London.

By this time, Russian settlement of the steppes was well underway. The Cossack population of the provinces of Akmolinsk and Semipolatinsk (two of the three provinces that made up the steppe at this time – the other was Semirecheye) was located in 149 settlements made up of

---

8. *Ibid*, p. 77

9. Atkinson wrote thus in the preface to his book: "I am deeply indebted to the late Emperor of Russia; for without his passport I should have been stopped at every government and insurmountable difficulties would have been thrown in my way. This slip of paper proved a talisman wherever presented in his dominions and swept down every obstacle raised to bar my progress." See T W Atkinson, *Oriental and Western Siberia*, Hurst & Blackett, London, 1858, p. vii.

87,723 combatants and 99,139 others. Another 25,000 combatants and a further population of 28,000 were living in the 54 settlements of the Irtysh Line, along the river, where they were originally settled to protect areas to the north from Kazakh raids. But there had been no such attacks for many years and the Cossacks were gradually turning into farmers, despite their obligation for military service. Lansdell called them 'warrior-farmers'.

It took four days to reach Semipolatinsk, a distance of 482 miles from Omsk, and required 134 horses and 44 drivers, at a total cost of just £6. Having arrived there on 24 August, Lansdell was well and truly in the regions of the Great Steppe. The province itself was the size of Spain – low, flat steppe to the north, rising gradually towards the south. Nomad encampments dotted the plains, with the needle-pointed Arkat Mountains in the distance. Scattered around the steppe were saltpans and brackish lakes. The Chingiz-Tau hills lay to the southwest, towards Lake Balkhash, with the Lake Nur Zaisan basin to the east and the Tarbagatai Mountains to the south. To the northeast stood the peaks of the Altai Mountains.

Lake Nur Zaisan, with a surface area of 700 sq miles, is described in some detail by Lansdell, who notes that in the 17th century it was called Lake Kyzalpu by the Siberians. The Mongols called it Kun-Bloti-Nor or the Lake of Bells because waves striking the reeds on the shore create a sound not unlike the tinkling of bells. Zaisan is a Kalmyk word that means "noble", as they were able to support themselves by fishing from it during a famine. There are two kinds of sturgeon and three kinds of sterlet in the lake, as well as salmon, grayling, trout, pike, roach, perch, carp and burbot. On its shores were to be found tigers – at that time they were also to be found around Lake Aral, Lake Balkhash and even the Caspian – leopards, lynx, Pallas' cat, bears, wolves, foxes, corsac foxes, wolverines, badgers, beavers, martens, squirrels, weasels, moles and ermine.

Throughout his travels Lansdell collected masses of data from every district through which he passed. Even in the 1880s the Russian authorities were collecting mountains of information, including details of crops sown and reaped, the varieties, numbers and circumstances of breeding of cattle, the value of wares purchased and sold, breakdowns of religious beliefs, taxes, duties, the number of hospitals, doctors, patients, diseases, crimes and prisons, schools, etc. He says that as the new report for the government of Semipolatinsk for 1881 was not quite ready at the time of his visit, it was later forwarded by officials to his English address.

He even included criminal statistics in his book, noting that it appeared that Russians committed more crimes per head of population than Kazakhs, a fact he explained by noting that the statistics did not include cases settled by native tribunals. In 1880, for example, 831 crimes were committed – one for every 552 persons. Offending rates were four times as great in the large Russian-dominated towns of Omsk and Petropavlovsk than in rural areas.

He observed that the Kazakhs watered three-quarters of their lands by damming up mountain streams and that this was more efficient than the efforts of Russian settlers. Crops grown included wheat, oats and millet (especially by the nomads), barley and spring rye. Locusts were a problem, destroying more than 4,400 acres of corn in one small area in 1880. Other crops grown by the Cossacks included tobacco, melons and hemp. As for animals, Lansdell gives the following figures for those owned by nomads: around 104,000 camels, 1.1 million horses, 483,000 cattle and 5.5 million sheep and goats. There were also over 5,000 beehives in the region.

As Lansdell headed south into the Great Steppe, the cost of provisions at the post-houses began to fall. He gives the following tariff: use of samovar, 2½d; portion of bread 2½d; pair of chickens 6d; a cooked fowl 10d; quart of milk 1¼d; ten eggs 4d.

More than half-a-million people lived in Semipolatinsk region in 1881, of whom more than 92 per cent were Muslims and the rest mostly Russian Orthodox, with a sprinkling of Old Believers, Jews, Catholics and pagans. Amongst the Kazakh population, 45 were nobles and 2,489 were descendants of sultans. About a third of the Kazakhs were nomadic, with the rest settled in towns and small villages. Each Kazakh *kibitka* (yurt) was liable for tax of 6 shillings a year, whereas town dwellers pad a land tax and a capitation tax.

Until just a few years before Lansdell made his journey, the border with China had been very much closer to Semipolatinsk. Lake Nur Zaisan had once been Chinese and there had been a border station at

Bukhtarminsk, where the Irtysh flows out of its northern shore. In the 18th century Chinese soldiers buying provisions and selling Djungarian captives had once been a common sight in the town.

It was not until the Treaty of Kuldja in 1851 that relations between Russia and China in this region were put on a legal footing. The Chinese province of Kuldja was thrown open to Russian trade and the right was acquired of appointing Russian consuls at Chuguchak on the border and at Kuldja.

The name Semipolatinsk means "Seven Palaces", the ruins of which had been seen by the German naturalist Johann Georg Gmelin (1709-55) during a visit to the region in 1734. They had originally been Buddhist temples built by the Kalmyks and one of them still contained statues of two bears.

Some of the first Tibetan Buddhist texts in Russian collections came from these temples at Semipolatinsk. They were brought to St Petersburg around 1718 as a gift to Peter the Great from the Siberian governor M. Gagarin. They were found by Cossacks while in the process of building fortresses along the Irtysh. Two years later, in late 1720, the soldiers founded Ust-Kamenskaya (Oskemen) fortress and nearby the following year they found another abandoned Djungar monastery called Ablaikit. Six folios from its rich library of Tibetan and Mongolian texts were first sent to St Petersburg and one of them was skilfully reproduced in *Acta Eruditorum*, an academic publication issued in Leipzig, thus becoming in 1722 the first Tibetan manuscript published in Europe.

According to the website of St Petersburg's Institute of Oriental Manuscripts of the Russian Academy of Science: "Many European scholars tried to translate it, but the first successful translation was only made a century later, by famous S Csoma Kőrősi. Around 1,500 folios were later transferred to St Petersburg from Ablaikit but the bulk of them were in Mongolian, about 200 folios from an unknown version of Tibetan Kagyur having been recently identified. During the 18th century, more Tibetan texts were acquired by the RAS from D Messerschmidt, G Müller, P Pallas, I Jährig and other sources."[10]

---

10. See http://www.orientalstudies.ru/eng/index.php?option=content&task=view&id=2065

Lansdell's next destination was Sergiopol – now called Ayaguz – 180 miles due south, past the Arkat Mountains painted by Thomas Atkinson and over the western spur of the Tarbagatai Mountains known as the Chingiz-Tau. At Ayaguz, where he arrived on 24 August, he slept in the post-house before making a visit to the local hospital, prison and barracks, where he was able to leave some of his religious tracts. In fact, he says he sold books in almost every post-house at which he stopped between Semipolatinsk and Ayaguz and usually enjoyed a good conversation with his customers. He also obtained a *kokoshnik* or traditional headdress from a young Cossack schoolmistress who came to buy books from him. She refused his offer to buy it, but graciously offered it as a gift. It is now in the collection of the British Museum.

Lansdell says that he had been preceded to Ayaguz by another Englishman, namely Edward Delmar Morgan (1840-1909), the translator of the Polish-born explorer Nikolai Przhevalsky, who had been there in 1880 on his way to the Chinese border.[11] At that point rumours of a Chinese invasion of Turkestan were rife, and Morgan, who was delayed in the town for three weeks due to bad weather, was witness to the preparations of the Cossacks who were being mobilised to meet any threat. Morgan had been brought up in Russia and spoke the language perfectly. The likelihood is that he was collecting information that would be useful to the British government – he was probably a spy.

Not far south from Ayaguz are the lakes Sassyk Kol and Ala Kol, the latter being the third largest lake in Central Asia. Lansdell provides detailed lists of the birds from the vicinity and fish from the lakes, and also the mammals, including Arctic hares, antelope, ibex, and the wild ass or *kulan*. He was now in Semirecheye – or Zhetysu as it is known in Kazakh, the land of the seven rivers. It is an area comprised of three basins – Lake Balkhash, Ala Kol and Issyk Kol in present-day

11. E Delmar Morgan, "A visit to Kuldja and the Russo-Chinese Frontier in 1880", *Journal of the Royal United Service Institution*, vol. 25, February 1881, pp. 261-81, which sets out very clearly the history of the changing border between Russia and China in Central Asia. Prior to Morgan, the only other British traveller who reached the Zhetysu, besides the Atkinsons, was Ashton Wentworth Dilke (1850-83), who made a journey to Kuldja from Bokhara in 1873. Kuldja had been occupied by the Russians in1871. Dilke presented a paper at the RGS which was later published. See "The Valley of the Ili and the Water-system of Russian Turkestan", *Geographical Magazine*, May 1874, pp. 84-6.

Kyrgyzstan, formed by the Tarbagatai Mountains in the north, the Djungar Alatau Mountains between Ala Kol and the River Ili; and to the south, the Trans-Ili Alatau, which is effectively the northern ridge of the Tian Shan mountain chain. As Lansdell says: "This mountain system, whether regard be had to its area or its length, the height of its crests, the abundance of its snows or the massiveness of its glaciers, is the grandest on the northern slope of the Asiatic continent".[12] It is, he says, 25 times the size of the Swiss Alps.

As to the seven rivers which are referred to in the name of the province, Lansdell says there is "some difference of opinion" as to which they are. He names the Ili, the Karatal and the Lepsa and also suggests the River Chu, which runs along the present border between Kazakhstan and Kyrgyzstan.

The most recent (but unpublished) census available to Lansdell dated from 1878 and showed a population for Semirecheye of 609,000, including the area around Lake Issyk Kul that is now in Kyrgyzstan. Of these, around 55,000 were settled and living in 8,000 houses and 553,000 were nomads living in 126,000 yurts. Settlement by Russians had been rapid since the establishment of the Turkistan district in 1867, their numbers rising from 30,000 in 20 settlements to 44,000 in 65 settlements, almost half of whom were Cossacks.

Not surprisingly, there was constant tension between the incomers and the nomads who had dwelt in these regions for generations. Disputes arose regularly over boundaries and water rights – issues which in 1916 contributed to a full-scale uprising against the settlers. There were also settlers from across the border in Kuldja, who arrived in 1867 after civil war broke out there. These *Taranchis* – Chinese converts to Islam – were settled mostly around the town of Sarcand, where they were given agricultural equipment and seed and a payment in cash, allowing them to develop into a thriving colony.

Lansdell left Ayaguz on 27 August, passing between Balkhash and Ala Kol, which Humboldt had once thought, erroneously, to be the centre of the volcanic activity that had created the Central Asian

---

12. Lansdell, *Russian Central Asia*, p. 152.

mountain chains. Both John de Piano Carpini in 1245 and Friar William de Rubruck around 20 years later passed through here on their journeys to meet the Mongol khans. Soon he had his first glimpse of Balkhash, lying around 20 miles to his west. Its southern shore, with its reeds standing at over five metres tall, provided winter homes for thousands of Kazakhs who each spring migrated into the Djungar Alatau Mountains with flocks and herds.

Before long Lansdell had reached Lepsinsk, one of the Cossack villages at the foot of the Djungar Alatau. He briefly considered crossing the mountains from there to Lake Sairam-Nor in Chinese Turkestan in order to shorten the route to Kuldja, but he was warned that it was not a good idea as the road was very poor. Instead he carried on, crossing the two branches of the Baskan river, then the Ak-Su before reaching Abakumovsky (today, Zhansugurov), where a post-road could be taken to Sarcand, famous, even then, for the local honey.

Lansdell says that the Djungar Alatau range of mountains corresponds nearly with the 45th parallel of latitude, with an almost unbroken line of snow peaks that stretches for 130 miles, some of which reach to almost 15,000 feet. From these run the Lepsa, Baskan, Sarkan and Ak-Su rivers from deep and almost impenetrable gorges into the plains below. It was this region that Thomas and Lucy Atkinson explored during the summer of 1849, being intent on visiting each of the river valleys and following them into the mountains as far as possible.

From Abakumovsky the old road rises up into the Gasfort (sometimes transliterated as Hasford) Pass before dropping down to Arasan and its famous hot springs. By the time Lansdell visited, there were already bathing houses, a garden and a small hotel for visitors at the springs. In the Soviet period a large sanatorium was built on the site, but in recent years it has fallen into disuse. From Arasan it was only a short distance to Kopal, the town where the Atkinsons spent the winter of 1848-49 and where their child Alatau was born. For a brief period it had been capital of the province, but once Vierney (Almaty) was founded in 1854 its importance began to decline. By the time Lansdell visited, it had a population of around 5,000, with two schools, two churches and a mosque.

He did not stop here but posted on along the base of the Djungar Alatau Mountains, to Altyn-Emel, where the road divided, one branch heading towards Vierney and the other to Kuldja, which is the direction he took. After an insurrection against the Chinese by Uighurs and Chinese Dungan Muslims that began in 1864 and lasted for several years, much of the region around Kuldja was in ruins, with tens of thousands of Chinese soldiers and settlers slaughtered. Later, fighting broke out between Turkic and Chinese Muslims. Fearful of the fighting spreading to its new territories in Central Asia, Russian troops invaded the Ili Valley and Kuldja in 1871, only handing these regions back to China in March 1883 under the terms of the Treaty of St Petersburg. During the decade or so that Kuldja was under Russian control, Cossack troops were stationed in the Ili Valley and a number of travellers, including Eugene Schuyler and Mme Marie de Ujfalvy-Bourdon and her husband, as well as the Britons Delmar Morgan and Dilke, were able to visit this remote area for the first time in recorded history. Dr Lansdell, travelling in 1882, was actually one of the last people to take advantage of this window of opportunity.

The Altyn-Emel (Golden Saddle) Pass reaches a height of around 5,500 ft as it cuts through a gorge. It is one of the easiest ways to cross the from high plateau of Chinese Central Asia into the steppes of Turkistan, and the oasis of Kuldja was often a resting and gathering place for the great hordes who passed through on their way to the west. In the 1880s many of the residents were Kazakhs. Lansdell provides a breakdown of the nomad population of Kuldja for 1878, as collected by Russian officials; in the five *volosts* of the northern and five of the southern divisions of the province there were 13,000 yurts with a population of 31,600 males, and 26,400 females. Of these, 36,000 were Kazakh and the remainder Tatars, Kalmyks and others. "So far as there are any grades among the nomads, one may distinguish in the province 14 sultan or aristocratic families, 4,000 *igintchas*, or poor, and 1,000 mullahs," he wrote. They owned 750,000 cattle – of which 107,000 died during the year. In addition, the settled inhabitants owned 182,000 cattle.

By 1 September Lansdell had reached Borokhudzir in the Ili Valley where he was struck by the abundance of game. He was told that this town would become a frontier fort once Russia had returned Kuldja to China. From here on towards Kuldja he witnessed the destruction caused by the insurrection, with wrecked canals and the scattered ruins of Chinese houses. Zharkent was in ruins. Close by lived a group of people called Solons, who were not a Djungarian race at all, but originated in northwestern Manchuria and were sent to the far west of the Chinese Empire in the middle of the 18th century. Most had fled north to Chuguchak or had converted to Christianity and moved to Sarcand in the Djungar Alatau region. Not far on from here was the River Khorgos, which marked the boundary between the Russian and Chinese Empires, as it still does today. Further on were the ruins of Tchimpantzi, where 50,000 Chinese had previously lived, and Ili, which was once the Chinese capital in the area and where reports suggested that 75,000 Chinese people had been butchered in a single day.

This area has always been strategically significant and has been important for the Chinese since at least the first century BC, when they began extracting tribute from the region. In 627 the Chinese Tang dynasty dispatched an army to strengthen the allegiance of the Uighurs. Later, it fell to the Tibetan tribes, the Arabs, the Kara-Khitai and then Genghis Khan.

After Genghis Khan it fell to the Kalmyks – known as the Western Oirats. They spread their influence over Mongolia and in 1450 conquered China. By the 18th century the Djungarian throne was seized by a usurper. It was then seized in 1756 by China whose troops slaughtered 600,000 Kalmyks in so doing. Then the region was divided into seven districts, three of which – Tarbagatai, Kurkara-Usun and Ili – made up the Viceroyalty of Ili.

China repopulated the empty land with Solons and Sibos from Dauria, Dungans from Kan-Su and Shen-Si and other Muslim settlers from Kashgaria known as Taranchis. In 1771 the remnants of the Torgut Kalmyks returned to this region from the Volga. Manchu Kuldja (Ili) became the regional capital.

In the 1864 insurrection the Dungans rebelled and killed all the Chinese and Manchus near Urumchi – around 130,000 in total. In Kuldja the Taranchis joined the Dungans in the massacres. Then they fell out and in April 1867 fought each other. The Dungans were beaten and the Taranchis became rulers. The Russians remained neutral at first. But when Kuldja was threatened by Yakub Beg, the Governor of Kashgar, the Russians stepped in and seized it, promising the Royal Court in Beijing that as soon as the Chinese could restore order and pay for the Russian troops, they would return it. This happened the year before Lansdell visited, although it was in a transitional state when he visited. The governor was Russian – General Friede. Russians and Chinese were negotiating the frontier.

Lansdell finally arrived in Kuldja, 1,800 miles from Omsk, after a journey that took two weeks. "There are no hotels at Kuldja, and as it was too late to present letters of introduction," he wrote, "I was glad enough to throw myself down on the bench in the dirty post-house and there to sleep until morning."

The Ili Valley was then, and remains today, a complex network of ethnic groups. Lansdell called it "a half-way house between the Turanian races of Central Asia and the Mongol races of China". Here he met Kazakhs, settled Muslim Taranchis and Dungans, Buddhist Sibo, Manchu and Chinese, as well as nomadic Kyrgyz and Lamaist Kalmyks. He obtained many interesting objects here, including a pair of Kashgar ladies' boots (*makhsa*), which are now in the British Museum, along with some Taranchi rings, silver hair pins and a single earring.

After a short stay, Lansdell left Kuldja on 5 September, having met the Manchu governor – the *Tsin-Tsiang* – in the town of Suidun, the only large town where Chinese survived the massacres of 1863-66. By 7 September he was back at Altyn-Emel and a few days later he was in Vierney, which then had a population of around 12,600. Alexander, the Russian Orthodox Archbishop of Turkistan and Tashkent, gave him some photos of Central Asia from his "splendid collection". Photography was of increasing interest to Lansdell, who took a camera with him on this journey. He also mentions the history of the translation of the Bible into Turkish and then Kazakh. He says it was finally completed by "Mr Brunton" and Charles Frazer, Scottish missionaries, in Orenburg in 1813.

Lansdell, who was particularly interested in the history of the regions through which he passed, gives a competent history of the Semirecheye region, noting that the Russian presence there was directly related to the needs of the Kazakh hordes to obtain protection from the raids of the Djungars residing on the other side of the Tian Shan

Mountains. He notes that it took less that 25 years for the Russians to push 600 miles south from Semipolatinsk into the Great Steppe. He makes a strong argument to suggest it was primarily Russia's growing interest in Central Asia that created the impetus for the formation of the Russian Geographical Society in 1845. They, in turn, funded Semenov's expedition into the Tian Shan Mountains in 1856.

The venerable doctor was also particularly interested in the Kazakhs, saying that they were closer to the original Hebrew patriarchs than any other living group. He writes that the area between the Oxus and Jaxartes (i.e. the Amu Darya and Syr Darya) had been conquered many times, but none of the conquering armies ever went beyond the latter river. Islam had barely penetrated these regions. The law and custom that still existed on the steppe, he said, obtained in the days of Moses and the great grandchildren of Abraham. He gives a breakdown of the three Kazakh hordes, which he said totalled around 2.3m people.

Further details follow about how the Kazakhs organise their livestock breeding, about marriage customs and inheritance laws. He explains how yurts are constructed and what one should expect to find within them. Descriptions of *kumyss* and of crime and punishment follow.

Leaving Vierney on 8 September, Lansdell headed off towards Aulie Ata, a distance of 507 *versts* along which were 22 post-houses. At one of them, Suigati, he witnessed the election for chief of the local *volost*. Nogai Bi was elected, from whom he received a ring that is now in the British Museum. As with other travellers at this time, his route took him to the River Chu, to Pishpek (now Bishkek, the capital of Kyrgyzstan), where he visited the Botanical Gardens run by Mr Fetisof, and then along the base of the Alexandrovsky Mountains to the village of Merke. By this time Lansdell's ability to travel for days on end had earned him, so he says, the nickname of "Ironpants".

His eventual arrival in Aulie-Ata (now known as Taraz) provided Lansdell with further opportunities to purchase goods, including earrings, tassels, a *tara* headgear for a woman, which hangs in a double row across the breast of an under-garment, and a *tchinikap* – a protective wooden case for a basin. He also mentions the tomb of Kara Khan, a descendant of Sheikh Ahmed Yesavi, who is the "holy father" of the town's name.

*

Having travelled out of Semirecheye, Lansdell travelled on to Samarkand and Bokhara and eventually back to England. It was not until six years later, in 1888, that he would return to the area again, as recorded in the final double-volume book, *Chinese Central Asia*, he published on his travels.[13] This last major journey was probably the toughest of his life in terms of physical hardship. His objective was to deliver a letter from the Archbishop of Canterbury to the Dalai Lama, which he hoped would grant him access to the then closed capital of Tibet at Lhasa. In the end he was unable to obtain the requisite permission.

During these latter travels Lansdell again started from Moscow, but headed first to the Crimea and then Baku, before crossing the Caspian to the Turkoman lands, passing through Akhal Tekke, home of the famous horses, and then Geok Tepe, Askhabad, Dushak and Merv. From here he travelled on the railway to Bokhara, Samarkand and Tashkent and then on to Lake Issyk Kul in present-day Kyrgyzstan, but then still part of the Russian province of Semirecheye.

He made it as far as the city of Karakol at the eastern end of Lake Issyk Kul, only the second English traveller – the first was Delmar Morgan – to reach this remote spot. There he stayed with Colonel Koroloff, with whose brother, the Governor of Samarkand, he had stayed in 1882. He had intended to travel from there via Chilik in the Ili Valley to Vierney but was unable to do so. On his previous visit he had arrived in Vierney from the northeast, having set out from Semipolatinsk, close to the Altai Mountains of southern Siberia.

In the meantime, on 9 June 1887, a year before his visit, the city had been hit by a massive earthquake. There were two quakes: the first lasted five seconds, followed by a much longer and stronger shock ten minutes later, said to be magnitude 7.3 on the Richter scale. "For some seconds the trembling ceased, but only to be renewed with fresh force, under which the walls began to fall and buildings to crack, whilst on

---

13. Henry Lansdell, *Chinese Central Asia: A Ride to Little Tibet*, Samson, Low, Marston & Co, London, 1893 (2 vols.).

all sides was heard the crash of tumbling houses. The town was covered with a cloud of dust so thick as to prevent any one seeing farther than from 30 to 40 steps and, to add to the confusion, the frightened animals – oxen, cows, dogs and horses – rushed pell-mell through the streets, making their way instinctively towards the Steppe," he was told.[14]

Lansdell said that the violent agitation lasted for about three minutes, almost without ceasing, after which the shocks became weaker and shorter and by 5.30 pm five his host and informant, Monsieur Gourdet, a French teacher and architect, was able to dress and look about the town. The least damaged were the wooden houses, but nonetheless 328 people were killed and 1,840 houses destroyed. The governor requisitioned hundreds of yurts from the nomads living nearby. "Things were still in a disorganised condition when we arrived on May 29th," wrote Lansdell. He was actually in the town on the first anniversary of the quake. Gourdet had kept a detailed record of the aftershocks which continued for the rest of the year. In fact, Gourdet continued to correspond with Lansdell and later wrote to tell him that on 30 June 1889 "we had a shock lasting 12 minutes, almost as strong as that of 1887".

On 13 June 1888 Lansdell left Vierney, driving eastwards across the steppe about 150 miles along the course of the River Almaty and at the foot of the Trans-Ili Alatau Mountains. From here he descended into the valley of the River Ili. He stopped at Illisk, where he met John Norman, a fellow Englishman. From Illisk the two men travelled together on to the east, to the post-station of Altyn-Emel and then Zharkent, which they reached on 16 June. Here he met Tochta Akhoun, who said he had been one of Przhevalsky's guides. He also met Przhevalsky's translator. In the market he decided to buy a large-wheeled *arba*, rigged with netting and three big draught horses, as well as a Kirghiz cob for his servant and a saddlehorse for himself. The total cost was £25, for which he changed some of his paper money to *yambus* – Chinese silver ingots.

As he approached the Russia-China border at the River Khorgos he must have been somewhat nervous. He says that all the advice he had received in England suggested that if he wanted to enter China from the

---

14. *Ibid*, p. 131.

west, he should first go to Beijing and see the foreign minister. Otherwise he was unlikely to be allowed in. In fact, although he had a Russian document allowing him to pass into China, he had no Chinese speakers with him, only a couple of Cossacks. "What the Cossacks said or did I know not; but the great doors, with 'warders' or painted dragons, flew open, my tarantass rolled majestically through, without my being stopped, or, so far as I remember, asked for my passport, and in five minutes we were calmly driving through the fields of the Flowery Land and among the Celestials, quizzing their pigtails and feeling on excellent terms with ourselves and the world in general. This was success 'number one' in China".[15]

A day or two later, on 21 June, after travelling for 5,000 miles across the Russian Empire over the course of 115 days, he arrived in Kuldja, which by this time had been returned to Chinese control. On the way he passed a place called Alimptu, which he thought might be the ancient city of Almalik, mentioned by many medieval travellers, where there was once a substantial Nestorian Christian community. Now, for the first time, Lansdell felt that he was really in China, although he was only midway between Moscow and Beijing.

His accommodation in Kuldja was basic, although it allowed him, for the first time, to erect the camp chair, table and bedstead he had brought with him. On the bedstead he was able to inflate his airbed and add a pair of sheets. He picked up from the post office the two dozen book packages – weighing more than 500 lb – he had sent ahead from London and was delighted to find that none had been stopped by the censor. The books were stacked in his room, "giving the establishment very much the appearance of a warehouse at one end and a compound dining, drawing, dressing and reading room at the other."[16]

Lansdell remarks that Kuldja had deteriorated since it had been handed back to the Chinese by the Russians, in part because they had moved the capital to Suidun. Chinese officials, he says, told him that their main objective was to make as much money as they could in the shortest possible time. They sent him visiting cards with his name expressed in

15. *Ibid*, p. 148.

16. *Ibid*, p. 173.

Chinese – *Lahn-sse-dur-rhe*. He made the journey back to Suidun to visit the Chinese *Tsian-Tsinn* (senior official) and passed through countryside that was almost empty, mentioning that "as a proof that travelling by night was a trifle dangerous, there were stuck up on poles, at various places along the road, small cages, each containing the head of a brigand."

Suidun itself was surrounded by a high wall and contained numerous bazaars and inns, although Lansdell admits that entering his first Chinese inn "made my flesh creep", even though it was said to be the best in the area. Foul straw and manure littered the yard, his room had no flooring or furniture and he was expected to sleep over a *kang* – a platform of loose boards over an ashpit where all kinds of rubbish had been burned. He was disturbed by endless hammering from the building next door: "This went on all day and what with the stench of manure, distracting noises, windows unglazed and inquisitive visitors, my lodging proved to be the worst I had ever had."

Dr Lansdell travelled on from Kuldja to Aksu and then Kashgar, before he made his way home via India – a total of 9,000 miles. Although he continued to travel for a few more years, his excursions were less extensive. It was the end of his peregrinations. From 1892 to 1912 he was chaplain at Morden College in Blackheath. He died in Blackheath, London, in October 1919.

He left behind him a major body of work on Central Asia and Siberia – probably a greater volume of work than almost any other British traveller. Throughout his journeys he had amassed huge amounts of information that he was only too glad to put in front of his readers. Although criticised by some for being uncritical of the Russian penal system, he was able to leave behind him some of the best descriptions of the Great Steppe and its inhabitants, and some of the earliest photographs. He never allowed his strong Christian beliefs to cloud his judgement and had a genuine respect for the tough nomads that lived in these remote places. The fact that he travelled – like the Atkinsons – as an independent person, not reliant on an institution, only added strength to his narrative. His collecting activity also enhanced the collections of numerous museums, where many items can still be seen to this day.

Samuel Turner.

BUSINESS – AND REVOLUTION – COMES TO THE STEPPE
Samuel Turner, E Nelson Fell, J H Wardell and Ralph Fox

—٨٨—

BY THE END OF THE 19TH CENTURY interest in the business prospects offered by the Great Steppe was growing. Geologists had revealed that there were minerals, including gold and silver, to be exploited and that agricultural production could flourish on the rich loams of the steppe. The real question was how valuable minerals and farm goods could be transported out of the steppe and sent to market. Part of the answer to that was through investment, to pay for better infrastructure, new equipment and more staff.

According to John McKay in his book *Pioneers for Profit*,[1] one of the most striking aspects of Russia's economic development in the decades before the First World War was the extent to which direct foreign investment fuelled industrial modernisation. In the years leading up to the outbreak of war the growth of heavy industries drew substantial British capital investments and personnel to the country. McKay says that foreign investment increased from 17 per cent of the capital of industrial corporations in Imperial Russia in 1880 to 47 per cent by 1914.

Despite the difficulties, foreign capital could see the potential of the steppes. Already, most of the machinery imported to Central Asia in parts on the backs of camels – including complete ocean-going ships and steam locomotives – came from British engineering workshops. By

---

1. John McKay, *Pioneers for Profit, Foreign Entrepreneurship and Russian Industrialization*, 1885-1913, University of Chicago Press, Chicago, 1970.

the end of the 19th century agricultural and mining companies were setting up business in the most remote areas.

So unusual was the experience of visiting the Kazakh Steppe that several of those who worked there wrote about it. Nor were these simply business stories. British, American and Australian engineers and mineralogists took the opportunity to travel across the steppe and record their experiences. Their accounts provide a fascinating picture of life before the great social convulsion of the Russian Revolution that would change the nomadic lifestyle of millions of people forever.

Typical of those accounts was Samuel Turner's fascinating book, *Siberia: A Record of Travel, Climbing and Exploration*,[2] about his experiences in the Altai Mountains. It was butter that brought Turner to the Altai region. Turner says that although his main object in visiting the region was business – specifically, the dairy business – having arrived close to the highest mountain range in South Central Asia, he decided to spend some time indulging in his favourite pastime of climbing. "It is my conviction that exploration and commerce should be in intimate relation, and that the explorer who fails to do something towards promoting the trade of the country he visits falls short of the main purpose of exploration", he wrote.[3]

His description of the growing importance of the dairy industry may come as something of a surprise to modern readers, who will find it hard to believe that thousands of tons of butter from the Kazakh steppes were exported to Western Europe, and particularly to Britain, in the years before the First World War. Prior to 1893 no butter was either exported or produced in Western Siberia. Turner says it was an Englishwoman, the wife of a Russian, who first began butter production in the Tyumen District, to the north of present-day Kazakhstan. The first exports were from Kurgan, again close to the present northern border of Kazakhstan. Business was slow at first, but government support for the formation of cooperative dairies and increased immigration of Russian peasants to Siberia and the steppelands led to increased production.

---

2. Samuel Turner, *Siberia: A Record of Travel Climbing and Exploration*, T Fisher Unwin, London, 1905.

3. Turner wrote more extensively about his climbing expeditions in *My Climbing Adventures in Four Continents*, T Fisher Unwin, London, 1911.

From 140 dairies and exports of 48,000 hundredweights (cwts) of butter in 1898, production rose rapidly. By 1904 there were 2,630 dairies and exports of 681,857 cwts. The areas around Barnaul and the Altai were particularly productive. "Altogether, between three and three and a half million sterling worth of butter is now exported annually from Siberia, which is more than double the value of the total quantity of wheat exported in 1900, the year of the last good harvest," Turner wrote.[4] He believed exports could continue to expand and that Siberia and the Altai could produce the best quality butter in the word. Only 22 lb of milk from Siberian cattle was needed to produce a pound of butter, compared to 28 lb from a Danish cow.

Incidentally, much of the butter marketed then as Danish butter, was actually from Siberia and simply repackaged in Denmark. Even in 1905 as much as 300 tons a week were arriving there from Siberia. And often 1,000 tons a week were being delivered directly to London. Turner notes that at least 11 large London importers had entered into direct business relations with the Siberian dairies: "It is British enterprise that rules the Siberian markets today." Every week up to nine trains of 35 refrigerated carriages brought butter from the steppes to Moscow for onward shipment to the Baltic ports. Much of it came to Hay's Wharf in Southwark, London. During the two years which ended with the winter of 1903 Siberia exported more butter than all the British colonies combined.

By this time, Russian colonisation of the steppe was proceeding apace under the protection of Cossack cavalry. Turner describes how the Siberian Cossacks were located in an almost unbroken line that started at the boundary of the region occupied by the Orenburg Cossacks, continued along the fringe of the Kazakh Steppe through the town of Petropavlovsk east towards Omsk and then in a westerly direction along the banks of the Irtysh – the so-called Irtysh Line. The Bysk Line ran through the government of Tomsk towards the north. Three Cossack Atamans constituted a Board of Military Affairs and commanded all the Cossacks.

Immigration was leading to the settlement of large parts of the traditional nomadic grazing lands, thus discouraging the traditional seasonal movement

---

4. Turner, *op. cit.*, p. 58.

of the Kazakhs. At the same time, much of the stockbreeding remained in the hands of Kazakhs, who found a ready market for their sheep, cattle and horses. In 1897, says Turner, in the Akmolinsk and Semipalatinsk regions alone there were 6.5 million head of cattle.

In late April 1903, having completed his business transactions, Turner decided to try his hand at climbing in the Altai Mountains, on the northeastern border of present-day Kazakhstan. He was already an experienced Alpinist, and even though it was very early in the season, he decided to try and conquer some of the highest peaks.

Snow still lay on the ground, so he travelled by sledge and cart southeast from Barnaul to Biysk and then into the foothills, via Altaiskoi, the Shemelovskaya Pass, Barancha, Tavourack and Chorni-Anni via the Yedtogol Pass. From here he travelled to Melia and then Ouskam. The journey was now through mountain valleys and over mountain passes. When his party got to Ouskam, they had difficulty getting replacement horses: "Most of the villages had gone after a pack of wolves that had, very inconsiderately, eaten two horses the previous night," Turner noted.[5]

The next post was Abbi and then on to Koksa, a total of 116 miles from Tavourack. From here Turner and his interpreter, a young Irishman called Cattley, went up to the Korgomsky Mountains and the going became much harder. They were now on the River Koksa and before long Mount Belukha, their objective, came into view, although still at a distance. Soon they were on the River Katun where they were strongly warned not to attempt to climb in the mountains so early in the year.

Undiscouraged, they travelled on to Katunda which lay surrounded by mountains. Here their hosts tried even harder to convince Turner not to attempt to climb Belukha, which stands at just over 14,700 ft: "All hope of persuading my interpreter to climb with me soon vanished, but I convinced the gentlemen that, at least, nothing would stop me, and repeated the argument, that as no one had ever been through the gorges and the passes in winter, it could not possibly be known if it were practicable to do so or not."[6] Turner was nothing if not confident.

---

5. *Ibid*, p. 164.

6. *Ibid*, p. 171.

He set off with Cattley, who lived in Siberia, and two guides and after a moderate climb reached the summit of Saptam, at 9,750 ft, before moving on alone to climb three more peaks at over 10,000 ft: "I enjoyed six hours of very interesting and difficult climbing, which was rendered the more difficult from the fact that, thinking only of ski practice, I had left my nailed boots behind." He descended in the moonlight, when the top layer of snow had frozen over into a slippery carpet and had several falls on the way down.

Nonetheless, he was completely exhilarated, suggesting that members of the Alpine Club should come to partake in "peak-bagging" the region's many unclimbed mountains: "There will be the uncertainty of ever gaining the summit and the possibility of meeting bears and other wild animals on the way. With these attractions the climber will require to add another to the many qualifications necessary for a successful mountaineer and be able to shoot well, both for protection and food."[7]

Saptam is about 40 miles from Belukha, which was Turner's main objective. He was determined to climb Belukha and was also convinced that he was the first European ever to attempt to do so. In this he was wrong, as we shall see. But that did not stop the press in England lionising Turner on his return to London. The *Daily Mail* reported on his climb on Belukha under the headline "Remarkable feat in the Altai Mountains":

The party moved off at eleven o'clock, and after they had gone over a very difficult moraine for two hours, it commenced to snow, with the result that it frightened the hunters, and they left Mr Turner alone on the mountain, on the distinct understanding that they would be up at his tent by four o'clock next morning. It was a lonely afternoon and night, but the next morning, the hunters not being visible, Mr Turner started off at 5am. The snow had stopped, and in four hours he reached the base of the actual peaks of Belukha. There are two peaks and a saddle between them, but he could only gain those ridges by a very difficult way.

7. *Ibid*, p. 173.

It had also begun to snow again, but he decided to push on.

At the top of the second ridge he measured 13,800 feet, and left his name in Russian and English under a large stone, and then continued until he came to an ice slope descending from the summit. Owing to the hardness of the ice it took half an hour to cut one step, and as 30 were necessary, the climber was compelled to pause and remodel his plans. He tried to go down the south side of the mountain, but the fresh-fallen snow on the ice slope slipped with him for about 60 feet, and he was glad to get back to the ridge again. Then a north wind sprang up, with all its bitterness, obliging him to beat a hasty retreat to his tent. Soon afterwards Mr Turner felt ill; he attributed it to having poisoned himself by drinking soup out of a tin, and to a diet of snow-water with black bread and dry rusks, and tinned articles. His hands and face were swollen and it was hopeless to go on. Mr Turner had intended going to find some thermometers which Professor Sapozhnikoff had placed on the south side of the mountain. In addition to this slight poisoning, he had sustained severe inflammation of the eyes through the intensely cold winds. The expedition had come to an abrupt close.

Mr Turner adds: "The view I shall never forget. Our third camp was on the side of a lake that had apparently frozen to the very bottom, as we dug down in the ice to about 6 feet and came to earth; this was about 12 feet from the edge of the lake. The mountains all round stood out like huge sentinels, but were scarcely as bold as the most massive group of the Alps." From the great difficulty of reaching there, it is not surprising to find that no European has tried to explore these mountains, and there is no literature on the subject in English, save a short translation of about 20 lines from a paper read before the Imperial Russian Geographical Society.[8]

Turner spoke specifically about the fact that he was the first European to visit the Altai and to climb there: "The indescribable beauty of

8. The *Daily Mail*, 1 June 1903.

the view before me and the consciousness that I was gazing upon a scene that had never yet been desecrated by the camera or described by any human being, was one of a lifetime, and amply repaid me for the difficulties and inconveniences I had experienced on my way. Here all was virgin ground. There were not passes known and labelled; no well-trodden routes to be followed; no Mark Twain had ever made the ascent of these peaks in imagination; no telescope had scaled their heights before my Zeiss binocular; no avalanche had hurled its hapless victims to an untimely death; no Alpine hut vulgarised the slopes or rides or obscured the view of the summit; no Baedeker enumerated the guides or reduced the glories of the ascent to a matter of pounds, shillings and pence."[9]

Except he was not the first person to climb in the Altai. Thomas Witlam Atkinson beat him to it by more than 50 years. Chapter 23 of Atkinson's first travel book, *Oriental and Western Siberia*, is entitled "Ascent of the Bielouka". Here Thomas describes a visit he made to the Altai in the late spring of 1852, during which he ascended the valley of the River Katounaia – now called the Katun – and made an attempt to climb the main peak of Belukha. In fact, he had made a previous attempt to conquer the peak on his second visit to the region in 1848, when travelling with his wife Lucy. He had also made extensive sketches of the mountains.

According to Thomas' account of the 1852 attempt, he ascended the mountain together with a Kalmyk hunter called Yepta, making good progress: "Having proceeded about five versts, we reached the bend in the valley, where Bielouka stood before us in all his grandeur. I lost no time in seeking out a good point whence to sketch this monarch of the Altai chain."[10] He reached the source of the Katounaia and the base of the mountain's twin peaks and began making his way up one of the spurs that runs towards the south: "When about half-way up, we came to a most effectual barrier – perpendicular rocks

---

9. Turner, *op. cit.*, p. 189.

10. Thomas Witlam Atkinson, *Oriental and Western Siberia*, Hurst & Blackett, London, 1858, p. 407.

283

about a hundred feet high. We now turned towards the east, riding along the foot of these precipices and shortly arrived at an opening; but so steep, that it was doubtful if we could get up on foot. Leaving two Kalmyks with the horses, Yepta and myself started, and shortly discovered that it was almost impossible to keep our feet; one slip and a roll to the bottom would have been our fate."[11]

With no mountaineering equipment at all, no maps or guides and the onset of bad weather, Thomas and Yepta decided to abandon their attempt on the summit, although not before accurately describing the route by which the mountain would eventually be climbed. Fifty years later, Turner failed in his attempt and in fact the peak was not climbed until 1914.[12]

MINERALS ON THE STEPPE

More than 500 miles south of the railhead at Petropavlovsk, northern Kazakhstan, and 150 miles southeast of the capital Nursultan, is the location of the remote Karagandy coal fields. Not far away the Spassky and Uspenssky copper mines had been worked since time immemorial by steppe nomads, before the first commercial workings were opened up during the second half of the 19th century. The closeness of the coal deposits to the rich seams of copper ore was particularly attractive to mining companies, which could use the coal to smelt the newly-mined ore.

According to Robert John Barrett,[13] who visited the mines at Spassky in 1908, they were first developed by a Russian called Stephen Popoff in the first half of the 19th century. He first started work on the silver and lead

---

11. *Ibid*, p. 409.

12. For a more detailed history of the attempts to climb Mount Belukha, see John Town, "In the Altai", in *Alpine Journal*, 1985, pp. 47-53: https://www.alpinejournal.org.uk/Contents/Contents_1985_files/AJ%201985%2047-53%20Town%20Altai.pdf

13. Robert John Barrett, *Russia's New Era: Being notes, impressions and experiences – personal, political, commercial and financial – of an extended tour in the Empire of the Tsar, with statistical tables, portraits, snapshots and other illustrations*, The Financier and Bullionist Ltd, London, 1908. Interestingly, Barrett mentions an Irishman, Mr P O'Cattley, working at the mines in 1907 as a translator. Was this person the same Mr Cattley, also Irish, who acted as translator for Samuel Turner on his attempt to climb Mt Belukha?

deposits, having obtained large contracts to supply lead to the Russian government during the Russo-Turkish War. Then came the Riazanov family from Ekaterinburg, who acquired properties from the local Kazakhs in 1864 and worked them until the mines were closed in 1898.

The mines are always referred to as Kalmyk workings, although the traces were always hard to see as the Kalmyks always filled up the excavations behind them. Early prospectors found them to be full of ore, which often assayed at 10-12 per cent. They could never go below 20-30 ft underground as they had no pumps to keep the mines dry. Even the Russians used primitive techniques, digging a large hole and lining it with timber in a log-cabin style. When it reached 40-50 ft it was abandoned. However, in some places the ore was very pure. Most copper mines at this time reckoned they could make a profit with ore that was 3 per cent pure. At the Uspenssky mine the ore reef was 70 ft wide and yielded ore that was often almost 70 per cent pure. That made it very profitable.

Modern operations started with the formation of the Spassky Copper Mine Ltd in July 1904. This Anglo-French company bought the freehold of the mine, which covered and area of around 100 sq miles, from the Riazanov family in Ekaterinburg for 200,000 roubles in cash. Founders included mining engineer E Nelson Fell and his brother (and company chairman) Arthur Fell MP.[14] Monsieur E Sadi Carnot, a son of the former French president, was vice-chairman. Other directors included Prince Khilkoff, formerly railways minister in Russia, and the Earl of Chesterfield.

The new company built a railroad from Karagandy to the Spassky mine, importing four six-wheeled locomotives from Leeds and building new blast furnaces, as well as a school, workers' houses and a hospital. The company was so profitable that it quickly paid off these costs and made a profit almost from day one.

Nelson Fell was director of operations at the mine from 1903 until 1908. He clearly enjoyed his time on the steppe and he took the

---

14. E Nelson Fell wrote a fascinating book about his experiences at the Spassky mine. See *Russian and Nomad: Tales of the Kirghiz Steppes*, Duckworth, London, 1916.

opportunity to learn about its original inhabitants: "To me a journey in Siberia had suggested the crossing of endless plains arid, desolate and forlorn. But the reality, in this part of Siberia, at any rate, is very different. Scarcely an hour passed without some object of interest coming into view. Now it would be a long prairie train of wagons, hauled by camels, horses or oxen, or by the three kinds of draught animals; a little later, close by the trail, there would be a Kazakh encampment, consisting of a few round tents. These strangely picturesque people are to be found more or less all over Siberia. For thousands of years they have led the strangely nomadic life they lead to-day. Untouched, unspoilt by civilisation, they were an endless source of interest to me. Never have I met a more kindly, gentle, hospitable race of people, and I found that this was the estimate in which they were generally held by the English mining people I met on my travels. Occasionally I passed great herds of cattle feeding on the country as they travelled on the way to Omsk."[15]

He described the important annual fair held close to Bayanaul and the standing stones that can be found all across the steppes. He also took an interest in the Kazakh tombs, which he refers to as 'moghila': "To an 'intelligent traveller' the really noteworthy feature of the work on these tombs in that it is carried out in precisely the form and method of construction of two thousand years ago. One form of brick ornamentation is particularly noticeable, because it is everywhere found in the work of people who came under the influence of the Greeks at the time of the expeditions of Alexander of Macedonia."[16]

By 1905 the mines employed close to 10,000 men, many of them migrants who had come from southern Russia and moved into the settler villages the Russian government had helped to create in the region. Such a large group of industrial workers, even hundreds of miles from a large city, was not immune to the turmoil that began to rock Russia at this time, exacerbated by the onset of the Russo-Japanese War. Disturbances began to break out, and in January 1906 the company received a demand from

---

15. *Ibid*, p. 188.

16. It may or may not be a coincidence that there is a town in Macedonia called Mogila, which in the local language (and Russian) means "tomb".

the workers at the Assumption Copper Mine for better living quarters and a resident doctor, otherwise they would strike and destroy the works.

The agitators leading these disturbances were Russians, and it seems that the local Kazakhs eventually turned against them, preferring to continue working. Within a short time the strike was called off and the mine management received an urgent request from the strike committee members asking for protection as they feared for their lives.

Fell contrasted the modern ways of working with the social organisation of the Kazakh nomads: "… the Kazakhs are extraordinarily clever along their own line of workmanship. The community starts with the camel, the sheep, the ox and the horse and from these, as they and their families wander over the Steppes, they evolve their tents, their clothes, their embroideries. Truly it seemed wonderful to us, with our machine-made, ready-to-use and ready-to-wear, ideas, to watch how the same results could be accomplished by skilful fingers without machines, and what an extraordinarily high standard of comfort and achievement could be attained with an astonishingly modest standard of cost."[17]

By June 1906 a new group of workers had been hired in Tomsk, but if anything, they were even more troublesome. The authorities there later admitted that they had sent all of these radicalised workers to the steppes. Instead of going on continuous strike, the workers decided instead to work-to-rule. Their contract stipulated that they were required to work for eight hours at standard rate and that overtime would be paid at double time. So they barely worked during their standard day and then did little more for another four hours, thus obtaining two days' pay for one very poor day of work.

Eventually, all these workers were dismissed and sent back to Siberia. But problems continued. The Kazakhs who worked at the mines or smelters received little more than US 25 cents per day, along with free coal, accommodation and water. After further reforms the plants got back to work, but the 1905 disturbances were merely a harbinger of what was to come only a decade or so later with the onset of the Russian Revolution.

---

17. Fell, *op. cit.*, p. 76.

Fell saw some remarkable sights during his stay at the Spassky mine. His book even contains a photograph of women taking part in traditional wrestling competitions. He also mentions eating competitions: "Every *aoul* of consequence has its eating champion, and, on festal occasions, the champions of different *aouls* are pitted against each other. The two champions sit down facing one another, and platter after platter of boiled meat (always without salt) is put in front of each man, who crams the meat into his mouth with his hands and gulps it down like a wolf. Bowl after bowl of *koumiss* and samovar after samovar of tea disappear in like manner. The quantity which these gastronomical giants are able to consume is astonishing. An ordinary accomplishment for one hero at a sitting is:

One entire sheep
Eight gallons of koumiss
Two gallons of tea.
Wonderful, but horrible."[18]

Fell also spent time on the northern shores of Lake Balkhash, where he hunted – unsuccessfully – for tigers. He also took part in a traditional hunt with eagles in the Kizil Tau Mountains. The first kill was of a large owl. The second quarry was a wolf: ""An anxious cry breaks from the Kazakhs: the quarry is a wolf, a dangerous foe even for an old and experienced eagle. Two miles from the hilltop the eagle drops. Its talons sink deep into the head of the flying wolf and bird and beast roll in the grass together. With whirling whips and frantic kicks, the Kazakhs beat their ponies to the battlefield. When they arrive, the wolf is almost overpowered; the eagle's beak is deeply imbedded in its brain and, though minus a few feathers, the gallant victor is an indomitable as ever. The efforts of three men scarcely suffice to extricate its claws, so ruthlessly are they implanted in its victim."[19]

---

18. *Ibid*, p. 152.

19. *Ibid*, pp. 198-9.

*

Even after Fell left the day-to-day management of the company in 1908, we are able to trace more of its history through the writings of John Wilford Wardell, who also ended up in this remote part of Central Asia. Wardell was a draughtsman from County Durham in the north of England. Having studied non-ferrous metallurgy in his spare time, he later joined the staff of Walter G Perkins, a consulting metallurgical engineer in London who had been asked to look at improving the output of the Spassky copper mines. When a job came up at the mine his application was successful and he finally reached the site on 2 June 1914, his birthday. As he later recollected in his memoir *In the Kirghiz Steppes,* published much later: "By good fortune or otherwise, my sojourn in southern Siberia coincided with one of the most critical periods in Russian history, when peace and war, revolution and counter-revolution passed in succession to that chaos from which a new Russia – since grown very powerful – ultimately emerged."[20]

When Wardell reached the mine it had a population of around 3,000, with around 1,500 Kazakhs and 300 Russians employed by the company, supervised by 18 foreigners, mostly Britons. The improvements he worked on included modernising the smelting plant, installing a concentrating plant and equipping new concentrating and smelting works at a new site at Atbazar. He signed up on a three-year contract, which allowed his wife to join him. The onset of the First World War made things much more difficult. Instead of a fortnight's journey from London to the mines, as could be done in peacetime, it was now an arduous four-month journey across land and sea. In the end Wardell did not return home until November 1919.

---

20. John Wilford Wardell, *In the Kirghiz Steppes*, Gallery Press, London, 1961. Wardell did not start to write the book until after he had retired in 1958, when he realised that he had been one of the last Englishmen to visit Kazakh territory since the Russian Revolution. Not until the 1990s did travellers once again venture into these regions. As he wrote in the introduction to his book: "As I was one of the last Englishmen to visit Kazakhstan – for few, if any, have been there since the Soviet Union was finally established – and as the conditions of life there have perhaps altered for ever, I think it is most desirable to save for history this account of the inhabitants of the country and how they had lived for hundreds of years before the great change. To this I have added a description of the country, its climate and other characteristics, and a record of the reactions of those five eventful years on the life of a British community isolated in this remote part of the world."

Wardell's journey out to the steppes was full of incident. Having reached Omsk in southern Siberia, he boarded a steamer on the Irtysh bound for Semipalatinsk, where he intended to take a *tarantass* to Pavlodar. Before he had left England, a friend of his mother had asked him to pass on greetings to her nephew, a Mr Rees. Incredibly, the only other cabin passenger on the steamer turned out to be Mr Rees, then returning from a trip to Riddersk in the Altai Mountains!

In 1914 the steppes were still full of Kazakhs with their large herds of animals, "each community following the patriarchal and pastoral life common to nomadic peoples with huge herds of horses, cattle, sheep, goats and camels." Once he reached the mine at Spassky, he found that the only regular means of transport was by animal; a light railway between the colliery and the smelter and the general manager's new automobile were the only exceptions. The British staff houses were in a large fenced-off area to the north of the works, built of stone due to the lack of wood in the area. The company also ran a farm for grazing animals and to grow oats and hay. Wardell's wife arrived in July 1914 and soon settled in. Within a few months he was taking part in local wolf hunts: "We set off at dawn, a cavalcade of 16 riders, and went into the hills to look for the wolves; but all the evidences of their existence that we could find were the places in the snow where they had slept and the bodies of two partly devoured colts."[21]

In August 1915 his first son was born – the first English child to be born at Spassky. Dick was aged four when they finally left the mine in 1919 to return to England and at that time spoke nothing but Russian, even though his parents always talked to him in English. By the time he was five he spoke only English and had forgotten all his Russian.

Despite the remoteness of the site, Wardell and the English community at the mine did not want for good food. They could feast on strawberries and the black- and redcurrants that were gathered by the Kazakhs in the upland valleys; raspberries, cranberries and bilberries were brought by Russians and Kazakhs from the woods to the east; and apples, which were grown in the Alatau Mountains to the south of Lake Balkash, arrived by traders' caravans. In September locally cultivated

---

21. *Ibid*, p. 47.

melons, marrows, cucumbers and tomatoes became available, along with potatoes, carrots, turnips, beetroots, onions, radishes and lettuce. Wheat, millet, oats, rye and maize gave good crops in the arable areas, and of these, wheat represented about two-thirds of the corn crop. Great fields of sunflowers were grown for their seeds. All this was a far cry from 50 years before when it would have been impossible to find any kind of cultivation on the steppes. Kazakhs, like most Central Asian nomads, held farmers in contempt. Overall, the mining operation at Spassky was entirely self-supporting, which was just as well, considering its remote location. The only imports were machinery and technical supplies and the only export was refined copper.

Surprisingly, considering the fact that he was an engineering draughtsman, Wardell took a great deal of interest in the Kazakhs who lived in the region. He provides a detailed description of their way of life. He noted, for example, the clothing worn by girls and young women: "A small pillbox-shaped hat, about six inches in diameter, made of velvet and decorated with owls' feathers, was perched on the front of the head. A three-quarter length velvet coat, close-fitting above the waist and very full below, was worn over an ankle-length sateen dress, which was so wide that it hung in folds. Hats, coats and dresses were of different and bright colours and it was evidently the fashion to have the three garments in hues that did not match. The coast and dress were sleeveless so as to display the long full sleeves of a white cotton undergarment and the coast was fastened up to the neck with silver or bone buttons. Leg boots of soft leather, which fit into hard leather shoes, were worn.

"Until the first child was born married girls wore red shawls as head and shoulder covering, but afterwards married women wore white cotton, nun-like headdresses and fronts, which covered the head and neck, but not the face, and hung down to the waist. These head and shoulder coverings were worn over full, long-sleeved silk or printed cotton gowns which extended to the ankles; footwear was similar to that worn by the girls. When out of doors women added velvet or cloth coats, like those of the girls but of duller colours. All females discarded skirts for trousers when travelling, because they always rode astride and they usually wore trousers and overcoats, like those of the men, in winter."[22] Like Thomas Atkinson before him, he noted that the better-off men used horse skins for winter coats.

As for the Kazakh diet, he noted, like E Nelson Fell, that the Kazakhs were great eaters, although they had a limited diet of meat, bread, cheese, milk and tea. The meat – usually mutton – was always boiled. Sheep was preferred to beef and horse to sheep. As winter approached, excess sheep were slaughtered and during this time men would often eat four lb of meat each day. Some would eat ten lb of mutton at a feast.

He writes that wealth was counted in terms of animals and that as soon as a Kazakh received cash he would try to convert it into stock. Some of the richest nomads owned tens of thousands of animals; they would employ poorer Kazakhs as stockmen, who would take their pay in food and clothing and also animals. In a small *aoul* of 20 yurts – say 100 people – there would be around 600 horses, 300 camels and cattle, and sheep and goats in substantial numbers. Artisans were to be found, especially those specialising in saddlery and metalwork. The typical greeting between nomads would be the phrase "How are your legs?", meaning that if a man could ride he had nothing to worry about.

Wardell also comments on the religious beliefs of the nomads he came into contact with. He says that despite their adoption of Islam, they had retained many shamanistic practices, particularly the art of divining the future from the cracks caused by burning a sheep's shoulder blade or in exorcising evil spirits, for which he provides the following account that he witnessed: "The shaman walked three times round the sick man, who lay on a felt mat near a fire of dried camel dung, strumming his *dumbra*, while his two seated assistants accompanied him on their guitars and continued playing after he had stopped and until the shaman had invoked the blue wolf genie which possessed the patient. As soon as the genie acknowledged his presence the assistants tied a rope round the shaman's waist and tightened the loop by means of a stick until the waist was reduced to half its circumference, by which time the shaman, who was supposed to be in a hypnotic trance, spun round, whirling an assistant on each arm while he argued with the evil spirit.

22. *Ibid*, pp. 90-91.

"Dropping the assistants, the shaman seized an axe, struck some near-hitting blows at the patient, and hit himself with the flat of the blade several times. Discarding the axe the shaman snatched burning coals from the fire and put them in his mouth with much rolling of eyes and twitching of shoulders, after which he filled his mouth with water and sprayed it across the bottom of a very hot frying-pan and the resulting steam indicated that the genie had been driven from the sick man's body. The shaman then collapsed and slept while his assistants massaged his stiff body, after which he drank a quart of sheep's fat oil and collected his fee."[23]

When it came to marriage, the bride price was paid by the groom's father. For a secondary chief's daughter, says Wardell, the price was around 40 horses. Poorer boys were often betrothed at 14 and girls at 12, but the actual marriage did not take place for another seven years. Ancestry was checked carefully to ensure that the prospective couple had no common ancestor for six generations. Divorce was almost unknown on the steppe, as wives were valuable assets in terms of managing large herds of animals. Their duties included childcare, cooking and serving food, milking all domestic animals except mares, making felt, weaving wool, erecting and dismantling yurts, fetching water and gathering and drying *argol* (dung) for fuel.

Wardell gives an interesting description of the way in which Kazakh nomads gave birth: "On her arrival the mother [of the pregnant woman] stretched a rope tightly across the interior of the tent about three feet above the floor, so that her daughter, when kneeling in front of the middle of it on a large square of soft felt with her arms over the rope to the armpits, was well supported. The mother then told her daughter to sway slowly backwards and forwards on the rope, inhaling on the backward stroke and exhaling and pressing heavily on the forward one, and gripping a skin bottle in both hands the while, until delivery took place."[24]

Children he says, "could ride sheep by the age of three, oxen by four and horses by five and both boys and girls were expert riders by the age of ten, when the former started herding duties." They played versions

23. *Ibid*, p. 103.

24. *Ibid*, p. 105.

of blindman's buff, hide and seek, and robbers and warriors. They were also taught to be very obedient, not speaking to their fathers unless spoken to first. Education was basic, usually involving being taught a few verses of the Koran by a mullah and the rudiments of arithmetic, local geography and the songs and sagas of tribal heroes.

Wardell's description of nomadic life shows that he spent a great deal of time in their company. He outlines the way the interior of a yurt is laid out, the way tea is prepared and how guests are entertained. He notes how Kazakhs sat on their horses, with high saddles and short stirrups, and the two paces to expect from Kazakh horses – a jolting springy walk and a mad gallop. They could easily cover 300 miles in a week on horses that could keep up a jog for days on end. In previous days they had set out on a *baranta* (raid), their main weapon being the battle axe, a formidable weapon with a 130-cm hardwood handle, iron rings for the grip and a leather wrist thong. For shooting they used a matchlock gun fired from the prone position, with a folding prong to hold the barrel off the ground.

Horses were central to Kazakh culture and played an important role in shamanistic rites. White horses were used for important sacrifices and the meat was offered to honoured guests. Treaties were sealed by parties dipping their hands into the blood of a white horse. Only men were allowed to milk mares. Buying and selling of horses was carried out in complete silence; the middleman squatted between the buyer and the seller, holding a hand of each hidden in his long sleeves, and transmitted bids and comments by gripping or bending certain fingers until the bargain was reached.

Kazakhs, then as today, loved to race their horses or to use them for the national sport of Kokpar, described by Wardell as Rugby Football played on horseback. The idea is to score by dumping a sheep carcass into a hole. There are precious few rules, meaning that the event often turns into a mounted brawl between the two teams, both of which use their whips liberally, often against competing riders. Horseracing, known as *Baiga*, involves horses racing over a 10-15-mile course across level country at top speed. Spectators would often join in, especially towards the end, when they would sometimes attach ropes to jaded horses and literally drag them over the finish line.

The other big sport on the steppe was wrestling. Competitors tried to force each other to fall on their backs by pushing, pulling and tripping their opponent. Sometimes it took place on horseback, but more usually on the ground. And as Nelson Fell noted, sometimes women took part in the competitions.

But supreme among all sporting activity for Kazakhs was hawking. Falcons were sometimes used, but mostly it was the golden eagle. These large birds – up to 10 kg in weight with a 2-m wingspan – are carried on a horse by using a special tee-headed stock, the lower end of which is socketed in the saddle near the rider's knee. The usual quarry was a wolf or fox. "When the wolf was found, the eagle was unhooded and cast off, rose in the air and sighted its prey and then, unhesitatingly swooping down with quietly flapping wings behind the unsuspecting quarry, it struck its great talons into the animal's neck behind the head, knocked the wolf over sideways and, baffling its defence with its powerful wings, tore out the victim's eyes with its great curved beak. A minute or so after the strike the wolf was dead, and then the watchers, who had dismounted downwind from the quarry when it was sighted, mounted and hurried to the scene of the conflict, where the owner re-hooded his eagle and, after skinning the prey, unhooded it again until it had satisfied some of its hunger on the carcass. The cavalcade then set off to find other game."[25]

Wardell describes the technique used to catch golden eagles for hunting. White string was pegged out on the ground in a complicated pattern at the beginning of winter. After the first snow, when the string was no longer visible, the hunter would tie a chicken to a stake and wait nearby in a hide. Once an eagle landed to kill the chicken, the strings would catch its legs and pull tight. The hunter would then break cover and throw a cloth over its head. Jesses were attached to the bird's legs and the cloth replaced by a hood. Now all that remained was to train the bird, which usually took several weeks.

This technique is different from that used by the Kazakh eagle hunters of Western Mongolia. There, the birds – invariably, the larger and more ferocious females – are taken directly from the nest at a very

---

25. *Ibid*, p. 112.

young age and brought up by the *berkutshiler* (eagle hunter) at home, where they usually live alongside the human inhabitants of the yurt. This allows a strong bond to develop between the eagle and its handler. However, in both cases the eagle is returned to the wild. Once it reaches sexual maturity at the age of seven or eight, an eagle will no longer hunt for its handler and so is released back into the wild. The owner will often leave a slaughtered sheep as a parting gift for all the good service the bird has provided.

Wardell devotes a chapter of his book to the Russian settlers of Kazakhstan. Men still wore the traditional peasant garb of peaked cap, shirt, belt, trousers, knee boots and cotton strips wound around the feet instead of socks. The women wore headscarves, a coloured blouse, petticoats and cotton chemises and ankle-length skirts. Often they were barefooted. Their houses usually consisted of two rooms with very small windows that were seldom opened. A large part of the kitchen area was taken up by a huge stove, generally built into the party wall, so that the bedroom was also heated. Children usually slept on top of the oven, while their parents slept on the floor.

Most peasants kept a few pigs, cows, horses, goats, chickens and geese. A kitchen garden and some grazing for the animals were usually nearby. Work on the surrounding fields was generally cooperative, with implements, labour and profits all being shared. Their food consisted mainly of soup, mutton, beef, salt pork, fish, eggs, rice, cucumbers, bread and tea. When jam was served it was usually put in the tea. Kvass, beer and vodka were the favoured beverages. Upper-class Russians ate like the French, says Wardell, and lower-class Russians ate like Germans.

As the First World War progressed, it became difficult for the foreigners to live in the mining camps. Wardell says he did not have any kind of a break for three years. The plant lost its chemist and the only replacement they could find was a German prisoner-of-war, transferred from the prison camp at Omsk. Food shortages increased in the towns and the Bolsheviks began to play a bigger role, organising strikes through the soviets they set up. It was some time before these changes became apparent on the steppes, but the establishment of the Provisional Government in March 1917 caused a stir.

By the end of 1917, two months after the October Revolution, things began to get difficult at the mines. By this time the workmen had obtained the eight-hour day and the six-day week. Wages had risen by 200 per cent. All of this was manageable, but the problem was the demands of the local soviet to become involved in the administration and operation of the works. "The Soviets were in perpetual session and whenever questions arose which the members thought necessary to put to the whole community, a general assembly was called, which meant serious interruption to the operation of the mines, smelter or mill. For these and similar reasons the production of the works and the efficiency of the labour became rapidly lower."[26]

Transportation routes throughout Siberia began to break down and it soon became impossible to obtain machinery and supplies. The local carters stopped transporting coal to the smelting plants and it soon became clear that operations would have to be suspended at some of them. Then, on 27 March 1918, all the Spassky mine properties were nationalised by decree from Moscow and the local committee took over the entire operation. Enemies of the soviets, whether real or imagined, were exiled from the plants. The English staff were not touched initially, although the German chemist was almost beaten up. One of the Cossacks, a foreman, quit the plant to fight in the hills as a guerrilla against the Bolsheviks.

By the time the plant was nationalised there were ten British men, five wives and seven children still left on the steppes. Unable to work, they decided they should try to leave by heading more than 500 miles north to Petropavlovsk and then by train to Moscow and the Arctic port of Archangel, where they hoped they could get a ship to England. The first party, including Wardell and his family, set off on 20 May 1918.

They reached Petropavlovsk after a week of travel. Here they arrived just as conflict was escalating between the Bolsheviks and the Czech Legion that was attempting to return to Europe to fight the Germans. Within a couple of days the Czechs had effectively liberated Petropavlovsk and many other towns along the Trans-Siberian Railway from Bolshevik control. White Guards arrived soon after and the town

---

26. *Ibid*, p. 144.

was secured. More of the staff from Spassky arrived, bringing the total number to 20, with only the general manager and his wife still to come.

All this was happening against a background of momentous events. Admiral Kolchak established the All-Siberian Government in Omsk on 12 June and became minister of war. Now there was a chance the British group could leave Siberia by way of Vladivostok. The children started to become ill with dysentery and scarlet fever and one of them sadly died. Wardell and the others stayed in Petropavlovsk until 30 September. By then the Whites had established control over much of Siberia, including the mines at Spassky. As a result, a decision was taken to return there. The engineers had done a remarkable job in getting the mines and smelters back into operation, although the workforce was sullen and resentful and blamed them for the collapse of their short-lived freedom. Having sold off most of their possessions before they left, the returnees were short of almost everything – although they managed to find a piano that no-one had been able to cart away. "Taking it from every angle," wrote Wardell, "this was the worst winter we had ever experienced."

Further north, the Whites were in control, but were becoming increasingly unpopular. Wardell claims that the White Terror in Eastern Siberia was worse than the Red had been. By May 1919 the Bolsheviks had mounted another offensive that opened up Siberia for reconquest. So after a winter spent on the steppe, on 21 July the British Consul in Omsk advised the British party to leave. Kolchak's forces were in disarray and town after town along the railway fell in succession.

It was now impossible to join the railway to the west of Omsk and so the party decided to head towards the River Irtysh at Ekibastuz and get aboard a steamer. To get there they had to convert hay carts into trek wagons – one for each family. The journey took five days, during which they met almost no-one on the road. They boarded the steamer on 14 August and arrived in Omsk two days later. Here they were able to obtain a Pullman car for the party, which now included three more British families from the Urals. There were British soldiers from the Hampshire and Middlesex regiments in the town, busy removing tens of millions of pounds worth of gold captured by Kolchak. The soldiers operated as guards on the railway all the way to Vladivostok but did not take part in any of the fighting.

It took six days to reach Irkutsk in eastern Siberia, travelling via Krasnoyarsk. The railway line was littered with wrecks from Bolshevik guerrilla operations and only a tenth of the rolling stock was still functioning. After a day in Irkutsk the group took another train to the south of Lake Baikal towards the frontier with Manchuria, north of the River Amur to Khabarovsk and then Vladivostok, where they arrived on 2 September after a 16-day journey from Omsk covering 3,300 miles.

After almost a month in Vladivostok part of the group – three families, including the Wardells – took a train for Shanghai where eventually they went on board the *Wallowra*, a 3,000-ton tramp steamer that took them to Marseille, where they arrived on 24 November. They landed in England two days later. All were relieved to get home. "Because of revolutions and other troubles, I had had no news from my parents for two and a half years, nor had my communications reached them during this time. They had been advised by the Company of our safe arrival in Vladivostok, and they had received my cable from Marseille, but prior to these notices they had given us up as lost in the Russian chaos."[27]

FAMINE RELIEF ON THE STEPPE

John Wardell rightly thought that he was one of the last outsiders to visit the Great Steppe prior to the break-up of the Soviet Union in 1991. He was certainly one of the last, but not the last. There was at least one later visitor, although he arrived only a few months after Wardell and his family left for Vladivostok.

Ralph Winston Fox, born in Halifax, Yorkshire, in March 1900, was a very different kind of visitor, one of many idealists who came to Russia to work in support of the fledgling Soviet state to alleviate the famine conditions by buying animals from the nomads of the steppe. Fox came from a middle-class family and after an education at Heath Grammar School and then Bradford Grammar School was clever enough to study modern languages at Oxford. There he joined an officers' cadet regiment and was commissioned as a lieutenant in

---

27. *Ibid*, p. 182.

the Devonshires but was too young to see active service before the war ended. Instead, in 1919, he became active as a campaigner against the British blockade and the military intervention aimed at overthrowing the Bolshevik government in Russia. At Oxford he was active in the "Hands off Russia" Committee and was a founder member of the newly formed Communist Party of Great Britain (CPGB).

In 1920, as the dust was settling from the Russian Civil War, Fox made a brief journey to Soviet Russia, an experience which further moved him towards lifelong identification with the communist political movement. After his return to Oxford, in 1922 he graduated with a first in modern languages. The following summer he returned to Soviet Russia, this time as a worker with the Friends Relief Mission based at Samara on the Volga.

The Friends Emergency and War Victims Relief Committee, as it is more properly known, was set up by Quakers at the beginning of the First World War, providing help to French communities destroyed by the fighting and helping interned Germans and other displaced people in Britain. After the Russian Revolution in 1917 it also began to organise aid there and in a joint operation with the Save the Children Fund was soon feeding 16,000 children in Moscow.

However, relief had only reached accessible places. When in 1921 committee member Anna Haines accompanied a Russian party to Buzuluk, close to Samara in the south of Russia, she found conditions so bad that food supplied by the Friends Relief Mission was diverted from Moscow to Samara town and district. Along with 30 wagons of government food, a kitchen that could prepare 5,000 ration meals, and a dispensary, Quaker relief work began in the area to alleviate what were famine conditions.

As more workers became available, they managed to distribute supplies across the wider region. Some journeys took two days; horses, weak from hunger, could hardly pull supplies and typhus was an ever-present risk. But eventually the FRC was able to set up 900 feeding points in 280 villages. The lack of doctors, nurses or medical supplies meant that famine-related diseases such as typhus and cholera spread quickly. Despite high numbers falling ill, disease was fought by elementary means such as cleaning and disinfecting houses. A dozen clinics were established and in one medical programme alone nearly 30,000 people received a course of quinine tablets. Feeding and medical schemes like these ensured that tens of thousands of Russian people were saved from starvation and disease.

Ralph Fox arrived in Samara in the summer of 1922, along with many other young idealists, keen to help the nascent Soviet Union. At the time, the second civil war was still in progress, following the defeat of the forces led by Kolchak and Denikin. The famine now evident across large parts of the Soviet Union – due in large part to the fighting that had been raging for almost three years – had led the Bolsheviks to introduce in March 1921 what was called the New Economic Policy. This represented a more market-oriented strategy aimed at strengthening the economy. The Soviet authorities partially revoked the complete nationalisation of industry (established during the period of War Communism of 1918 to 1921) and introduced a system of mixed economy which allowed private individuals to own small enterprises, while the state continued to control banks, foreign trade and large industries. In addition, the NEP abolished forced grain-requisition and introduced a tax on farmers, payable in the form of raw agricultural product.

As Fox put it himself: "In the summer of 1922 a little band of Anglo-Saxon oddities was islanded in a small town upon the far south-eastern plain of Russia. Pacifists, Socialists, faithful Christians, rootless Intellectuals, misunderstood and misunderstanding, they were engaged in giving relief to the stricken peasants of the district."[28] One of his first jobs was to find a member of their team who had disappeared after travelling to "Bouz", near Aralsk on the Aral Sea to buy horses, needed to replace those that had died of starvation in the famine, or been eaten for want of anything else. Fox travelled from Samara on the Tashkent train, first visiting Orenburg, and carrying some £3,000 in his pocket for the purchase of horses.

"We saw men from Khiva, tall and clean-limbed, in blue felt *khalats*, their heads crowned with beautiful round hats of fox-fur. There were Kazakhs in drab camel cloth, each one carrying his short horseman's whip, their headgear a summer one of white felt, in shape like an Elizabethan pikeman's helmet and embroidered in blue or red. Bokhara Jews, dirty but curiously dignified, wearing *khalats* of silk and embroidered skull-caps,

---

28   Ralph Fox, *People of the Steppes*, London, Constable & Co, 1925, p. 1.

hurried along the platform, kettle in hand, seeking the hot-water tap. Out on the tracks to the right two devout Sarts from the cities of the south, "divine Bokhara or happy Samarkand", had spread their carpets between the metals and were saying the first evening prayer, calm and unhurried."

For the first time, he saw through the windows of the train the yurts of the nomads, "shaped like broad beehives". He saw the women in their white headdresses, with long smocks reaching to the ground and often he caught a passing glimpse of entire groups on the road, "the elders and children perched above their household goods on the beautiful shaggy Bactrian camels, the youths on horseback, small, sturdy ponies."[29]

Finally, he reached the coast of the Aral Sea, where "Bouz" turned out to be Turksoyuz, a trading organisation based in Tashkent. A colleague had been in the town for a month trying to buy horses to replace those which had died during the famine further north, but had only succeeded in finding 28. After little luck in finding horses here, Fox decided that the best way to fulfil his quota of a thousand horses was to ride out into the steppe, to the estuary of the Syr Darya, where the Junior Horde of the Kazakhs made its winter encampments.

Eventually they reached Kamyslybas, which is today in Kazakhstan's Kyzyl Orda oblast, where there is a large saltwater lake connected to the delta of the Syr Darya by a canal. It was a remote place but known to be a gathering place for the nomadic Kazakhs who migrated here for the winter from more northerly regions. Soon Fox had settled into a routine. Every day at 10am the Kazakhs would arrive, driving large numbers of horses for inspection. "Then started a duel of words in Kazakh. 'Kansha?' (How much?) 'Iki Juz' (200) or 'Tort Juz' (400) was the reply, the numerals referring to millions of roubles. That was the salute, as it were, before the fight began. For as sure as the Kazakh called out his price the answer came from Yaganov in a string of uncomplimentary epithets applied to horse and owner. Out shot the chubby brown hand and '120' he would bid against 200. The Kazakh would stare a minute, burst into a torrent of protest and smite away the hand, calling out vehemently '195'."[30]

---

29. *Ibid*, p. 9.

30. *Ibid*, p. 58.

Another five minutes and the bargain would be struck at 165, or something close. The horses would be corralled and after five days in the village, the train arrived ready to take the horses they had purchased back to Orenburg. Meanwhile Fox himself had succumbed to malaria and had to return to Moscow for three weeks for treatment.

On his return to the steppe he found chaos: "Indeed we were soon in trouble on all sides. Steklov tried to back out of his agreement with us, the people whose house we used tried to extort a monstrous rent, the railway authorities demanded bribes before they furnished wagons, the Ispolkom (Petrograd Soviet) accused us of buying without permits and Sam discovered attempts had been made to substitute bad horses for his good ones on the steppe. Two of the horses Bill had bought died of old age, many others proved unsatisfactory in various ways and rumours came to us from all sides that he had been taking bribes from the Kazakhs."[31]

Amidst all this chaos Fox took the opportunity to learn something of the Kazakhs with whom he dwelt. He argues that they are made up of fragments from all the tribes of Central Asia. "How else can be explain the existence among them of tribal names such as Naiman, Kipchak, Kirei, Kankly and Kungrad? Must it not be that wandering fragments of these defeated nations preserved the old names when they joined forces with the Kazakhs?"[32]

He explains the structure of the Kazakh tribal society, its division into four hordes, and many more clans and subtribes, making up a nation of around three million at that time, scattered across a territory the size of Europe. He also notes the fact that each clan has its private mark, called a *tamga*, used for a seal to sign important documents. Some clans actually use the cross as their *tamga*, harking back to the days when Nestorian Christians were as common in this region as Muslims. There are separate *tamgas* for the noble families descended from sultans and also for the *khodjas*, the caste of saintly warriors who are the councillors of the nation. Most of the khans, he notes, claim descent from Genghis Khan or Timur.

---

31. *Ibid*, p. 76.

32. *Ibid.*, p137.

Fox suggests that the Kazakhs were already a nation before the Mongol invasion and it was probably the case that the remnants of the great empires of the Kara-Khitai and Khorazm (Khiva), destroyed so completely by the Mongols and Timur, threw their lot in with them. Their very existence was unknown, even to the Russians, until 1534, although as early as 1573 the Strogonov merchant family urged Ivan Grosni (the Terrible) to send envoys to the Blue Sea (the Aral) to open up trading negotiations with their khans. They expanded into Siberia and south to the great city of Turkestan, which holds the shrine of their greatest saint, Khoja Ahmed Yasawi. Turkestan became the capital of the Kazakh khanate in the 16th century and the mausoleum is considered to be one of the greatest in the Islamic world.

As Fox wrote, Soviet plans for Central Asia were still in flux. The capital of the Soviet Republic of Turkestan was Orenburg – since then returned to Russia – and the terrible disaster of the Great Famine of the early 1930s had not yet occurred. As a committed communist he sang the praises of the Soviets. "The people of the steppe, as so often before in history, are on the march again," he wrote.

Like some of the other writers mentioned in this chapter, Fox gives detailed descriptions of the Kazakhs' nomadic lifestyle, their love of horseracing and Kokpar, wrestling and stockbreeding. He asks what will become of them and their steppelands. But his stay in the steppes was over almost before it began. By the beginning of 1923 he was back in Britain, where he went to work as a functionary for the CPGB in its propaganda department and to study at the School of Oriental Languages in his spare time. Soon after, in 1925, he published *People of the Steppes*.

In 1925 Fox returned once again to Moscow, this time to work in the apparatus of the Communist International. He met his wife in the Soviet Union and married in the spring of 1926. Two years later he returned to London to join the staff of the *Sunday Worker*, the high-profile weekly predecessor of the *Daily Worker*, launched in 1930. Fox and his wife returned once again to the Soviet Union in 1929, where he became a librarian at the Marx-Engels Institute in Moscow, and where he began a detailed study of Asiatic economic development as reflected in the writings of Karl Marx. He published an article on the topic, "The

Views of Marx and Engels on the Asiatic Mode of Production and Their Sources", in the journal *Letopisi marksizma* in 1930.

Fox returned once again to England in 1932, going to work for the *Daily Worker* as a columnist and writing several pamphlets and books for the communist press, including a biography of Genghis Khan. When the Spanish Civil War started in 1936, he made his way to Paris and signed up to join the International Brigades. On his arrival in Spain at he was sent to be trained in Albacete and was assigned to the 121st Battalion of the XIV Brigade as a political commissar.

After some weeks as a political commissar at the base, Fox was sent to the front in one of the first operations in which the Brigades were involved. He died not far from Cordoba at the Battle of Lopera in January 1937 after barely six weeks in the country.

Ralph Fox was probably the last English person to travel freely on the steppes and to report on what he found. Soon the Soviet authorities would stop any outsiders from travelling to these remote areas.[33] They had their own problems to deal with, not least the tricky ideological question of how to fit nomads into the straitjacket of Marxist theory. It was to result in one of the worst crimes of the Soviet era – the near-complete obliteration of the nomadic way of life in much of Central Asia. Anyone owning a couple of cattle and a handful of sheep – which was most of the population – was classified as a *kulak* – a rich peasant.

By the beginning of the 1930s hundreds of thousands of nomads, deprived of their animals and the freedom to roam the steppes, were dying of starvation. Thousands of others, unable to identify with the aspirations of a workers' state, were shot as counter-revolutionaries. According to a recent book by Susan Cameron, more than 1.5 million people perished in this famine, a quarter of Kazakhstan's population.

---

33. There is one further account of life on the steppes during the 1940s and 1950s. Nicholas Bethell's *The Long Journey Home: the memoirs of Flora Leipman*, Bantam Press, London, 1987, tells the tragic story of a young Scotswoman whose mother took her to the Soviet Union as a child, only for her to be arrested and sentenced to hard labour in a work camp on the Kazakh Steppe. She was sent to work in the coalmines at Karaganda – the same mines that were once owned by British companies and which are described above in the books of E Nelson Fell and John Wardell.

"In its staggering human toll, the Kazakh famine was certainly one of the most heinous crimes of the Stalinist regime," writes Cameron.[34]

Little more was to be heard of the Kazakh steppe for most of the rest of the 20th century. It became, in parts of the northeast, a rocket launch site and a testing ground for Soviet atomic weapons, while other closed cities held thousands of Stalin's deportees from the Caucasus or from the German villages along the Volga. Other prisoners came from Japan and Korea. Kazakhs became a minority in their own land. Only by the time of the 1989 census did Kazakhs outnumber Russians again – by 39.7 per cent to 37.8 per cent – and it was not until 1999 that Kazakhs made up more than 50 per cent of the population.

Right: Rider carrying a goat carcass on horseback during the traditional sport of *kokpar*.

34. Sarah Cameron, *The Hungry Steppe: Famine, Violence and the Making of Soviet Kazakhstan*, Cornell University Press, Ithaca and London, 2018, p. 2.

POSTSCRIPT

—ɯ—

AFTER THE MID-1920S THERE WERE FEW VISITORS TO THE GREAT STEPPE UNTIL THE 1990S. Owen and Eleanor Lattimore passed through in the late 1920s,[1] as did the much-travelled missionary sisters Francesca and Evangeline French and their companion Mildred Cable.[2] Douglas Carruthers published *Beyond the Caspian* in 1949,[3] having spent a bitterly cold winter in the Ili Valley in what is now Eastern Kazakhstan and the Xinjiang region of China. But other than these few hardy travellers, the vast steppelands remained off-limits to outsiders.

One reason for this was the massive programme of atomic tests conducted in an area known as the Semipalatinsk Test Site (STS) or "The Polygon", located about 150 km west of the city of Semey in northeast Kazakhstan. Between 1949 and 1989 the Soviet Union conducted 456 nuclear tests in this 18,000 sq km area with little regard for their effect on the local people or environment. The full impact of radiation exposure was hidden for many years by the Soviet authorities and has only come to light since the test site closed for good in 1991. From 1996 to 2012, a secret joint operation by Kazakh, Russian, and American nuclear scientists and engineers cleared up what they could and ensured the security of the waste plutonium that had been abandoned at the site.

Since its closure, the STS has become the best-researched atomic test

---

1. See Eleanor Holgate Lattimore, *Turkestan Reunion*, Hurst and Blackett, London, 1935, and Owen Lattimore, *The Desert Road to Turkestan*, Little Brown & Co, Boston, 1929.

2. See for example, Evangeline French, Mildred Cable & Francesca French, *A Desert Journal: Letters from Central Asia*, Constable & Co, London, 1934.

3 Douglas Carruthers, *Beyond the Caspian: A Naturalist in Central Asia*, Oliver & Boyd, London, 1949.

site in the world, and the only one open to the public. Ironically, it has actually become a tourist destination in its own right.

Following the collapse of the Soviet Union and Kazakhstan's declaration of independence in December 1991, the Great Steppe has once again become accessible to travellers. Yet, this vast country, the ninth largest in the world with an area of more than 2.7 million sq km, still remains a challenge to even the hardiest adventurer. The deserts are now crossed by road and rail, and massive infrastructure spending is changing the landscape. But huge regions in the interior of the country and the mountainous regions of the Altai, the Tarbagatai, the Alatau Mountain chain, not to mention parts of the Caspian seaboard and vast swathes of the interior, still offer a challenge to all travellers.

I have travelled widely in many parts of Central Asia – Kyrgyzstan, Mongolia, Uzbekistan, Tajikistan and Tuva – but I arrived in Kazakhstan for the first time only in 2014, determined to trace the routes taken by Thomas and Lucy Atkinson during their extensive stay in the country from March 1848 to September 1849. My first objective was to locate and visit Kopal – now usually called Kapal – where the Atkinsons had been based during their stay. With logistical support from Kazgeo – the Kazakh Geographic Society – I visited the town and its famous Tamchiboulac spring. My wife and I also crossed over the mountain ridges into the impressive Kora Valley directly south of Kapal in an effort to locate the giant standing stones described by Atkinson as the "Tombs of the Genie". The stones are no longer standing, but their remains, knocked over and shattered, lie on the valley floor.

On that journey we also tried to ascend the Ak Su river as far as possible, only turning around when the path alongside this bustling white water river disappeared as it entered a gorge.

The following year I returned, this time starting at Oskemen in the far northeast of the country and making my way southwards, visiting Lake Zaisan and the Tarbagatai Mountains and then Lake Ala Kol. From here my companion Vladimir Gostyevsky and I travelled to the town of Sarcand where we entered the Djungar Alatau National Park. On our first day we rode up on horseback to Zhassyl Kol lake, a beautiful turquoise blue lake set in apple forests in the mountains. From there we visited the valley of the Big Bascan river before making our way to Tekeli and then Almaty.

In 2016, with support from the Kazakh government and again from KazGeo, I brought a group of ten descendants of the Atkinsons to the Zhetysu region to visit the places associated with their ancestors. Members of the group came from England, America and New Zealand and were received everywhere like long lost relatives. The prime minister met the group, as did the Governor of Almaty region and many other dignitaries. In Kapal the whole town put on a huge show for their honoured guests and unveiled a five-ton memorial stone that commemorates the birth of Alatau Atkinson in the town. Singing and dancing followed, as well as a musical play performed by a theatre company.

Since then I have continued visiting this region of Kazakhstan each summer, setting off on horseback into the mountains to trace as closely as possible the routes taken by the Atkinsons, systematically visiting all the river valleys that flow from the Djungar Alatau Mountains towards Lake Baikal. In 2018, along with KazGeo, we again visited the valley of the Big Bascan before heading up to above 3000 m in the mountains, covering more than 100 miles. In 2019 we visited the River Sarcan as well as the Little and the Big Bascan. We also reached the Schumsky Glacier at the base of Peak Tianshansky, the tallest mountain in the range.

These river valleys and uplands have scarcely changed since the days of the Atkinsons although large caravans of nomads no longer take their flocks and herds into the high pastures for the summer. In fact, for the most part one sees few other humans. During the Soviet period winter sports and mountaineering were popular, but whatever facilities existed then have all but disappeared. Wooden bridges have rotted away and old tracks are slowly disappearing beneath the vegetation. Bears, ibex, Maral deer, antelope, marmots, lynx, wolves and even snow leopards flourish.

There is still much more to do in this region. When I suggested to local park rangers that we should attempt to repeat a horseback journey undertaken by the Atkinsons from the town of Lepsinsk to Lake Ala Kol

– a distance of around 120 miles through an untracked wilderness – I was told that no-one had done this journey in recent history and that it would be very dangerous. As for the Tarbagatai Mountains that lie on the other side of Lake Ala Kol, they have scarcely been visited by anyone and I cannot find any recent accounts of their exploration. One has to go back to the Russian explorers Karelin and Kirilov (see Chapter 6) in the 1840s for any detailed information.

Being larger than Europe it is not surprising that there are still large areas of the Great Steppe that are little known to outsiders. My hope is that this book and the stories it contains will stimulate further exploration of this beautiful and exciting region.

—ɯ—

INDEX

—✺—